Asian Security in the Age of Globalization

This book examines the security challenges and opportunities that the nation-states of Asia confront in an era of globalization.

With consideration of the increasingly border-less nature of international relations via the integrative process of globalization, this book explores the emerging threats to regional and national security in Asia. It looks beyond traditional military threats, analysing non-traditional aspects of security including economic, social, environmental, transnational, energy, health concerns and threats posed by organized-crime groups. Its approach is organized both theoretically and, in a country-specific, case study form which provides contemporary examples of the threats faced in the region. By acknowledging that contemporary Asian security has become much more complex and complicated, it highlights the uncertainty and instability that the nation-states of the Indo-Pacific region confront.

Presenting both a globally oriented and expanded vision of Asian security, this book is an excellent resource for scholars and students of Asian Studies, International Relations and Global Studies.

Lui Hebron is a Faculty Affairs Specialist at the California State University, USA. His research focuses on the areas of political economy (Globalization), international relations (ethnicity, conflict and war, security studies), and Asian studies (Pacific Rim, China).

Asian Security in the Age of Globalization

**Edited by
Lui Hebron**

Routledge
Taylor & Francis Group
NEW YORK AND LONDON

Designed cover image: Getty Images - Skegbydave

First published 2024
by Routledge
605 Third Avenue, New York, NY 10158

and by Routledge
4 Park Square, Milton Park, Abingdon, Oxon OX14 4RN

Routledge is an imprint of the Taylor & Francis Group, an informa business

© 2024 selection and editorial matter, Lui Hebron; individual chapters, the contributors

The right of Lui Hebron to be identified as the author of the editorial material, and of the authors for their individual chapters, has been asserted in accordance with sections 77 and 78 of the Copyright, Designs and Patents Act 1988.

All rights reserved. No part of this book may be reprinted or reproduced or utilised in any form or by any electronic, mechanical, or other means, now known or hereafter invented, including photocopying and recording, or in any information storage or retrieval system, without permission in writing from the publishers.

Trademark notice: Product or corporate names may be trademarks or registered trademarks, and are used only for identification and explanation without intent to infringe.

Library of Congress Cataloging-in-Publication Data
Names: Hebron, Lui, editor.
Title: Asian security in the age of globalization / Edited by Lui Hebron.
Description: Abingdon, Oxon ; New York, NY : Routledge, 2024. | Includes bibliographical references and index.
Identifiers: LCCN 2023052468 (print) | LCCN 2023052469 (ebook) | ISBN 9781032752815 (hardback) | ISBN 9780813344607 (paperback) | ISBN 9781003473206 (ebook)
Subjects: LCSH: Security, International--Asia. | Globalization. | National security--Asia.
Classification: LCC JZ6009.A75 A765 2024 (print) | LCC JZ6009.A75 (ebook) | DDC 327.5--dc23/eng/20240205
LC record available at https://lccn.loc.gov/2023052468
LC ebook record available at https://lccn.loc.gov/2023052469

ISBN: 978-1-032-75281-5 (hbk)
ISBN: 978-0-8133-4460-7 (pbk)
ISBN: 978-1-003-47320-6 (ebk)

DOI: 10.4324/9781003473206

Typeset in Times New Roman
by Taylor & Francis Books

**Dedicated to Patrick James
Mentor, Collaborator, Friend**

Contents

List of illustrations	viii
List of acronyms	ix
List of contributors	xi
Acknowledgments	xv

1	Asia Security Today: State of the Field LUI HEBRON	1
2	Asia after the Cold War: Back to the Future ENYU ZHANG, YITAN LI AND PATRICK JAMES	14
3	Military Threats to Security HYUN JI RIM	33
4	Terrorists Threats to Security MARIA ORTUOSTE AND CAMERON OLSON	51
5	Economic Threats to Security SHU FUKUYA AND ZONGYUAN ZOE LIU	70
6	Criminal Threats to Security JOEL R. CAMPBELL	87
7	Environmental Threats to Security LUBA LEVIN-BANCHIK	104
8	Health Threats to Security JEREMY YOUDE	131
9	Towards Regional Security Cooperation JANICKE STRAMER-SMITH	146

Index	164

Illustrations

Figures

2.1	Map of Asia	18
2.2	A Systemist Graphic Summary	29
3.1	The Republic of China (Taiwan)	43
7.1.	KOF Globalization Score for Countries in Asia	108
7.2	Total greenhouse gas emissions by countries in Asia in 2020	110
7.3	The Share of Most Polluting Countries in Asia Compared with the Rest of the Region	111
7.4	The Share of Most Polluting Countries in the Asia Compared with the Rest of the World	112
7.5	Changes in globalization and greenhouse gas emissions in Asia, from 1990 to 2020	113
7.6	Relationship between globalization and greenhouse gas emissions in Asia 1990	114
7.7	Relationship between globalization and greenhouse gas emissions in Asia 2020	114
7.8	Countries with highest emmission CO2 change from 1990 to 2020	115

Table

2.1	Systemist Notation	16

Acronyms

A2AD	Anti Access Area Denial
AMF	Asian Monetary Fund
APEC	Asia-Pacific Economic Cooperation
ARF	ASEAN Regional Forum
ASEAN	Association of Southeast Asian Nations
ASEAN+3	ASEAN plus China, Japan, South Korea
ASEAN+6	ASEAN plus Australia, China, India, Japan, South Korea, New Zealand
ASG	Abu Sayyaf Group
BARMM	Bangsamoro Autonomous Region in Muslim Mindanao
BIFF	Bangsamoro Islamic Freedom Fighters
BKI	Babbar Khalsa International
BRICS	Brazil, Russia, India, China, South Africa
CBRNE	Chemical, biological, radioactive, nuclear, and explosive weapons
CEPEA	Comprehensive Economic Partnership for East Asia
Counterforce	Chinese term for A2AD
CPI	Maoist Communist Party of India
CPTPP	Comprehensive and Progressive Agreement for Trans-Pacific Partnership
EAEC	East Asian Economic Caucus
EAFTA	East Asia Free Trade Agreement
EAS	East Asia Summit
FATA	Federally Administered Tribal Areas
FATF	Financial Action Task Force
FTA	Free Trade Agreement
FTAAP	Free Trade Area of the Asia-Pacific
GATT	General Agreement on Tariffs and Trade
GWoT	Global War on Terror
IHR	International Health Regulations
IPEF	Indo-Pacific Economic Framework
ISA	Internal Security Act
ISK	Islamic State-Khorasan Province

JVP	Jantha Vimukthi Peramuna
LeT	Lashkar-e-Taiba
LTTE	Liberation Tigers of Tamil Eelam
MERS	Middle Eastern Respiratory Syndrome
MFC	Military-Civil Fusion
MILF	Moro Islamic Liberation Front
NATO	North Atlantic Treaty Organization
NLD	National League for Democracy
NPA	New People's Army
NPT	Nuclear Non-Proliferation Treaty
NSCN-IM	Nationalist Socialist Council of Nagaland-Isak-Muivah
NTS	Non-Traditional Security
OPM	Free Papua Movement
PSI	Proliferation Security Initiative
Quad	Quadrilateral Security Dialogue
RCEP	Regional Comprehensive Economic Partnership
SARS	Severe Acute Respiratory Syndrome
SEARCCT	Southeast Asian Regional Center for Counter-Terrorism
SEATO	Southeast Asian Treaty Organization
TAC	ASEAN Treaty of Amity and Cooperation
TCO	Transnational Criminal Organization
TECRO	Taipei Economic and Cultural Representative Office in the United States
TPP	Trans-Pacific Partnership Agreement
TRA	Taiwan Relations Act
USTR	U.S. Trade Representative
WMDs	Weapons of Mass Destruction

Contributors

Joel Campbell – Associate Professor of Political Science at Troy University Global Campus Program (USA). He has published extensively on the politics and political economy of Northeast Asia, along with technology policy, international security, and film and politics. His recent publications include *The Politics and International Relations of Fantasy Films and Television: To Win or Die* (2023), *Politics Go to the Movies: International Relations and Politics in Genre Films and Television* (2022) and is currently writing a book on the politics and international relations of the *Second Golden Age of Television*, to be published in 2024. He earned his PhD in Political Science at Miami University (Ohio).

Shu Fukuya – Deputy Director of the Strategic Research Department at the Japan Bank for International Cooperation (Japan). His research areas of focus include international political economy, global financial markets, and development finance. He holds a Doctorate degree in International Affairs from Johns Hopkins SAIS.

Lui Hebron – Faculty Affairs Specialist at the California State University, (USA). His research focuses on the areas of political economy (Globalization), international relations (ethnicity, conflict and war, security studies), and Asian studies (Pacific Rim, China). His publications include three co-authored books, two co-edited volumes, and numerous articles and book chapters. He holds a PhD in Political Science from Florida State University.

Patrick James – Dean's Professor of International Relations at the University of Southern California (USA). He is the author or editor of over 30 books and more than 170 articles and book chapters. He is the Editor-in-Chief of the Oxford Bibliographies in International Relations and also served a five-year term as Editor of International Studies Quarterly. He earned a PhD in Political Science from the University of Maryland, College Park.

Luba Levin-Banchik – Associate Professor in the Department of Political Science at California State University, San Bernardino (USA). Her expertise is in the fields of global and national security, international crises, conflict processes, geopolitics, and international affairs broadly defined. Her research has been published in *Conflict Management and Peace Science*, PS: Political Science and Politics, *Terrorism and Political Violence, Studies in Conflict and Terrorism, Media, War & Conflict*, and *Journal of Political Science Education*. She is a co-author of World Politics Simulations in a Global Information Age (2015). She is an associate editor of *CSU Global Journal*, which aims to promote the scholarship and study of globalization. She earned a PhD from the Department of Political Studies at Bar Ilan University in Israel.

Yitan Li – Professor and Chair of Political Science and Director of Asian Studies at Seattle University (USA). His research focuses on international relations, foreign policy analysis, international conflict and security, international political economy, comparative politics, and Chinese and East Asian politics. He has published in *Applied Economics, Asian Affairs, Asian Perspective, Canadian Journal of Political Science, Foreign Policy Analysis, Fudan Journal of the Humanities and Social Sciences, International Studies Perspectives, Journal of Chinese Political Science, Journal of Contemporary China, Journal of East Asian Studies, Journal of Territorial and Maritime Studies, Nationalism and Ethnic Politics*, and *Political Research Quarterly*. His recent book (co-authored with Scott Gartner, Chin-Hao Huang and Patrick James) is entitled: *Identity in the Shadow of a Giant: How the Rise of China is Changing Taiwan*. He is currently serving as the editor of the *Journal of Chinese Political Science*. He holds a PhD in Politics and International Relations from the University of Southern California.

Zongyuan Zoe Liu – Maurice R. Greenberg fellow for China studies at the Council on Foreign Relations (USA). Her work focuses on international political economy, global financial markets, and energy and climate change policy. Her regional expertise is in East Asia, specifically China and Japan, and the Middle East, with a focus on Gulf Cooperation Council countries. She is the author of *Can BRICS De-dollarize the Global Financial System?* (2022) and *Sovereign Funds: How the Communist Party of China Finances its Global Ambitions* (2023). She earned a PhD in Politics and International Relations from the University of Southern California.

Maria Ortuoste – Professor of Political Science at the California State University, East Bay (USA). Her research focuses on international relations of the Indo-Pacific, alliances, non-traditional security, and state-building. her most recent publications include "Philippines in the South China Sea" Co-authored with Zenel Garcia. In *The South China Sea: Contemporary Security Dynamics, Part III – Contemporary National Interests, Objectives and Strategies*, edited by Howard M. Hensel and Amit Gupta. Routledge; and *Maritime Space and Security in the Building of Southeast Asian States* (Routledge). She received her PhD in Political Science from Arizona State University.

Cameron Olson – Graduate Researcher at the California State University, Fullerton (USA). His areas of research include, post-colonial development, international security, public policy, economic development, and 20th century history. He is a Masters student at CSU Fullerton.

Hyun Ji Rim – Adjunct Professor at the Johns Hopkins University's School of Advanced International Studies (SAIS) and a Non-Resident Scholar at SAIS's Edwin O. Reischauer Center for East Asian Studies (USA). Dr. Rim is also a Research Associate at University of Missouri – Kansas City and an adjunct lecturer at Kansas State University. She writes extensively on extended deterrence, Indo-Pacific strategy, East Asian security dynamics, emerging technologies, and alliance politics. Her writings have appeared in *Pacific Review, Journal of Indo-Pacific Affairs, Asian Perspective, International Journal of Conflict Management*, and *International Journal of Korean Unification Studies*, among others. She edited and contributed to a forthcoming book: *Indo-Pacific Strategy and Foreign Policy Challenges*. She received her PhD in International Relations from Johns Hopkins University, SAIS.

Janicke Stramer-Smith – Assistant Professor and Director of Political Science at Weber State University (USA). Her research focus is on international security, civil-military relations, labour movements, and political transitions. Her most recent publications include "Securitising the new Egypt: Partisan vs. revolutionary demands" in the *Journal of North African Studies* (April 2020) and "Socio-economic factors and political mobilization in the Maghreb: Lessons from the Arab Spring" in Eds. *Entanglements of Maghreb: Cultural and Political Aspects of a Region in Motion*. Germany: Transcript Verlag (2021). She is currently working on a book project examining link between the military's economic interests and its political behavior in the Greater Middle East. She earned her PhD in Political Science at the University of Nevada, Reno.

Jeremy Youde – Dean of the College of Arts, Humanities, and Social Sciences at the University of Minnesota, Duluth (USA). A specialist in global health politics and global health governance, he is the author of five books, co-editor of two volumes, and author of more than 40 peer-reviewed journal articles. He is also frequently invited to serve as a commentator on global health politics issues for national and international media outlets. He holds a PhD in Political Science with emphases in international relations and comparative politics from the University of Iowa.

Enyu Zhang – Associate Professor of International Studies and Acting Director of Asian Studies at Seattle University (USA). She specializes in international relations, foreign policy analysis, international security, and comparative politics with a focus on East Asia. Her research has been published in reputable academic journals and publishers, including the

Canadian Journal of Political Science, Chinese Political Science Review, Foreign Policy Analysis, Journal of Chinese Political Science, Journal of Territorial and Maritime Studies, Ashgate, Blackwell Publishing, Lexington Books, Routledge, etc. She earned her PhD in Political Science from the University of Missouri, Columbia.

Acknowledgments

I owe a great debt of gratitude to the editorial board at Routledge, who graciously and patiently waited for this project to be completed. My sincere thanks to an amazing team of people including Andrew Leach (Senior Editorial Assistant), Philip Stirups (Senior Production Editor), Ravinder Dhindsa (Copy Editor), TBD (Indexer) who worked on this project.

I would like to thank the anonymous reviewers for their insightful feedback and constructive suggestions in helping to make the chapters that much stronger, theoretically and analytically.

I would like to give a special shout-out to Amy Below (California State University, East Bay), Gigi Gokcek (Dominican University of California), and Jeff Pickering (Kansas State University) for their assistance in helping me to assemble a fine group of scholars to contribute to this volume.

1 Asia Security Today
State of the Field

Lui Hebron

Introduction and Overview

As the title indicates, the topic of this book focuses on Asian security within the context of globalization. It does so by addressing important questions and issues about threats to security such as 1) to what extent has globalization impacted the security of states, societies, groups, and individuals in the Indo-Pacific/Asian-Pacific/East Asian[1] region, 2) how have security threats evolved, and 3) what are prospects for greater security cooperation? The purpose of this volume is to examine the changes that have taken place in international relations (geopolitics) and international political economy (geoeconomics) and to offer a framework to a better understanding of security within a neo-liberal world order guided and driven by globalization. The basic theme of the book is to undertake an expansive and inclusive definition of the challenges to security that goes beyond military threats. Specifically, given the increasingly borderless landscape of the globalized world order, threats to national, regional, and international security need to be examined beyond a strict state-centric perspective and take into account the risks and dangers relating to natural, societal and criminal threats. By acknowledging that contemporary Asian security has become much more complex and complicated, this volume examines the uncertainty and instability that the nation-states of the Indo-Pacific region confront in an era of globalization.

The term "Asian Security" refers to the threats that are indigenous (rooted in local security conditions and dynamics) to the South, Southeast, and East Asian sub-regions as well as a sub-category of international security studies. The Asian-Pacific regional focus on East Asia (China, Japan, Korea, Mongolia, Taiwan), Southeast Asia (Brunei, Cambodia, Indonesia, Laos, Malaysia, Myanmar/Burma, Philippines, Singapore, Thailand, Timor-Leste, Vietnam) and South Asia (Bangladesh, Bhutan, India, Nepal, Pakistan, Sri Lanka) is at once somewhat subjective and arbitrary as well as historically grounded based on common political perceptions and popular usage. These three sub-regions encompass the full spectrum of nation-state evolution politically (authoritarian to democratic regimes), economically (underdeveloped/developing/emerging to advanced industrial

DOI: 10.4324/9781003473206-1

states), militarily (conventional to nuclear powers), and culturally (multitude of ethnic, linguistic, racial, and religious diversity). Western Asia (normally analyzed and grouped with Middle Eastern studies) and Central Asia (the "-stans" and usually associated former Soviet Republics) are not examined in this volume. It should be noted that Australia, New Zealand, Canada, Chile, Mexico, and Peru are included in the analysis of some chapters by virtue of their participation in the various economic and trade communities centered in the Asian-Pacific region.

Asia is the central focus for a number of reasons. First, with its highly educated and predominately young population, unprecedented economic growth and development, prolific industrial output, energetic technological prowess, creative engineering marvels, and growing military capabilities, Asia has emerged as a legitimate power center – joining the US/North America and Europe in guiding regional and global political/military and economic relations. Indeed, if the nation-states of the region are able to prevail over their historical enmity and incessant grievances and can resolve their differences by focusing on their shared values and working together for the common and greater good, the Indo-Pacific is poised to become a formidable third axis of geopolitical/geoeconomic power and influence in numerous issue areas such as, for example, decreasing political–military conflicts though enhanced transparencies/mutual openness and increasing economic cooperation by means of a "collaborative culture" that overrides narrowly defined national self-interests.

Second, the Asian-Pacific is one of the most volatile regions in terms of 1) natural threats – environmental issues (climate change/catastrophe, global warming, rising sea levels, degradation/pollution, ecosystem collapse, illegal hunting, fishing, logging, resource access and depletion); 2) societal threats – economic uncertainty/instability (sustainable development, social justice, income gap, poverty, winners vs. losers), health and safety concerns (infectious diseases/HIV-AIDS,[2] epidemic/SARS,[3] pandemic/COVID[4]), cultural conflicts (ethnic, racial, and religious disputes, irredentism, revanchism, separatist and secession movements), and terrorism (deliberate and indiscriminate violence towards civilians by non-state actors disgruntled about their current state of affairs operating within and across national boundaries); and 3) criminal threats – transnational organized crime (trafficking of counterfeit goods, illegal drugs, weapons, and humans, sea piracy) in addition to 4) traditional security threats – political/military discord (military and strategic conflicts, territorial antagonism, arms buildup, domestic insurgencies, and militarized interstate disputes).

Lastly, the region is also on the brink to becoming the primary arena for a new regional and global strategic (geopolitical and geoeconomic) competition between China and the US/West stemming from the Peoples Republic's dramatic rise in its economic, political, and military power and influence. Evidence of this potential return to a bipolar world order and a new Cold War can be seen by China's policies and actions – economically (China's Belt and Road Initiative,[5] Asian Infrastructure Investment Bank,[6] Beijing Consensus[7]), politically (China Threat Theory[8]), militarily (China's build up of its Blue-Water Navy[9]), and culturally (China's Confucius Institutes[10]) – that seeks to refashion the international order more in alignment with its interests, objectives, and goals (Hebron, 2011, 2012). Beijing's imperialistic ambitions pose a direct challenge to the current global order established and dominated by the United States. China has, in no uncertain terms, made clear its dissatisfaction with and intention to challenge US hegemony on the regional and global stage (de Graaff et al., 2020).

The chapter is organized as follows: It begins with a reappraisal of the traditional conception of security located within its conventional state-centric, military power framework of analysis. This traditional approach tends to focus myopically on external and internal military-based concerns and thereby overlooks transnational non-military threats. Next, taking into account the changing complexion of international relations/international political-economic affairs as driven by globalization, a more comprehensive conception of security that takes into account the insecurities generated from the proliferation of these threats by drawing on theoretical insights beyond realist-based security studies is presented. This expanded and inclusive perspective of security that is mindful of the impact of non-traditional, transnational threats to human and global security would be especially useful in developing a truly accurate definition of security. After establishing the theoretical orientation for analysis, the chapter surveys the various military and non-military threats to international, regional, and national security. The study concludes with an exploration of the potential for greater regional security cooperation as well as a brief overview of the chapters.

Theoretical Foundations

Drawing on theoretical insights from International Relations (geopolitics), International Political Economy (geo-economics), and Globalization (integration, interdependence, connectivity, openness), this chapter makes a case for a more inclusive, expansive and thereby realistic and accurate conceptualization of national security defined as ensuring a high probability of achieving the primary goal of a country's leadership in securing the territorial integrity of the state as well as providing for the safety of its denizens (citizens, foreign nationals, visitors). In so doing, it supports calls for a comprehensive and eclectic approach to conceptualizing national security, a methodological stand that acknowledges that a range of understandings, concerns, and responses to the problem of national security exist depending on the historical, political, and social contexts of states and their societies as well as the strategic environment in which they find themselves.

In today's contemporary globalizing world, security threats can no longer be viewed and examined as primarily of a military nature because dangers and risks have become much more complex due to the heightened openness, greater interconnection, increased interdependence, and enhanced integration of the relations between and among nation-states, society, groups, and individuals (Ullman, 1983; Matthews, 1989; Tickner, 1995; Baldwin, 1997; Buzan et al., 1998). This state of affairs in which many more factors now constitute potential dangers to security warrants the need to examine the expanded spectrum of threats in a multidimensional manner – i.e., its traditional, non-traditional, external, internal, national, regional, international, human, and global conceptions and dimensions.

Traditional Security Threats

The number one responsibility of a country's leadership is its national security. In its most basic form, national security revolves around the defense of a nation-state's territorial borders, the preservation of its independence, and the maintenance of its sovereignty as well as the physical protection and economic well-being of its population (Hebron, 2022). This prime directive assigned to a regime to provide for the fundamental conditions of a nation-state's secure existence holds true irrespective of a country's political system (totalitarian, authoritarian, oligarchy, theocracy, monarchy, democracy), economic structure (Communist, Socialist, Planned, Capitalist/Market, Autarchy), growth and development stage (emerging, advanced industrial) or societal make-up (cultural, ethnic, linguistic, racial, religious tribal identities).

According to the traditional, realist/neorealist, nationalist, state-centric view of security, military, "hard power," threats emanating from another country is one of the greatest dangers facing all states because this external intrusion threatens a state's independence and endangers its internal order (Waltz, 1979; Mearsheimer, 2001; Russett and O'Neal, 2001). This external threat of violence is ever present due to the anarchic configuration of international relations (Buzan et al., 1993). The absence of a central authority ("global government") to regulate or control the behavior of states entails that each member of the community of states must constantly be vigilant and responsible for its own security. This realpolitik framework of security has a very narrow conception of threat focused mainly on militarized interstate disputes and as such does not take into account non-military, "soft power" (Nye, 1990, 2008, 2017), sources of threats or what is to be protected and defended beyond the territorial state.

In the context of Asian security, though the threat of interstate conflicts and wars have lessened due to both strong military deterrence (via national defense capabilities, balance-of-power, alliances, and collective security) as well as powerful economic disincentives (financial and trade interdependence via globalization), the possibility of an militarized interstate dispute breaking out remains a very real possibility. Potential threats of war include: 1) the People's Republic of China and the Republic of China deadlocked dispute regarding the status of Taiwan; 2) China's and India's long-standing tension due to lingering disputed territory along their shared border; 3) India's and Pakistan's ethno-religious military tension and periodic border skirmishes over Kashmir; 4) the unresolved war (stalemate) between the two Koreas operating under a precarious armistice; 5) North Korea's unpredictable militarism and Pyongyang's rouge nuclear weapons program; 6) China's and Japan's sovereignty claims over the Senkaku (Diaoyu in Chinese) Islands in the East China Sea; 7) maritime disputes involving China, Taiwan, Brunei, Malaysia, the Philippines, and Vietnam over conflicting borders and island ownership claims in the South China Sea; and 8) the economic and political-military rise of China as a regional and global power ,which poses as a direct challenge to the United States' preeminent great power position with the potential of another Cold War. Of particular significance is the potential for some these border tensions to escalate into a nuclear confrontation.

Traditional notions of security must also contend with internal disturbances such as public disobedience, domestic strife and political instability that threatens the disintegration of the state or the overthrow of the regime from within. In an ironic twist, the relative "peace" of the bipolar Cold War period was shattered by the resurgence of ethnic and religious driven militarized conflicts of the multipolar world order that followed. These threats may be brought about by competing extremist ideologies, ethnic conflict, religious rivalry, social and cultural chaos, economic grievances, civilian–military power struggle or ineffective governance. Such threats to internal peace and order can involve violence by non-state actors and takes the form of coups, civil wars, armed insurgencies, terrorism, irredentism/revanchism, and separatist or secessionist movements aimed at either revolt (change in political leadership) or revolution (territorial ambitions for a change to the status quo – e.g., splitting off a part of the existing state or annexation of territory from a neighboring state to establish their own independent, sovereignty nation-state).

In the Asian security theatre, there are numerous internally driven threats: 1) China's revanchist claims on Taiwan; 2) ethno-religious strife in the Chinese regions of Xinjiang and Tibet; 3) Christian-Muslim clashes in the Indonesian regions of Aceh, Ambon, Irian Jaya, the Maluku Islands as well as Sunni-Shiite conflict in Riau and East Java; 4) Islamic-separatist terrorist movement demanding independence for the Moro Muslims in the Philippine island of Mindanao; 5) Muslim extremist, militant groups in Malaysia (Kumpulan Mujahideen) and Indonesia (Jemaah Islamiah) want to establish a pan-regional Islamic state in Southeast Asia that encompasses Malaysia, Indonesia, and the southern parts of Thailand and the Philippines; 6) over 50 ethnic armies (e.g., Karens, Kachins, Shans) plus two non-indigenous religious groups (Rohingya and Muslims) are fighting for greater autonomy, self-determination or equal rights in Mynamar (Burma); 7) irredentist insurgent Muslims in Kashmir, India; 8) and disaffected Indian Tamils in Sri Lanka due to systematic discrimination and repression.

Non-traditional (Contemporary) Security Threats

In the current neoliberal-based world order, three developments related to the globalizing process have transpired, which has fundamentally altered the state of affairs of national, regional, and international security. First, since globalization is predominantly an economically driven process, geoeconomics has been elevated and become geopolitics' "co-pilots" as the dual orientations and main analytical tools of policymakers (Luttwak, 1990). Many security scholars of globalization would agree that one of the benefits of a globalized world order is its deterrence property due to the economic interdependence between and among nation-states. The greater the depth and breadth of economic connections between states, the greater the disincentive to engage in militarized interstate disputes. Second, though globalization is mainly focused and driven by the economic component of the process, the underlying leitmotif of its proceedings is the "construction" of a "borderless" world. Any conception of security that does not take into consideration the prevailing transnational structural condition of globalization would be counter to the realities of contemporary life. Third, globalization has witnessed the rise in power and influence of non-state actors at the international level to the point in which their activities pose a serious threat (direct and indirect) to global stability. The addition of globalization to the security studies discourse has brought forth a paradigm shift that evaluates threats in a more holistic and organic manner by taking into consideration the depth and breadth of the globalizing processes' deepening web of interdependence as well as the expansion of actors and diversification of dangers that challenges and risks world peace. As Dominique Moïsi (2001) succinctly observed: "Globalization in this context means complexity, interaction and simultaneity."

Non-traditional notions of security have clearly emerged as a response to the changing milieu of world politics (Caballero-Anthony et al., 2006; Caballero-Anthony, 2016; Martel, 2017; Gong and Li, 2021). With the end of the Cold War and subsequent "resumption" of globalization, the vast majority of risks and dangers to national and international security have come not from external and internal threats of violence (insurgences, civil and interstate wars), but rather from a wider spectrum of increasingly more prominent non-military hazards stemming from political, economic, social, cultural, health, and environmental challenges and crises that endanger human life. As a consequence, a situation in one issue area has the potential to seriously impact circumstances in other areas due to the interconnected nature of the global environment. In a similar manner, the focus on security concerns has been redefined to become more people-centered (focused on the physical, economic, mental, emotional, and cultural well-being of individuals, groups, and society) rather than directed primarily on the protection of the state (consequences for a state's territorial integrity and sovereignty). This human condition ("civil") approach to security incorporates shielding people from significant and inescapable crises, misfortune, suffering and anxiety in addition to traditional military factors.

This more comprehensive, liberalist/internationalist perspective of security also takes into account the impact of a globalizing world and the accompanying transnational threats. The key distinguishing characteristic of globalization relevant to security include, 1) the free flow of goods, services, information, technology, and people between and among states; 2) the growing irrelevance of borders due to porous frontiers; 3) the breakdown of the distinction between domestic and foreign affairs; and 4) forces beyond the capacity of an individual state to deal with solely. This "transparency" of state borders has several implications and consequences. First, the benefits of free trade, open markets, integrated communications networks, and widely diffused and easily accessible technologies providing greater and cheaper consumer goods, services, and global travel can also be used by international drug dealers, arms merchants, and human traffickers for nefarious purposes – e.g., the unlawful production and world-wide distribution of narcotics, the illicit manufacture and global sale of weapons, and the smuggling of illegal immigrants across state borders – and in the process giving disgruntled and anti-status quo individuals and groups the power to disrupt global affairs. Second, the globalizing process challenges the traditional paradigm of strict state control of borders as no longer an accurate mode of thinking about security because threats can quickly and easily spread from one country to another without regard to prescribed boundaries. Third, this "open" state of relations between and among countries has the potential to escalate (spillover) a national security threat into an international security calamity. In sum, globalization's borderless world order means that security threats and destructive forces – such as international terrorism, interstate criminal organizations, trade wars, cultural clashes, global warming, and world-wide epidemics and pandemics – can now more easily transcend national boundaries.

Let's briefly examine these threats more closely. Natural and man-made threats (environmental issues and disasters) include rising greenhouse gas emissions from the region's dependence on fossil fuels (coal, crude oil, and natural gas) due to the industrialization of emerging markets throughout the Indo-Pacific. Five of the top 10 of the world's biggest carbon polluters are in Asia - China (1st), India (3rd), and Indonesia (9th) along with Japan (5th) and South Korea (10th) (Statista.com, 2023).[11] The Asia Pacific is "one of the world's most disaster prone and most heavily climate change-affected regions" (World Bank, 2023). Overfishing is another bone of contention between neighboring states with disputes between China, Japan, and Korea in the East China Sea (SIPRI, 2023) and among China, Indonesia, Malaysia, the Philippines, and Vietnam in the South China Sea (CFR, 2023). Finally, water insecurity due to population growth, urbanization, agricultural consumption, and pollution poses an imminent threat and crisis for the countries and peoples of the Indo-Pacific region with "approximately 500 million individuals still lack access to basic water supplies in Asia and the Pacific, while 1.14 billion lack access to basic sanitation" (Savoy and Bryja, 2023). Societal threats encompasses – economic problems (poverty,[12] wealth gap[13]), health concerns (infectious diseases/HIV-AIDs, epidemic/SARs, pandemic/COVID), cultural conflicts (ethnic and religious disputes, irredentism, revanchism, separatist and secession movements), and terrorism. Criminal threats (transnational organized crime syndicates) include the Chinese Triads and Japanese Yakuza as well as smaller "mafia" groups from

North and South Korea, Laos, the Philippines, Taiwan, Thailand, and Vietnam. These criminal organizations constitute a security threat due to the extreme violence in which they conduct their illegal activities that challenges and undermines state authority and non-recognition of national boundaries.

Given the greater stress on the human condition ("protection of people") within countries and elevated impact of globalization, non-traditional threats to security have been labeled as "Human Security" (Acharya, 2001) and/or "Global Security." The key point and commonality that binds these two categories is the understanding that in a globalizing world, security is best defined in terms of personal security with people at the center of analysis and that individual, group, national, and regional insecurity must be addressed not as isolated, mutually exclusive problems, but as part and parcel of an interdependent global village since self-interest and mutual interests have become one and the same. Hence, the transnational scope of threats requires an integrated, international response across borders between and among nation-states.

Human security comprises of seven sub-components of common concern to humankind and most relevant threats to the average person – personal (physical) security, economic security, health security, food security, community security, political security, and environmental security – according to the United Nations Development Program's 1994 Human Development Report (UNDP, 1994). The ascension of Global Security was a response to the growing world-wide natural threats (e.g., global warming) societal threats (e.g., transnational epidemics/pandemics), and criminal threats (e.g., international organized crime networks) to both state and society that transcend state boundaries and therefore requires a concerted global effort to address. These topic areas are once an indication of the stability of the state system as well the continuing challenges to human security that needs international and transnational solutions.

Conclusion: Regional Security Amid a Changing Security Environment

The new geopolitical/geoeconomic/globalization dynamics have three implications for security cooperation in the Indo-Pacific region. First, traditional security challenges and risks will always be of utmost concern to a nation-state's leadership and continue to threaten countries that are politically and economically weak and/or governed by incompetent or corrupt governments who lose control over the population and thereby are susceptible to disruption. Second, the rise of a more diverse, wider range of non-traditional hazards not only pose dangers to societies and creates challenges that undermine effective governance around the region, but these threats pose unprecedented challenges for the Asian-Pacific community of nation-states in an increasingly open, interconnected, interdependent world order. Third, the combination of threats and instability that arise from the evolving world order have increasingly become such a central disruptive force to a country's peace and stability that every responsible government must take into account as part of their security framework and policymaking.

With military and economic power no longer sufficient to guarantee the security of an individual state due to the transnational nature of global affairs, regional and international cooperation will clearly be required to withstand and deal with many of these traditional and non-traditional security threats. Depending on the nature of the threat as well as the capability, willingness, and commitment of a country to respond either nationally or internationally, these cooperative efforts may be conducted bilaterally, regionally, or globally.

By taking a globally oriented and expanded vision of Asian security, this volume would contribute to both the breadth and depth of international and regional security studies. Specifically, it examines the trends and transformations currently underway in the Asian region within the context of the globalizing world order. Moreover, this book cast a more inclusive and expansive perspective by examining the non-traditional aspects of security.

Scope and Structure of Book

The scholarships undertaken in this book will cover both the traditional (military/political) as well as the non-traditional/contemporary (human and global) security issues. Security for the Asian-Pacific region will be examined and organized both in an issue-specific approach and in country-specific/regional case study form.

This in-depth examination of Asian security begins with a discussion on post-Cold War Asia by Zhang, Li, and James. Chapter 2 provides an overview of political, economic, geographical, and socio-cultural developments since the end of the Cold War in 1991. Taking as its point of departure the understanding that Asia after the Cold War is living through an era of possibly unparalleled uncertainty, the chapter proceeds as follows: First, the chapter will establish the guiding theoretical framework of systemism, which emphasizes a graphic approach toward communication. Second, the strategic terrain and historical context of the security architecture of Asia will be identified. Drawing from the key points in these two sections, the third section will zoom in on Asian security after the Cold War. Put simply, there is a new Cold War in the era of deglobalization. Sino-US rivalry, the principal source of rising tensions, could lead to armed conflict in the near future if not managed well. Section four will address future prospects for Asian security. The fifth and final section, which includes a systemist graphic summary, will sum up what has been accomplished in this chapter.

Rim tackles the subject of traditional military threats. Chapter 3 contends that the rise of Chinese military power, especially in the security realm, is a concerning aspect of the strategic competition in the Indo-Pacific region. Increasingly more complex geopolitical calculations of states are leading stronger emphasis on military power in the theatre. On the backdrop of intensifying military buildup and modernization in the theatre, this chapter explores the role of military power and its relations to states' grand strategy. Through examining key issue areas of arms race, weapons proliferation, and security dilemma as well as a case study of the cross-strait crisis, it draws implications for power alignment in East Asia, and the potential role of multilateral regional defense for Southeast Asia.

Non-state political threats are scrutinized by Ortuoste and Olsen. Chapter 4 situates terrorism within the political violence that is used to build Westphalian states. It shows the different trajectories of terrorism in South and Southeast Asia, later converging with the creation of al Qaeda. The different reasons for militancy – ethno-nationalism, secular or religious ideological, among others – persist due to structural conditions that also underpin the motivations for terrorism. The historical and comparative approach in this chapter also examines the lessons from anti-terrorist measures such as the Global War on Terror, domestic laws, and joint operations in the face of resilient militant groups.

Liu and Fukuya explore economic threats. Chapter 5 focuses on three main areas of economic security for the Asian region: 1) After the end of the Cold War, East Asia witnessed the rise of regionalism, with the Asia-Pacific Economic Cooperation (APEC) forum functioning as a platform for cooperation among diverse nations, including China, Japan, ASEAN members, the United States, and Russia. APEC's goal is to navigate the complexity of extensive multilateralism in a region characterized by differences in political systems and economic disparities. 2) Economies in East Asia often deviate from strict market capitalism, and establishing a regional security community in East Asia requires the development of social institutions and recognition of shared geographic and ecological characteristics. However, challenges arise from differing priorities among major East Asian countries like Japan and China. 3) Importantly, changes in U.S. trade policies and priorities in East Asia over the past 30 years, influenced by factors such as China's rise and regional dynamics, have led to shifts in regional alliances and agreements. The regional order in East Asia is at a significant turning point, with the potential for transition and evolving dynamics.

Transnational criminal threats is investigated by Campbell. Chapter 6 examines how organized crime has become a major threat to security of Asian countries. Globalization, the COVID-19 epidemic, and the internationalization of the Chinese underworld have contributed to regionalization of local criminal organizations and transnational organized crime. Much of the recent increase in organized crime is centered on poorer Asian countries: Cambodia, Laos, and especially Burma/Myanmar. The lack of effective central governance and franchising of criminal activities means that several criminal enclaves have been set up. Crimes involving illegal sales of methamphetamines, weapons, rare animals, or animal products, along with human trafficking and maritime piracy (in the island states) have greatly increased, and governments have limited resources with which to attack criminal organizations. Underlying it all is rampant corruption in Southeast Asia. To take on organized crime more effectively, Asian governments need both enhanced policing and better cooperation across borders. This analysis uses constructivist and other IR theory to explain the comeback of Asian organized crime.

Levin-Banchik analyses how environmental threats affect all people and nation-states. The leaders of Asian countries commonly describe it as the gravest, even existential, threat. Chapter 7 probes this emerging and urgent threat to Asian security in two ways. The first part of the chapter provides a theoretical framework for the discussion of environmental threats in Asia, surveys existing research on the topic, and analyzes data on the links between globalization and the environment in the region. The second part of the chapter provides a detailed discussion of a sample of three environmental threats. In particular, it discusses food and water security in the regional context and examines the phenomena of rising sea-level to illustrate how slow-onset events associated with climate change affect various aspects of security in Asia. The chapter concludes with a discussion of prospects for managing and containing regional environmental threats in the increasingly globalized world.

The various health threats are examined by Youde. Chapter 8 posits that global health and disease, security, and globalization are inextricably interconnected in both positive and negative ways, and this is particularly true in Asia. The ease and speed with which people and goods can cross borders create deep relationships throughout the region, but ill health can also use these same connections to spread rapidly. This chapter demonstrates the interplay between health, security, and globalization in Asia by first examining the concepts of health security and the securitization of health. It then presents three brief case studies of SARS, non-communicable diseases, and COVID-19 to examine the successes and failures of individual governments and regional organizations to address health challenges. In particular, the case studies illustrate the ongoing collaborations and challenges faced by governments throughout Asia as they attempt to put health security into practice. The concluding section discusses the future of health security in Asia and how states within the region might address these ongoing challenges in the future.

Stramer-Smith appraisal of the potential for greater regional security cooperation closes the volume. Chapter 9 begins with an examination of the evolution of security cooperation in the Asia-Pacific region, with a focus on the post-Cold War security challenges both traditional and non-traditional security (NTS). It argues the "Asian way" of informality, consultation, and non-interference has enjoyed limited success. While there have been fewer military confrontations between regional powers, the "Asian way" delimits the Asian states' ability to meet future security challenges. The second part of the chapter consists of a case study of the ASEAN Regional Forum (ARF) and the Asian Pacific Economic Cooperation (APEC). While ARF and APEC are not designed to facilitate ambitious security cooperation, APEC, with its focus on economic security, is better situated to deal with an expanded set of security challenges than ARF, with its focus on political issues. The concluding section discusses security challenges facing the region with the inevitable rise of China in this age of globalization and whether the existing network of multilateral security cooperation is robust enough to create pathways for peace and cooperation.

Notes

1 The terms – Indo-Pacific, Asian-Pacific, and East Asian – will be used interchangeably throughout the volume.
2 HIV: Human Immunodeficiency Virus; AIDS: Acquired Immunodeciency Syndrome.
3 SARS: Severe Acute Respiratory Syndrome.
4 COVID: Coronavirus.
5 Belt and Road Initiative (BRI): Beijing's multibillion dollar infrastructure project expand China's global political-economic power and influence by connecting Asia, Africa, and Europe (21st Century Silk Road).
6 Asian Infrastructure Investment Bank (AIIB): A multilateral development bank launched by China as an alternative (potential rival) to the World Bank and the International Monetary Fund.
7 Beijing Consensus: An alternative to the Washington Consensus as a growth and development model.
8 China Threat Theory: Fear, anxiety, and uncertainty brought about by the rise of China's economic and military power and influence.
9 Blue-Water Navy: China has built the largest naval force in the world giving it the capability to project its power and protect its interest on a global scale.
10 Confucius Institutes: China funded language schools located throughout the world to promote Chinese language and culture.
11 The most updated data is from 2021.
12 "Asia's Poor Grew by 68 Million People After Pandemic, Report Says" *Al Jazeera* August 24, 2023.
13 Cambodia ($1,826), Laos ($1,866), Myanmar ($1,372), Nepal ($1,338), North Korea ($642), Pakistan ($1,416), Timor-Leste ($1,487) are the poorest countries in Asia by GDP (PPP) and GNI per capita (World Population Review, 2023).

References

Acharya, Amitav. 2001. "Human Security: East versus West." *International Journal* 56 (3): 442–460.
Al Jazeera. 2023. "Asia's Poor Grew by 68 Million People After Pandemic, Report Says." *Al Jazeera*, August 24, 2023. https://www.aljazeera.com/economy/2023/8/24/asias-poor-grew-by-68-million-people-after-pandemic-report-says
Baldwin, David A. 1997. "The Concept of Security." *Review of International Studies* 23: 5–26.
Buzan, Barry, Charles Jones and Richard Little. 1993. *The Logic of Anarchy: Neorealism to Structural Realism*. New York: Columbia University Press.
Buzan, Barry, Ole Wæver, and Jaap de Wilde. 1998. *Security—A New Framework for Analysis*. Boulder, CO: Lynne Rienner.
Caballero-Anthony, Mely, Ralf Emmers, and Amitav Acharya. 2006. *Non-traditional Security in Asia: Dilemmas in Securitization*. Hampshire, UK: Routledge.
Caballero-Anthony, Mely. 2016. "Understanding Non-traditional Security." in Mely Caballero-Anthony ed. *An Introduction to Non-traditional Security Studies: A Transnational Approach*. London: Sage.
CFR. 2023. "Territorial Disputes in the South China Sea" https://www.cfr.org/global-conflict-tracker/conflict/territorial-disputes-south-china-sea.
de Graaff, Nana, Tobias ten Brink and Inderjeet Parmar. 2020. "China's Rise in a Liberal World Order in Transition – Introduction to the FORUM" *Review of International Political Economy* 27 (2): 191–207.

Gong, Lina and Mingjiang Li. 2021. "China–Southeast Asian Nontraditional Security Engagement" *China Review* 21 (4): 1–9.
Hebron, Lui. 2022. "International (Global) Political Economy" in R. Joseph Huddleston, Thomas Jamieson, and Patrick James eds. *Handbook of Research Methods in International Relations.* Cheltenham: Edward Elgar.
Hebron, Lui. 2012. "China and Globalization" in Emilian Kavalski, ed. *Research Companion on Chinese Foreign Policy* London: Ashgate Publishing.
Hebron, Lui. 2011. "The Evolution of China's Grand Strategy with the Developing World" in Carrie Liu Currier and Manochehr Dorraj eds. *China's Energy Relations with the Global South.* New York: Continuum Publishers.
Luttwak, Edward. 1990. "From Geo-politics to Geo-economics" *The National Interest*, Summer: 17–23.
Martel, Stéphanie. 2017. "From Ambiguity to Contestation: Discourse(s) of Nontraditional Security in the ASEAN Community." *Pacific Review* 30 (4): 549–565.
Matthews, Jessica Tuchman. 1989. "Redefining Security," *Foreign Affairs* 68 (2): 162–177.
Mearsheimer, John J. 2001. *The Tragedy of Great Power Politics.* New York: Norton.
Moïsi, Dominique. October 21, 2001. "The West must Temper Strength with Generosity" *Financial Times.*
Nye, Jr., Joseph S. 2017. "Soft Power: The Origins and Political Progress of a Concept" *Palgrave Communications* 3 (1): 1–3.
Nye, Jr., Joseph S. 2008. "Public Diplomacy and Soft Power" *The Annals of the American Academy of Political and Social Science* 616 (1): 94–109.
Nye, Jr., Joseph S. 1990. *Bound to Lead: The Changing Nature of American Power.* Basic Books: New York.
Russett, Bruce, and John R. O'Neal. 2001. *Triangulating Peace: Democracy, Interdependence, and International Organizations.* New York: Norton.
Savoy, Connor M. and Bryja, Thomas. 2023. Challenges and Opportunities in the Indo-Pacific Water Sector. Center for Strategic and International Studies (CSIS). April 18, 2023. https://www.csis.org/analysis/challenges-and-opportunities-indo-pacific-water-sector
SIPRI. 2023. "Promoting crisis management in the East China Sea" https://www.sipri.org/research/conflict-peace-and-security/asia/promoting-crisis-management-east-china-sea.
Statista.com 2023. "The Largest Emitters of CO2 in the World" https://www.statista.com/statistics/271748/the-largest-emitters-of-co2-in-the-world/.
Tickner, J. Ann. 1995. "Re-visioning Security" in Ken Booth and Steve Smith eds. *International Relations Theory Today.* Pennsylvania: Pennsylvania State University Press.
Ullman, Richard H. 1983. "Redefining Security," *International Security*, 8 (1): 123–129.
UNDP. 1994. *Human Development Report 1994 New Dimensions of Human Security.* United Nations, https://hdr.undp.org/content/human-development-report-1994
Waltz, Kenneth N. 1979. *Theory of International Politics.* New York: McGraw-Hill.
World Bank, 2023. Climate Action in East Asia and Pacific Urgent Challenges, Innovative Solutions. https://www.worldbank.org/en/news/immersive-story/2023/11/28/climate-action-in-east-asia-and-pacific
World Population Review. 2023. "GDP Ranked by Country 2023." https://worldpopulationreview.com/countries/by-gdp

2 Asia after the Cold War
Back to the Future

Enyu Zhang, Yitan Li and Patrick James

Introduction and Overview

Asia has risen to the forefront of the global economy in the early post-Cold War period of the 1990s–2000s while descending into the whirlpool of great power competition since the 2010s. Put simply, Asia after the Cold War is living through an era of possibly unparalleled uncertainty, and this chapter will assess its security environment under these challenging conditions.

Up until September 11, 2001, post-Cold War Asia had been both contributing to and benefiting from globalization. Traditional security issues had seemed to increasingly take a backseat to non-traditional ones, such as human security, environmental security, piracy, migration, etc. While 9/11, as it became known, may signal the start of a global trend of anti/de-globalization, it was not until China's rapid rise and Obama's "Pivot to Asia" strategic shift that traditional security was brought back to the center of Asia's power reconfiguration.

This trend toward confrontation has intensified under the Trump and Biden Administrations and accelerated by the COVID-19 pandemic and the ongoing Russo–Ukrainian War. China's continued rise under Xi Jinping's more ambitious and assertive foreign policy and the United States's (US) seeming decline are the main driving forces in Asian security today. Rising nationalism, isolationism, and China's shift to a more authoritarian path coupled with its growing economic and military strengths, also affect how security is re-oriented back to traditional geopolitical struggle. Meanwhile, Asia as a region has not completed its security reconfiguration yet. The lack of legalist and institutional traditions (Henry, 2007; Goh, 2003), whether by choice (Acharya, 1997) or not, and the Sinocentric nature of the regional order, must be taken into consideration.

This chapter contextualizes the traditional and non-traditional security threats in Asia with an overview of political, economic, geographical, and socio-cultural developments since the end of the Cold War in 1991. It also assesses the impact of regionalism as part of globalization and US–China rivalry on East Asian security. The chapter culminates in a systemist graphic that is intended to enhance comprehension and retention of its arguments.

Asia After the Cold War 15

This chapter proceeds in the following sections. First, the chapter will establish the guiding theoretical framework of systemism, which emphasizes a graphic approach toward communication. Second, the strategic terrain and historical context of the security architecture of Asia will be identified. Drawing from the key points in these two sections, the third section will zoom in on Asian security after the Cold War. Put simply, there is a new Cold War in the era of deglobalization. Sino–US rivalry, the principal source of rising tensions, could lead to armed conflict in the near future if not managed well. Section four will address future prospects for Asian security. The fifth and final section, which includes a systemist graphic summary, will sum up what has been accomplished in this chapter.

Systemism

Conveyance of theories in a way that facilitates and elevates the potential for comparison and criticism by means of a visual approach is the primary goal of systemism.[1] As such, implementation of systemism can help the discipline of International Relations (IR)[2] (and other fields) grapple with longstanding challenges in research and teaching and promote both knowledge acquisition and retention. The systemist approach has its roots in the philosophy of inquiry, with its essence best conveyed by the most longstanding exponent, Bunge (1996): a commitment to building theories that are both comprehensive and logically consistent. In doing so, systemism renounces theorizing that occurs exclusively at the level of the system (holism) or its components (reductionism) alone. Systemism transcends both approaches by allowing for linkages operating at macro- and micro-levels as well as interactions between and among them.[3] Designation of a system on the basis of an expected level of content relative to its environment is an essential aspect as well.[4]

Systemism thereby facilitates the comparison of alternative visions regarding cause and effect through an emphasis on clear and comprehensive presentation. Consequently, systemism is both an approach and a method aimed at a diagrammatic exposition of cause and effect to promote clarity and completeness that will benefit any discipline as a whole.

Table 2.1 illustrates the notation used in the process of creating systemist figures. Before any connections are introduced in a diagram, the starting point is the designation of a diagram's system, recognizable visually as its "inner box," and the corresponding environment being the diagram's "outer box," in which the system is embedded. For example, the discipline of "International Relations" can serve as the system, with the "World Beyond" as its environment. Within "International Relations," the macro level (the upper part of the system with variables in all upper-case characters) would be the discipline as a whole, while the micro level (with variables in all lower-case characters found in the lower part of the system) consists of the activities of individual scholars.

Over 800 systemist diagrams now appear in the archive of the Visual International Relations Project (VIRP) (www.visualinternationalrelationsproject.com).

Table 2.1 Systemist Notation

Initial Variable		The start point of a series of relationships.
Generic Variable		A step in the process being depicted.
Divergent Variable		Multiple pathways are created from a single linkage.
Convergent Variable		A single pathway is created from multiple linkages.
Nodal Variable		Multiple pathways are created from multiple linkages.
Co-constitutive Variable		Two variables that are mutually contingent upon each other.
Terminal Variable		The end point of a series of relationships.
Connection Stated in study	⟶	A linkage explicitly made by the author.
Connection Crossing Over		Two separate linkages that do not interact.
Connection Inferred from Study	┈┈⟶	A linkage inferred by the reader but is not made explicit by the author.
Interaction Effect	⟵⟶	Two variables that depend upon the effect of each other.

Source: Created by the Author.

These graphics cover a wide range of publications in terms of subject matter, theoretical perspective, and methods. The VIRP archive is intended to serve multiple purposes in scholarship and teaching.[5] Note also that while IR has been the starting point for the application of systemist graphics, work from any and all academic disciplines can be represented via this approach.

Strategic Terrain and Security Architecture of the Cold War

Strategic Terrain

Asia is the world's largest and most populous continent, home to the world's fastest-growing economies and the center of the modern global supply (and value-added) chain. As Kamphausen (2014: 17) noted, beyond the Himalayan mountain ranges and the Gobi Desert on the vast Asian landmass, the most strategically significant terrain of Asia is "the aggregate of the island chain facing the eastern edge of the Asian landmass and straits that provide access to the Western Pacific and that extend laterally between the marginal seas." Included are Kamchatka, the Kuriles, the Korean Peninsula, the Ryukyus, the strategic maritime chokepoints along the western Pacific, including the Tsugaru Strait, the Ishigaki Strait, the Taiwan Strait, the Luzon Strait, the Strait of Malacca, the Lombok and Sunda Straits, among others. These form the strategic contours of the island chains that have shaped the imagination and security strategies of the great powers in the Asia-Pacific region. According to the US Indo-Pacific Command (n.d.), Asia is one of the world's most diverse regions—culturally, socially, economically, and geopolitically:

> The 36 nations comprising the Asia-Pacific region are home to more than 50% of the world's population... several of the world's largest militaries, and five nations allied with the U.S. through mutual defense treaties. Two of the three largest economies are located in the Asia-Pacific. The [region] includes the most populous nation in the world, the largest democracy, and the largest Muslim-majority nation.... The region is a vital driver of the global economy and includes the world's busiest international sea lanes and nine of the ten largest ports. The Asia-Pacific is also a heavily militarized region, with seven of the world's ten largest standing militaries and five of the world's declared nuclear nations.
>
> Given these conditions, the strategic complexity facing the region is unique.

Furthermore, Asia is a politically contested arena between (illiberal) democracies and authoritarian regimes. It is the world's most concentrated region of post-Soviet communist regimes (China, North Korea, Vietnam, and Laos) while democratization has swept the other parts of Asia. Taken together, it would be difficult to imagine a more complex system to maintain in a way that manages issues, short of escalation to war.

Figure 2.1 is a map of Asia, and it facilitates understanding of the geostrategic importance of the locations just enumerated. The map reveals that the openness and security of sea lanes across Asia are key geographic enablers of economic globalization, setting the foundation for the Asia-centered maritime trade and global supply chain in the age of globalization. And all of that leads, naturally, to a review of Asian security architecture.

Security Architecture

Since the end of World War II, heightened tension and intense competition for influence and control between the capitalist camp led by the US and the communist camp led by the Soviet Union predominantly shaped and drove the security dynamics in Asia. The remnants of the Chinese Civil War

18 *Enyu Zhang et al.*

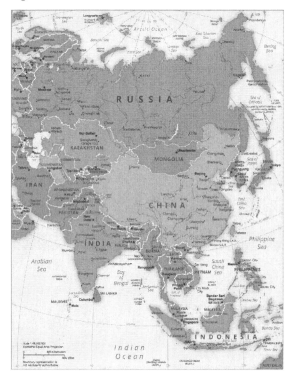

Figure 2.1 Map of Asia
Source: CIA World Factbook.

profoundly shaped the security and economic policies of the US, leading to a divided China between the Chinese mainland led by the People's Republic of China (PRC) and the island of Taiwan led by the Republic of China (ROC). The entire region quickly became the ideological battleground between the two that led to some of the greatest human sufferings in the 20th century. The complex and multifaceted competition for influence in Asia during the Cold War included military and security alliances, arms races, proxy wars, and efforts to gain the support of non-aligned states in the region.

The Cold War had a significant impact on the security and stability of Asia, and several countries were directly involved in hot wars and divided lands along ideological fault lines. The Korean War (1950–1953) was a major war that was fought between the Democratic People's Republic of Korea (DPRK) or North Korea (backed by the Soviet Union and China) and the Republic of Korea (ROK) or South Korea (backed by the US and its allies under the banner of the United Nations). The Vietnam War (1955–1975) was another major war between North Vietnam (backed by the Soviet Union and China) and South Vietnam (backed by the US and its allies). Two major legacies of the Cold War, the DPRK and ROK separation and the Taiwan question, have not been permanently settled, making them major flashpoints of conflict from the perspective of traditional security.

As the Cold War intensified in Europe, Washington established the US-centered security structure in Asia to contain the spread of communism like the falling dominos across the region. On 8 September 1951, right after Japan signed the peace treaty with the Allied countries in San Francisco to normalize relations with its former enemies in World War II, the US started constructing the hub-and-spokes bilateral security structure in Asia, also known as the San Francisco System, with the US as the hub and parallel bilateral security alliances through a series of bilateral security treaties with Japan (1951), South Korea (1953), the Philippines (1951), Thailand (1954), and Taiwan (1954–1979). The US led the founding of a NATO-like multilateral security organization through the Southeast Asian Treaty Organization (SEATO), headquartered in Bangkok, with the Manila Pact signed in September 1954. The SEATO included eight founding members: the US, France, Great Britain, New Zealand, Australia, the Philippines, Thailand, and Pakistan, along with South Vietnam, Cambodia, and Laos added later as observers (Cheng-Chwee, 2022).

The US's security strategy during the Cold War also had an economic counterpart. With Washington's financial backing and technological support, along with the stimulus of wartime production during the Korean War, Japan became the first Asian economy to quickly recover and take off from the ruins of World War II. The ROC in Taiwan also benefited from the Korean War, which, as a by-product, discouraged military takeover by the Chinese Communists due to the American military intervention. Economic assistance from Washington also helped the ROC avoid a recession and set a solid foundation for its later economic takeoff.

Since the 1960s, Asia has been filled with economic dynamism and success. The "flying geese" formation led by Japan's economic miracle propelled the rise of the four "Asian Tigers"—South Korea, Taiwan, Hong Kong, and Singapore from the 1960s to the 1980s. Since the late 1970s, China also has followed suit with its economic reforms and opening. With an unparalleled average of 10% annual growth from 1980 to 2010, China surpassed Japan to become Asia's largest economy and the world's second-largest economy, after the US, in 2010. China's GDP accounts for 47% of Asia's total GDP, followed by Japan, India, South Korea, and Indonesia (Lincoln, 2022). These all drove a fast integration of the majority of Northeast Asian and the Association of Southeast Asian Nations (ASEAN) economies into the global supply chain on an unprecedented scale.

The Cold War also coincided with the waves of decolonization and national independence across Asia. After Japan's defeat in World War II, the people of former colonies in Indonesia, Malaysia, Vietnam, Cambodia, Laos, and Singapore, among others, started fighting for their national independence. Along with communist influence around the region, many of these civil wars also became communist insurrections and proxy wars as part of the Cold War.

Cross-pollination of national independence movements and communist insurrections further complicated the security dynamics in the region.

In addition to these direct military conflicts, the Cold War in Asia also manifested in a series of proxy wars and armed conflicts, including the civil wars in Laos and Cambodia and the communist insurrections in Malaysia and the Philippines. The Cold War also had a profound impact on the internal security and stability of many countries in the region, as governments sought to suppress internal opposition and maintain control over their populations. Indonesia under Sukharno would be just one memorable example.

While the two nuclear-armed superpowers—the US and the Soviet Union—managed to avoid a direct military confrontation in proxy wars in other regions, the Cold War, in fact, was not so "cold" in Asia. US forces directly and actively participated in the Korean and Vietnam Wars. As the leader of the communist camp, the Soviet Union also was directly involved in the two "hot" wars. Soviet leader Joseph Stalin and Chinese leader Mao Zedong played key roles in greenlighting North Korea's decision to invade its southern nemesis in 1950. The Soviet Union discreetly avoided direct participation in the battlefields on the Korean Peninsula, but it provided crucial economic, military, and medical aid to the North Korean leader Kim Il-sung.

Similar dynamics moved the complex situation in Indochina—a subregion caught between anti-colonial, nationalist movements, and the ideological struggle between the two superpowers. Many smaller, post-colonial states—such as the newly independent Cambodia and Laos—were caught in the crosshairs and involuntarily turned into the battlegrounds of those wars. For instance, the multilateral security alliance, SEATO, functioned nothing like NATO and had to be dissolved in 1977, largely due to the end of the Vietnam War (which provided the legal framework for the US military intervention in Vietnam) and the suspicion that the alliance represented a new form of Western colonialism and imperialism in the wave of the Non-Aligned Movement.

After the Soviet leader Joseph Stalin's death, the seemingly monolithic communist bloc became locked in an unparalleled ideological struggle between the USSR and the PRC, commonly known as the Sino-Soviet Split, about which was the revisionist veering away from the orthodox communist path. This development, along with the protracted conflict in Indochina, presented a rare opportunity for strategic realignment and diplomatic rapprochement between the US and China, which Richard Nixon and Mao Zedong seized during the former's historic visit to China in 1972. Japan, Thailand, and the Philippines soon followed suit to normalize relations with the PRC. South Korea, Singapore, Malaysia, and Brunei, among other Asian states, also normalized their relations with the PRC in the late 1980s and early 1990s.

At the end of 1979, the Soviet Union made the strategic mistake of militarily intervening in the Afghan civil war. Moscow tried unsuccessfully to prop up a socialist government to maintain its strategic foothold in Central Asia and South Asia. While the Soviet Union under Mikhail Gorbachev managed to improve relations with both the US and China, events in Afghanistan soon exposed the military weaknesses of the USSR and turned into a decade-long bloody war, contributing to the eventual downfall of the communist bloc.[6]

After the disintegration of the USSR in 1991, US unipolarity and even hyperpower ensued, and high-level confrontation in the international system diminished significantly. While the Korean Peninsula remained divided, the two Koreas managed to improve bilateral relations and simultaneously joined the United Nations on 17 September 1991. Beijing's renewed commitment to market-oriented reforms and further opening to the global economy after the political crisis of 1989 convinced the Clinton Administration about the potential value of constructive engagement, paving the way for China to join the (World Trade Organization) WTO. The US-centered San Francisco System remained the core of Asian security architecture that further consolidated American dominance in the region. North Korea's isolation and nuclear crises in 1994 and 2003 and the growing tensions across the Taiwan Strait—with the PRC's military modernization and the rise of pro-independent parties in the democratized Taiwan—strengthened the US security ties with South Korea and Japan, respectively.[7]

The end of the Cold War has produced significant "peace dividends" in Asia. With democracy flourishing in several countries in the region, it was as if the "End of History" (Fukuyama, 1989) had come. Liberal institutionalism, liberal republicanism, and liberal commercialism, in particular, seemed to be the defining factors of a new security order known among academics as the Kantian triangle of peace (Russett and Oneal, 2001). Asia experienced two decades of unprecedented peace, reconciliation, economic growth, and integration. With growing economic interdependence through trade and investment, traditional military security was sent from the driver's seat to the back seat.

Although the US has maintained its dominance in the regional security architecture and economic development during this period, China and India as rising economic powers, and ASEAN-center regional institutions, have increasingly reshaped, and sometimes challenged, the regional order. This has taken place via their norm entrepreneurship, growing collective economic clout, and ever-closer regional economic networks at the center of the global supply chain.

In Southeast Asia, post-colonial states shelved their cultural and political differences and resorted to regional multilateralism in expanding ASEAN. ASEAN countries have intentionally avoided an EU-style, legally binding approach. Instead, the "ASEAN way" features an adaptive multilateral institutional process of "cooperative security," "open regionalism," "soft regionalism," and "flexible consensus" to build mutual trust and confidence and to manage crises involving traditional and non-traditional issues both within ASEAN and with extra-regional players, such as China, Japan, the US, etc. (Acharya, 1997, 1998; Cheng-Chwee, 2022).

By the early 1990s, however, Asia's economic giant during the Cold War—Japan—fell to decades of economic stagnation. Financial security and demographic crises, such as low birth rates and aging, played a significant role in

Japan's economic decline. Soon after, South Korea and Southeast Asia started to exhibit similar challenges, particularly during the 1997 Asian Financial Crisis. While the upward momentum of China's rise remains the dominant force since then, it has also started to show signs of economic slowdown (e.g., the average annual GDP growth rate fell to 7.7% in the 2010s), particularly while approaching domestic growth saturation. Some of the same demographic and socioeconomic challenges seen in Japan and South Korea have also started to appear in China but on a much larger scale. These long-term challenges coincide with the growing strategic rivalry between the US and China, shifting the regional security dynamics into uncharted territory.

How, then, to sum up the security architecture of Asia in the Cold War? The era molded the political, economic, and cultural relations among the countries of the region in significant and far-reaching ways. Despite the end of the Cold War over three decades ago, the legacy of that period continues to influence the security and stability of the region to this day. To sum up, Soviet-American rivalry played a central role in Asian security throughout the Cold War. Soviet-American détente pivoted the US–China strategic realignment in the last phase of the Cold War. The Soviet disintegration paradoxically pushed US–China relations back to high political tensions and strategic rivalry, despite deeply interdependent economic relations through trade and investment. This set the stage for confrontational politics between the US and China, a new challenger for leadership in the region. An ongoing culture of confrontation, albeit with some elements of cooperation, prevented anything on the scale of the EU or NATO from emerging within Asia.

The New Cold War in the Era of Deglobalization

Any number of questions arise in the face of deglobalization and a renewed Cold War that features the US and China as adversaries. What, for instance, are the patterns of strategic and security interactions in Asia today? How are the cross-cutting dynamics of regionalization, globalization, along with some significant signs of de-globalization in the 21st century, playing out? More specifically, as Asian economies have grown increasingly interdependent, is regional security moving to a "New Cold War" featuring US–China competition? How has the recent trend of economic de-coupling between the two dominant players of Asia affected regional security dynamics, especially the countries that have been deeply integrated into the Sinocentric regional economic ecosystem? Or is a multipolar order with several powers balancing against one another, including China, Japan, and Korea, among other regional powers, emerging?

Before September 11, 2001, globalization had been the dominant trend of world order, with East Asia at the forefront. Rapid industrialization and export-driven economic growth, along with growing intra-regional trade—a dominant theme of globalization in East Asia, has molded a distinct form of regionalism, with multiple regional institutions anchored in ASEAN. Given the lack of legalist traditions (Henry, 2007), the unique strategic culture of embodying "preferences for informal and bilateral" engagements instead of formal institutionalism (Johnston, 1995: 64), and the Sino-centric tributary historical tradition in the region (Kang, 2003; Qin, 2018), post-Cold War Asia has not formed a clear and consistent pattern of regionalism as seen in the case of the EU, either from the traditional or non-traditional sense of security (Goh, 2003; Goh, 2007).

This form of regionalism, known as the "ASEAN Way," is informal, loosely institutionalized, consensus-based, dialogue-driven, non-confrontational, and led by ASEAN and its ten member states (Goh, 2003). The post-Cold War era has witnessed the rise of more diverse, overlapping, complementing, and occasionally competing, modes of multilateral economic and security dialogues and cooperation mechanisms anchored in the ideals of regional economic cooperation and integration. Internally and externally, the "ASEAN Way" allows its member states and partners with diverse cultures, regimes, and economies to co-exist and collaborate for peace and prosperity. It also relies on the collective, normative, and persuasive power of the middle and small powers of Southeast Asia to socialize the great powers, such as China, Japan, South Korea, the US, and Russia, into specific sets of jointly agreed norms and rules of conduct intended to enhance mutual understanding and reduce the risk of conflict and war (Cheng-Chwee, 2022).

After the September 11 terrorist attacks, the US focused on the Global War on Terror in Afghanistan and Iraq. It not only diverted US attention and resources away from Asia but also provided a strategic opportunity for Beijing to cooperate with Washington on counterterrorism and intelligence sharing. More importantly, the 2001 accession to the WTO that had been negotiated under the Clinton Administration further allowed China to quickly integrate with the global economy. Asia, up until the mid-2010s, continued to ride the wave as both a benefactor and beneficiary of globalization, but several major events around the late 2000s started to rewrite the globalization-dominated regional order.

First and foremost, the dominance of the US in Asian security has been challenged by the US's weakening position and China's persistent military modernization and expansion since the 1990s, which was propelled by the latter's market-oriented economic reforms and integration into the global economy. Contrary to what the modernization theorists (Lipset, 1959) had predicted, China's economic development not only failed to nudge China onto the road of democratization; instead, the regime has gone in the opposite direction and become visibly more authoritarian.

The US's hegemonic position both globally and regionally was further undermined by the 9/11 terrorist attacks and the 2007/2008 financial crisis that originated in the US housing sector. The US's decline, China's rising economic strength, and increasing authoritarianism have created the perfect storm to redefine security concerns in Asia.

Strategic competition between China and the US has intensified in almost all areas; and the risk of war is growing higher as their relative capabilities are rapidly approaching parity (Organski and Kugler, 1980; Zhang and James, 2023). The COVID-19 pandemic has undoubtedly accelerated the reconfiguration of the security structure in Asia. Will the rise of China bring Asia back to the future of Europe's past in which the balance of power among the great powers sought to keep any rising power from growing into a hegemon (Friedberg, 2011) or back to the future of Asia's past in which Imperial China dominated a hierarchical but relatively stable system of tributary relations with its neighbors (Kang, 2009)?

Heightened nationalism across the region (e.g., China, Japan, South Korea, the Philippines, etc.) would seem to point in the direction of instability, especially given the unsettling shifts in US foreign policy orientation across the most recent Administrations. In the US, the election of Donald Trump ushered in a shift from decades of norms and practices based on the peace dividends derived from globalization to nationalist-driven deglobalization. With his campaign slogans "Make America Great Again" and "America First," competition with China was a major driving force of Trump's Asian policy. One of Trump's very first unprecedented moves was to take a congratulatory yet protocol-breaking telephone call from Tsai Ing-wen on December 2, 2016, breaking the tradition of not having any direct communication between US and Taiwanese presidents since official ties were severed in 1979 (Bader, 2016; Gartner et al., 2021). The incident immediately heightened the tensions between China and the US. Soon after Trump officially took office, a major US–China trade war followed.

According to the Peterson Institute for International Economics data, the US–China trade war unfolded in five stages between 2018 and 2022.

> The first six months of 2018 featured only a moderate increase in tariffs. The months of July through September 2018 resulted in a sharp tariff increase on both sides: US average tariffs increased from 3.8 percent to 12.0 percent, and China's average tariffs increased from 7.2 percent to 18.3 percent. In stage three, there was an 8-month period (September 25, 2018, through June 2019) of little change in tariffs. From June to September 2019, another set of tariff increases kicked in. In the current stage five, and despite the phase one agreement, tariffs between the two countries remain elevated and are the new normal
>
> (Bown, 2023)

Chinese economic policies provide a background explanation for why Beijing might end up in a trade war with Washington. Since 2015, China has been developing strategies and policies to escape the "Middle Income Trap" (e.g., Cai, 2012; Liu et al., 2017) by transforming its economy from a labor-intensive manufacturing-oriented economy to a technology-rich economy so its GDP per capita can take a great leap from $8,016 that had been reached in 2015. To do so, under the ten-year industrial strategy called "Made in China 2025," China had been heavily investing in high-tech sectors, such as telecommunication, aerospace, solar energy, electric vehicles, and battery technology, etc. One of the strategies China has adopted involved "forced technology transfer" acquiring technology from foreign companies or requiring foreign companies to transfer technology to their Chinese counterparts (Huang, 2021).

The Trump Administration quickly responded to China's state-led industrial policy with a series of sanctions (or threat of sanctions) and licensing restrictions to prevent China from acquiring advanced technologies from US companies and other multinational corporations. For example, Chinese companies Huawei and ZTE were banned from entering the US 5G mobile network industry and from importing advanced semiconductors and tools for manufacturing those semiconductors. These decisions have been continued under the Biden Administration and further contributed to the momentum of decoupling the two economies and escalating the trade war.[8]

The breadth and depth of economic ties China has established with other regional powers have formed a sharp contrast to the relative decline of the US's economic influence, becoming a source of major concern for US policymakers. From the US perspective, much of China's recent activism amounts to a direct challenge to the rule-based liberal international order Washington established after World War II.

Since the Trump Administration, exacerbated by the COVID-19 pandemic, the bipartisan consensus has focused on an increasingly hardline strategy against China. On March 28, 2023, the Heritage Foundation in Washington released its 143-page special report about how the US should counter its adversary—China—and win in the New Cold War (Carafano et al. 2023). With rising tensions in the US–China rivalry, the US under the Biden Administration has taken a multidimensional approach to be "competitive where it should be, cooperative where it can be, and adversarial where it must be" (Blinken, 2021) vis-à-vis China. As a strategic balance against China's advancement in the South China Sea, the newly announced basing agreement marked the expanded return of the US to the Philippines. AUKUS—the US and the United Kingdom agreed to share their nuclear submarine technologies with Australia. The relocation of the Taiwan Semiconductor Manufacturing Company (TSMC) and the US restriction on exports of semiconductors and relevant hardware and technologies to China have further escalated the bilateral strategic competition.

At the same time, the Biden Administration has sought to cooperate with China where it can, establish "guardrails" to manage the risks of armed conflict, and contain China's growing influence. The guardrails—channels of communication (e.g., hotlines, embassies, etc.)—entail a mechanism to manage and defuse heightened tensions and prevent escalation in a time of crisis. However, given persistent mistrust and growing suspicion, Beijing has not reciprocated Washington's approach to compartmentalizing areas of strategic competition, crisis management, and cooperation.

Years leading up to the present have included a wide range of developments that complicate Sino–US relations. Obvious examples include rising nationalism and xenophobia, major global supply-chaining restructuring, and COVID-19-induced interruption of travel and transportation. All of these developments reinforced a shift away from economic globalization to concerns about traditional national security.

Moreover, with Xi Jinping's third term confirmed in 2022/2023, China has become more authoritarian at home and assertive abroad. The most visible manifestations have included the closing of respective consulates in July 2020, unofficial support for the Russian invasion of Ukraine in 2022, and the bizarre flying of a spy balloon across the entire continental US that began in January 2023. China, in sum, appears to be re-rallying with Russia due to shared grievances against the US-led world order (Zhao, 2023). In response, the US-led hub-and-spokes security system has been broadened to include more like-minded security partners, such as Malaysia, Singapore, Australia, and Vietnam, in a concentric manner beyond the US treaty allies (Auslin, 2014).

The most difficult aspect of Asian security concerns sovereignty, territorial integrity, and maritime security. In 2019, most notably, Xi Jinping's major speeches and the PRC's Defense White Paper all stressed the centrality of Taiwan and the South China Sea as the core of China's national interests to maintain its sovereignty and territorial integrity. Beyond the uncompromising rhetoric, the PLA has modernized into the largest fleets of aviation forces, including advanced 5th-generation fighter jets in its air force and blue-water fleets and three aircraft carriers, along with full-range missiles and expanding nuclear arsenal.

With China's growing clout and connections across Asia through Xi Jinping's signature Belt and Road Initiative and intensified diplomacy through the more recent Global Security Initiative and the China-Central Asia Summit, China is trying to reshape the regional order centering around its national interests and strategic preferences. Trade growth within Asia in the last two decades largely came from trade with China while Japan has declined as a major trading partner of its Asian neighbors (Lincoln, 2022).

Risk of armed conflict over China's territorial claim over Taiwan has intensified, especially since Russia's invasion of Ukraine, Nancy Pelosi's high-profile visit to Taiwan, and Tsai Ying-wen's meeting with US House Speaker Kevin McCarthy in California. Influential think tanks in the US, such as the Center for Strategic and International Studies (CSIS), have started to simulate wargames as the potential war in the Taiwan Strait may be imminent (Cancian et al., 2023). The US continues its arms sales to Taiwan and is expected to increase US troops to 100–200. These moves were meant to help Taiwan focus on tactics and weapon systems that would make the island harder to assault (Youssef and Gordon, 2023).

The multilateral and multifaceted sovereignty and maritime disputes in the South China Sea combined to create another security flashpoint that potentially can lead to direct armed conflict between the US and China. Although the US is not a claimant of the rocks and reefs under dispute, Washington has broader strategic interests in the freedom of navigation of commercial and military vessels in the disputed exclusive economic zones—given that China's

Nine Dash Line claims approximately 90% of the South China Sea. Therefore, it is no surprise that the US has been strengthening security cooperation with Vietnam and the Philippines, two of the claimants that have clashed with China in the Paracel and Spratly Islands.

Beyond the US treaty allies, most of the Asian countries have sought to maintain strategic autonomy and equidistance with a hedging strategy of refusing to take sides. For instance, the Philippines, after the 2016 arbitration case over its disputes in the South China Sea, quietly set the legal ruling aside while moving closer to Beijing with economic deals. While Vietnam remains confrontational with China about the overlapping claims in the South China Sea, the Communist Party of Vietnam continues to cultivate cooperation with its Chinese counterpart. Leading countries in ASEAN, such as Indonesia and Singapore, have shown similar preferences. In a persistent effort to reduce tension over the South China Sea, ASEAN has engaged in a new round of negotiations with China on a Code of Conduct (COC) to manage the norms of behavior around disputed waters.

Conclusion and Future Prospects

Asymmetry, uncertainty, and high tension are central characteristics of Asian security in an era of deglobalization and renewed Cold War. This chapter has made some progress in answering attendant questions about the future of the region: What do the preceding changes mean for the key players and stakeholders of Asia and their respective strategic policies when they navigate these undercurrents in the 21st century? How can great power rivalry be strategically managed to maintain regional peace and prosperity? Three basic points can be offered in response to these interconnected queries about the future.

First, strategic flexibility and risk management will be a key priority for Asia, particularly between the US and China. As the world recovers from the COVID-19 pandemic and reorients for a New Cold War, states and multinational corporations with significant stakes in the peace and prosperity of Asia have made significant adjustments to manage the risks exposed to the disruption of the global supply chain. These actors also seek diplomatic and economic opportunities in a seemingly increasingly rigid strategic environment dominated by the US–China rivalry, particularly regarding Taiwan and the South China Sea. Variegated but sometimes harsh lockdowns in different parts of China during the COVID-19 pandemic severely strained the global supply chain and stimulated the relocation and diversification of suppliers from China to Vietnam and other Southeast Asian states.

Second, tension for strategic competition and armed conflict may rise in the short term since both the US and China have renewed their strategic and diplomatic offense to bolster their alliances while the bilateral relationship continued to follow a downward trajectory, especially after the spy balloon incident noted above. In short, the way in which the US and China manage their rivalry will shape the future of Asia (Allison, 2018; Rudd, 2022).

Third, most Asian states continue to hedge against the pressures from Beijing and Washington to take sides in the ongoing US–China rivalry while managing the geopolitical uncertainty and diverse challenges at home. This has been the dominant approach for most of the middle and small powers in the region to navigate the Cold War and will remain the dominant approach to maintain their strategic autonomy through the New Cold War. Meanwhile, the ASEAN and its member states will continue to rely on their normative power of multilateral regional institutionalism to manage risks and uncertainties—especially regarding the maritime disputes over the South China Sea.

Finally, Figure 2.2 conveys a systemist graphic that summarizes the arguments of this chapter. The system is Asia, with the International System as its environment. Within Asia, the micro and macro levels correspond, respectively, to individual actors and the region as a whole. A total of 20 components appear in the diagram—sufficient to convey the basics but not overwhelming in terms of complexity. This graphic, therefore, is well-suited to be used as a memory aid if, for example, the chapter is to be referenced in a classroom lecture, research publication, or some other context.

Among the variables, 17 of 20 appear within Asia, confirming it as the appropriate choice for the designation of a system. Within the 17 components that appear in Asia, 14 are macro and 3 are micro. This also seems valid because the principal focus of the chapter has been on processes in Asia rather than individual states. At the same time, note that the argument starts in the International System with "INTENSE COMPETITION AFTER WORLD WAR II: US AND SOVIET COALITIONS" and eventually reaches terminal points at the micro level of Asia: "democratization flourishes in several states' and 'most states seek to maintain strategic autonomy – hedging strategy." Processes in between occur primarily at the level of Asia as a system.

One way to think about the identity of the diagram as a whole is in reference to the idea of the "second image reversed" (Gourevitch, 1978). In that exposition, Gourevitch (1978) drew attention to how forces from beyond the state can impact what goes on within it—a reversal of the second image from the classic Waltzian framework. Outside actors, notably the US, have impacted upon Asia as a system, which in turn has reverberations for individual states. One effect on individual states is on regime type—an increase in democracy—and the other is on policies pursued—a shift toward strategic autonomy vis-à-vis the Sino–US rivalry.

Finally, the figure facilitates thinking about what might happen next. How might the analysis be extended a year or even a decade from now? In closing, the systemist approach facilitates understanding and retention of complex arguments, such as those conveyed in the present chapter about Asia after the Cold War.

Asia After the Cold War 29

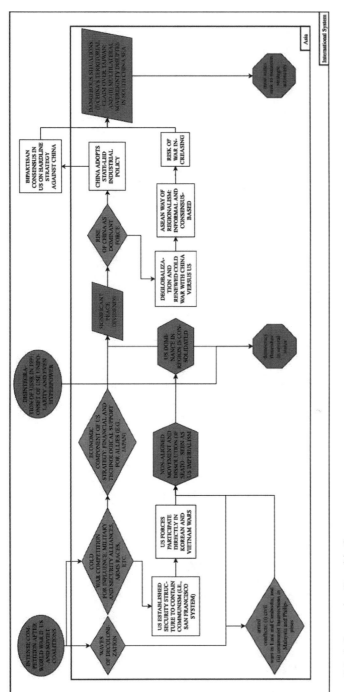

Figure 2.2 A Systemist Graphic Summary
Source: Created by the author.

Notes

1 The overview of systemism that follows is based primarily on Gansen and James (2022a).
2 As is conventional within the field, 'International Relations' refers to the academic discipline while 'international relations' concerns its subject matter.
3 Designation of a system and its environment applies basic set theory. The system is a set and the environment is its complement.
4 For example, a study of Cambodia likely would designate that state as the system and the rest of the world as its environment. Likewise, a focus on an academic discipline would make that field, such as International Relations, the system, with the world beyond designated as its environment.
5 A detailed treatment of applications appears in Gansen and James (2022b).
6 The US played a crucial but covert role by secretly supporting the anti-Soviet Islamist guerrilla forces of the Afghan Mujahadeen.
7 In Southeast Asia, however, the US security alliance with the Philippines was significantly weakened when the Aquino Administration ordered the US forces to withdraw from the Subic Bay Naval Base, Clark Air Base, and other military bases, which was completed by November 24, 1992. As tension has risen in the East and South China Seas since the 2010s, the Philippines regranted access to five of its military bases to the US under the 2014 Enhanced Defense Cooperation Agreement that was updated in 2023.
8 From the standpoint of China, any number of initiatives under the Trump Administration seemed to aim at containment and even antagonism. While a full treatment is beyond the scope of the present exposition, the most prominent instances would include the QUAD, Free and Open Indo-Pacific (FOIP), and Five-Eye Alliance to cooperate on intelligence sharing.

References

Acharya, Amitav. 1997. "Ideas, identity, and institution-building: From the 'ASEAN way' to the 'Asia-Pacific way'?" *The Pacific Review* 10 (3): 319–346.

Allison, Graham. 2018. *Destined for War: Can America and China Escape Thucydides's Trap?* New York: HarperCollins.

Auslin, Michael R. 2014. "The US Alliance Structure in Asia." In Mahnken, Thomas G., and Blumenthal, Dan, eds. *Strategy in Asia: The Past, Present, and Future of Regional Security.* Palo Alto, CA: Stanford University Press.

Bader, Jeffrey. 2016. "Trump, Taiwan, and a Break in a Long Tradition." Order from Chaos [BLOG]. The Brookings Institution, last modified December 3, 2016, https://search.proquest.com/docview/1845445492

Blinken, Antony. 2021. "A Foreign Policy for the American People." US Fed News Service, Including US State News, Mar 3, 2021.

Bown, Chad. 2023. "US-China Trade War Tariffs: An Up-to-Date Chart," last modified April 6, 2023, https://www.piie.com/research/piie-charts/us-china-trade-war-tariffs-date-chart

Bunge, Mario. 1996. *Finding Philosophy in Social Science.* New Haven, CT: Yale University Press.

Cai, Fang. 2012. "Is There a 'Middle-income Trap'? Theories, Experiences and Relevance to China." *China & World Economy* 20 (1): 49–61.

Cancian, Mark F., Matthew Cancian, and Eric Heginbotham. 2023. "First Battle of NextWar: Wargaming Chinese Invasion of Taiwan," *Center for Strategic &*

International Studies, https://www.csis.org/analysis/first-battle-next-war-.wargaming-chinese-invasion-taiwan.

Carafano, James, J., Pillsbury, Michael, Smith, Jeff M., and Harding, Andrew J. 2023. *Winning the New Cold War: A Plan for Countering China.* https://www.heritage.org/asia/report/winning-the-new-cold-war-plan-countering-.china

Cheng-Chwee, Kuik. 2022. *Southeast Asian States and ASEAN.* In D. Shambaugh (Ed.), *International Relations of Asia* (3rd edition, pp. 189–228). Rowman and Littlefield.

Friedberg, Aaron L. 2011. *A Contest for Supremacy: China, America, and the Struggle for Mastery in Asia.* New York: W. W. Norton.

Fukuyama, Francis. 1989. "The End of History." *The National Interest* 16 (Summer): 3–18.

Gansen, Sarah, and Patrick James. 2022a. "The Russo-Ukrainian War: Insights from Systemism in a Pedagogical Setting." *New Area Studies* 3 (1).

Gansen, Sarah, and Patrick James. 2022b. "Systems Analysis: Systemism and the Visual International Relations Project." In R. Joseph Huddleston, Thomas Jamieson and Patrick James, eds. *Handbook of Research Methods in International Relations.* Cheltenham, UK: Edward Elgar, pp. 89–115.

Gartner, Scott Sigmund, Huang, Chin-Hao, Li, Yitan, and James, Patrick. 2021. *Identityin the Shadow of a Giant: How the Rise of China is Changing Taiwan.* Bristol University Press.

Goh, Evelyn. 2007. "Great Powers and Hierarchical Order in Southeast Asia: Analyzing Regional Security Strategies." *International Security* 32 (3) (Dec 1): 113–157.

Goh, Gillian. 2003. "The 'ASEAN Way': Non-Intervention and ASEAN's Role in Conflict Management." *Stanford Journal of East Asian Affairs* 3: 113–117.

Gourevitch, Peter. 1978. "The Second Image Reversed: The International Sources of Domestic Politics." *International Organization* 32: 881–912.

Henry, Laurence. 2007. "The ASEAN Way and Community Integration: Two DifferentModels of Regionalism." *European Law Journal: Review of European Law in Context* 13 (6) (Nov):857–879.

Huang, Yukon. 2021. "The U.S.-China Trade War Has Become a Cold War." (September 16) https://carnegieendowment.org/2021/09/16/u.s.-china-trade-.war-has-become-cold-war-pub-85352.

Huntington, Samuel P. 1993. "The Clash of Civilizations?" *Foreign Affairs* 72 (3): 22–49.

Johnston, Alastair I. 1995. "Thinking about Strategic Culture." *International Security* 19 (4): 32–64.

Kamphausen, Roy. 2014. "Asia as a Warfighting Environment." In Mahnken, Thomas G., and Blumenthal, Dan, eds. 2014. *Strategy in Asia: The Past, Present, and Future of Regional Security.* Palo Alto: Stanford University Press.

Kang, David C. 2009. *China Rising: Peace, Power, and Order in East Asia.* New York, NY: Columbia University Press.

Kang, David C. 2003. "Getting Asia Wrong: The Need for New Analytical Frameworks." *International Security* 27 (4): 57–85.

Lincoln, Edward J. 2022. "The Asian Regional Economy." In D. Shambaugh (Ed.), *International Relations of Asia* (3rd edition, pp. 339–364). Lanham, MD: Rowman and Littlefield.

Lipset, Seymour Martin. 1959. "Some Social Requisites of Democracy: Economic Development and Political Legitimacy." *The American Political Science Review* 53 (1): 69–105.

Liu, Xielin, Sylvia Schwaag Serger, Ulrike Tagscherer, and Amber Y.Chang. 2017. "Beyond Catch-up—Can a New Innovation Policy Help China Overcome the Middle Income Trap?" *Science and Public Policy* 44 (5): 656–669.

Organski, A. F. K., and Jacek Kugler. 1980. *The War Ledger*. Chicago, IL: University of Chicago Press.

Qin, Yaqing. 2018. "A Multiverse of Knowledge: Cultures and IR Theories." *The Chinese Journal of International Politics* 11 (4) (Dec 1): 415–434.

Rudd, Kevin. 2022. *The Avoidable War: The Dangers of a Catastrophic Conflict between the US and Xi Jinping's China*. Public Affairs.

Russett, Bruce and Oneal, John R. 2001. *Triangulating Peace: Democracy, Interdependence, and International Organizations*. New York: W. W. Norton.

US Indo-Pacific Command (n.d.), USINDOPAC Areas of Responsibility, https://www.pacom.mil/About-USINDOPACOM/USPACOM-Area-of-Responsibility.

Youssef, Nancy A. and Gordon Lubold, 2023. "U.S. to Expand Troop Presence in Taiwan for Training Against China Threat; the Pentagon is Helping Taiwan Focus on Tactics and Weapon Systems that would make the Island Harder to Assault," *The Wall Street Journal*, Eastern edition, February 24. https://search.proquest.com/docview/2779141295.

Zhang, Enyu and Patrick James. 2023. "All Roads Lead to Beijing: *Systemism*, Power Transition, and the Belt and Road Initiative." *Chinese Political Science Review* 8: 18–44.

Zhao, Suisheng. 2023. *The Dragon Roars Back: Transformational Leaders and Dynamics of Chinese Foreign Policy*. Stanford, California: Stanford University Press.

3 Military Threats to Security

Hyun Ji Rim

Introduction and Overview: An Evolving Milieu

In the post-Cold War Asia, we are witnessing rising tensions as US–China strategic competition deepens. Some refer to the competition as a New Cold War and much research in the field is re-examining Cold War history and the lessons from the past for dealing with the present challenges. Despite the similarities between the "old" and "new" Cold War of being a bipolar great power competition in nature, there are differences that make the ongoing competition a much more complex dynamic.

Asia has inherited a regional economic cooperative network and US alliance structures from the US–Soviet rivalry that contributed to high interdependence among local states. In addition, owing to communications networks and technologies, states enjoy a much higher level of policy cooperation. This interdependence in the region is the key environment for shaping alliance paths and forming partnerships for both the United States and China, thus, carries strategic importance in obtaining more favorable conditions in rivalry for both Washington and Beijing.

The rise of Chinese military power, especially its offensive and defensive capabilities, is a concerning aspect of the strategic competition in the Asia-Pacific region. China is strengthening its "strategic deterrent capabilities" with an estimated operational nuclear warhead stocked pie of over 400 warheads and continued expansion that will reach 1500 warheads by 2035 (DOD, 2022). China's military spending has increased exponentially over the last 30 years: USD 28 billion in 1993; USD 67.18 billion in 2003; USD 183.36 billion in 2013; and over USD 297.99 billion in 2022 (Tian and Su, 2021).

Other countries have been investing in military modernization to keep up with such trends as well. Military modernization that elevates a state's tactical advantage through adopting new technologies that advance intelligence, surveillance, and reconnaissance (ISR) capabilities, precision strike capabilities, is a global trend. Developing countries in Asia have also picked up on this trend, and the diffusion of military power is likely to contribute to a more complicated regional security dynamic with more capable actors involved in shaping regional order and stability in the face of rising conflicts. For this

DOI: 10.4324/9781003473206-3

reason, globalized Asia is now facing a fog of war. Clausewitz perhaps best captured this eternal state of affairs in international relations when he observed:

> War is the realm of uncertainty; three-quarters of the factors on which action in war is based are wrapped in a fog of greater or lesser uncertainty. A sensitive and discriminating judgment is called for; a skilled intelligence to scent out the truth.
>
> (Von Clausewitz, 1950: 101)

Increasingly more complex geopolitical calculations of states are leading towards a stronger emphasis on military power (Huminski, 2022) in the theatre. Against the backdrop of intensifying military buildup and modernization in the theatre, this chapter explores the role of military power and its relations to states' grand strategy. This chapter consists of four sections. Section one examines the theoretical background of military power in the evolving security settings including the degree of political power of military on various domains, the role of military power in the domestic and international arena, and the expanding military influence in states' strategic calculations. Section two surveys key issue areas related to military threat to security such as arms race, weapons proliferation, deterrence, and security dilemma. Section three investigates the cross-strait crisis to show the military power confrontation and security concerns in the theatre; and draws implications for power alignment in East Asia, and the potential role of multilateral regional defense for Southeast Asia. Section four concludes the chapter exploring future prospect of the deepening great power competition, complex strategic calculations and multilayered security dynamics.

Understanding Security: Theoretical Orientation

Military power for security may be portrayed differently affected by national interest and the core values it pursues, and these elements are closely linked to what states view as threats as well as their advantage in power distribution.[1] Along with economic wealth and political skill, military power is one of the three fungible assets of states (Art, 2009). Military power in the extant literature affects many domains, and "[a]t the minimum, … is fungible to a degree because its physical use, its threatened use, or simply its mere presence structure expectations and influence the political calculation of actors" (Art, 2009: 6).

In addition to its status and role as a defensive and offensive force, there are varied explanations for what decides the degree of political power a state's military capabilities and influence have on other domains. Alagappa's (2001) examination of coercion in governance argues that a high level of coercion in a state's governance leads to a higher level of political power in the military. The coercion in governance may be lowered as economic development is further achieved, then the political power of the military, thus will decrease. While his argument in part explains the dynamic of military influence, it fails, however, to capture more recent developments in Asia. With economic development, China seems to exhibit stronger coercive governance to pursue its grand strategic goals. In addition, the rising Southeast Asian countries are strengthening their military owing to economic development, and with states' heavy investment in military power is triggering closer civil–military relations and fortifying the political power of the military.

Others offer individual-level analysis where key leaders' pursuit of their strategic interest determines the stability of civilian governance—not threatened by the military—in a state, and not economic factors (Mietzner, 2009). This is based on a theory that military influence and civilian or democratic control of the military has a negative correlation (Cottey, Edmunds, Foster, 2002).

To varying degrees, military power is an integral component of statecraft that engages society and plays two main roles. In the domestic arena, the military exercises political power that affects stability. We have seen in many cases how the excessive political power of the military led to social instability in Asia. Myanmar/Burma was a pariah state under a military junta between 1962 and 2011, liberalized by Aung San Suu Kyi in 2015 only to undergo horrific atrocities against the Rohingya in 2017, followed by a military coup in 2021. In Thailand, a military coup that demanded the resignation of Prime Minister Thaksin Shinawatra in 2006 and again in 2010 recorded mass casualties of civil war. In 2001, Philippine President, Joseph Estrada, was removed by a violent military uprising. East Timor also went through a military division that led to violence across the country in 2006.

On the world stage, military power plays a critical role in setting the rules of the game in international politics and bringing order to the system. This perspective is more dominant in realist literature that assumes an anarchic nature of the international system. Through the forceful use of military power—i.e., waging war or threatening to go to war—states shape the international order and engage in a power play for self-help.

From defending itself by more actively pursuing its national interest in the long-term, military power is a quintessential component of states' grand strategy. In the cases where economic development and a more stable government are present, a viable military would also be constructed as the state matures, rendering it as an established military power. States further utilize their military power to protect global commons via international networks such as anti-piracy networks, humanitarian disaster relief (HDR), UN peacekeeping, etc.

Today we are witnessing the expansion of potential military influence over various domains, and it is due to the following aspects of the evolving security environment.

First, more players means more calculations: Due to an increase in the number of actors who possess enhanced military capability, the security dynamic and risk calculation in the theatre is becoming more complex. The US extended its nuclear deterrence (umbrella) to protect its allies—Japan, South Korea, and the Philippines—in the region. Thailand is undergoing upgrades as its allies become more militarily capable via a higher defense budget, advanced technology application, and newly established states' strategy. In addition to the alliance network, other members of ASEAN are also investing in their military strategy and capacity to counter potential conflicts in the South China Sea.

Second, the rise of overall regional military power: In addition to the increase in the number of actors in the theatre and their individual enhanced-military capability, the larger aggregate military power in the theater calls for more sophisticated communications among states to avoid any inadvertent escalations. As a result, the region has greater military power in terms of military capacity and capability with a greater number of conventional and non-conventional weapons, and is the reason why the Indo-Pacific is becoming a priority theater for many around the globe.

Third, the deepening strategic competition between the United States and China that many are calling the new Cold War: This course of intensifying relations between great powers—which may include Russia as well—signify that things are at a higher stake. Rather than being a limited local conflict, if it were to take place, an armed dispute between/among great powers will have a global impact, one that would leave a grave footprint on the map of international relations and states' national security, much like the Cold War did in the past.

Lastly, advanced technologies and their dual use: It is harder these days to clearly separate defensive capabilities from offensive capabilities owing much to emerging technologies. Technologies have always been one of the major factors that decide the fate of an arms race, symmetry-asymmetry, and a state's strategic advantage. Emerging technologies such as artificial intelligence (AI), lethal autonomous weapons (LAWS), hypersonic, directed energy, quantum technologies, cyber and undersea capabilities, mentioned in US Indo-Pacific Strategy (The White House, 2022) and US National Defense Science and Technology Strategy (US Department of Defense, 2023), are open to dual use, and are hard to draw the line between defensive capabilities and offensive capabilities. In this context, Roberts (2021: 5) argues that "emerging and disruptive technologies" deepen "multi-domain complexity bearing on strategic stability." As Art (2009: 83) states, "Peace, in short, may depend less on the ingenuity of rival statesmen than upon the ingenuity of the rival scientists," and as such technological innovation will be an essential aspect of the future military power that is linked to the avoidance of war.

With heightening regional tension, rising regional powers, and great power competition in addition to the expanding role of the military in non-military areas, the rise of military power and its influence is becoming a crucial factor in understanding the ongoing power game in the Asia-Pacific theater.

Military Threats and Key Issue Areas

To understand the military threat to security, this section explores three issue areas of arms race and weapons proliferation, deterrence, and security dilemma.

Military power may help states achieve national security, at the same time, however, one's security can be perceived by other states as a threat factor, by its very nature.[2] The balance of power approach to security seeks a power balance among states and considers bipolar symmetry as the ideal state of affairs that is stable and sustainable. This was the rationale of the Cold War which was contained from going "hot." In this realist conception of international relations, military power is the key component in deciding the use of a state's power in its competition with others. In this context, one's military power—an aggregate of military doctrine, leadership, and capabilities—is the source of threat for other members of the international community of states.

The notion of military threat changes when placed in the context of collective security or collective defense. The North Atlantic Treaty Organization (NATO) is an example of this concept. This view considers a multipolar system to be more stable than a bipolar security structure. Collective security posits that "an attack on one is an attack on all" type of thinking[3] as its casus foederis.[4] In this pluralist perspective, a multilateral defense alliance against an adversary or adversaries provides a much more stable environment for states' international affairs. This suggests that military threat is a shared concern for all alliance members.

Traditionally, the Asian security structure has been greatly influenced by the great power politics of the West, and the US hub-and-spokes system of the Washington Consensus[5] remains the key driver of regional security dynamics. Coming out of the Cold War, however, the bipolar dominant regional structure has moved onto the US hegemonic alliance system. Now, with a rising China and rising ASEAN nations, a US hub-and-spokes system, multilateral regional orders like ASEAN and Quad, and high economic interdependence among states, we see a mix of various security structures in the Asia-Pacific theater.

Arms Race and Weapons Proliferation

The "arms race" and its link to war has been widely researched in the context of its cause and consequences. Huntington defines an arms race as "a progressive, competitive peacetime increase in armaments by two states or coalition of states resulting from conflicting purposes or mutual fear" (Huntington, 1958: 41). As its name suggests, an arms race implies an antagonistic competition perceived by all parties (Gray, 1971: 41). On the causes of an arms race, scholars from different schools utilize to varying lenses to explain key drivers. The realist Action-reaction model suggests that external factors or perceptions of these factors, like political and military threats, trigger states' armament (Buzan and Herring, 2011: 203; Gray, 1974: 71; Kydd, 1997). The spiral model by Jervis, also in this context, explains how adversaries' arms buildup can initiate an aggregate competitive arms buildup increasing tension and leading to war (Jervis 1976; Singer, 1958). Others find internal factors such as political and military leadership, technological momentum, government structure, and domestic political structural dynamics as the drivers (Fearon, 1998; Manken, 2014; Buzan and Herring, 1998).

The causes of an arms race is a critical element in determining policy direction since it is closely linked to the consequences of an arms race (Glaser, 2000). In a spiral model and armament-tension dilemma Singer (1958) suggests that states fall into a security dilemma (Jervis, 1976; Glaser, 1997) where two parties expose themselves to a higher risk of conflict by continually pursuing ever higher levels of security. In this scenario, the recommended policy solution would be arms control. The Preparedness model, on the other hand, would prescribe arms buildup in preparation for war; supported by the "you prepare for war to avoid war" type of thinking. Although an arms race and its association to war is a heavily studied topic in international politics, many agree that the two are correlated but do not always exhibit causality: an arms race sometimes end in war, but other times does not (Hammond, 1993; Sample, 1998; Rider, Findley, and Diehl, 2011) suggests that the dynamic is much more complex and case-specific.

This distinct form of international rivalry deals with military components of international politics and generates a security setting that promotes severe competition that is prone to crisis escalation—intentional or inadvertent, possible preventive war if not all, heightened tension at the least. It is in this context that an arms race can potentially cause insecurity and stir up international stability. This potential military threat to security—states' acquisition of new weapons/weapon systems or restructuring military forces and increasing their size—however, needs to be understood in a broader context of states' strategic goals, resource endowment, and geopolitical environment (Glaser, 2000). The series of interrelated increases in states' armament, thus, may be a tool that each state is applying to achieve a political goal (Hammond, 1993).

The US–China strategic competition exhibits this arms race dynamic, where China is a late-comer catching up with the United States in terms of high-tech capabilities—counterforce, i.e., Anti-Access Area Denial (A2AD) capabilities in particular—and military strategy across multiple domains including maritime, cyber, space. Supported by high economic growth and nuclear weapons, Beijing is pursuing information and emerging technologies to sharpen its strategic edge over Washington (Rim, 2023) since introducing the "International Situation and the Military Strategic Guidelines" in 1993 (Finkelstein, 2007: 69). This great power competition is triggering an arms race dynamic that may lead to an inadvertent escalation of hostilities that could have global implications.

Deterrence

Deterrence is one of the classic military strategies of warfare history. It was the central concept for security strategy during the Cold War enforced by the absolute weapon (Brodie and Dunn, 1946), nuclear bombs, as well as the "high risk of utter catastrophe" (Freedman, 2004: 10) of its possible use.

Generally, deterrence is a type of coercion made by a state using its power to discourage and dissuade an adversary from initiating a targeted move. There are deterrence by denial and deterrence by punishment (Snyder, 1959). The former focuses on denying potential gains of an adversary's initiating an action while the latter uses more traditional means, "the threat of retaliation to forestall a military attack" (Paul et al., 2009: 35). For example, we have witnessed how deterrence worked when two great powers—the United States and the Soviet Union—threatened each other with nuclear weapons capable of mutually assured destruction (MAD) if one were to launch such an attack during the Cold War.

There are also general deterrence and immediate deterrence (Morgan, 1997)—immediate deterrence will follow only when general deterrence fails—and both forms of deterrence "assume that adversaries are most likely to resort to force or threatening military deployment when they judge the military balance favorable and question the defender's resolve" (Lebow and Stein, 1989: 49). Thus, it entails risk calculation or cost-benefit analysis for the potential adversary; and such calculation is heavily influenced by the perception of threat, cost of credibility, and assumed rationality of states involved in the dynamic.

In addition to deterrence that limits its resources to military factors, we see "non-limitation to military factors" that Snyder argued in 1961, similar to Knopf's (2010) argument that explores the strategy in asymmetric settings like what we see today, a second nuclear age (Bracken, 2012) or an Asian Nuclear Age (Delpech, 2012: 5). As new nuclear powers, like North Korea, emerge and a more complex mix of offensive and defensive means are readily available for states in the Asian-Pacific, deterrence strategy is also adapting.

Moreover, extended deterrence and bilateral alliance structure in the region is also a critical component of a state's military power. The United States provides security guarantees, its extended nuclear deterrence, to its allies: the United States promises its allies that it will provide security protection should they come under attack and will retaliate on their behalf. With alliance politics and dynamics added to already sophisticated deterrence calculations, extended deterrence is another complex dimension of the regional security dynamic. Many countries, such as Japan, South Korea, the Philippines, Thailand, Australia, New Zealand, and to a limited extent Taiwan, build their military posture and strategy centered around the US nuclear umbrella.

Security Dilemma

As the states in the region pursue military modernization and capacity build-up, concerns for security dilemmas also rise. In addressing security in our times, Booth (1991: 318) notes:

> the greater awareness of the pressures of the security dilemma, the growing appreciation of security interdependence, the wide recognition that the arms race has produced a higher level of destructive power but not

commensurate growth of security, and the realization of the heavy burden on economies of extravagant defense spending.

Though it was a different time during the Cold War, the description of the current situation in the Asia-Pacific region sounds hauntingly familiar to what we are facing today. Here, the security dilemma occurs when "an increase in one state's security decreases the security of others" (Jervis, 1978: 186), and is also closely related to states' military expansion.

In the context of alliance politics, security dilemmas can occur in two phases—alliance formation and post-formation (Snyder, 1984). In explaining alliance politics, how and why alliances are formed in a multipolar system, Snyder shows how states bear more burden and risks by forming an alliance, thus, "the outcome could be worse than all-around abstention because each state has incurred the risks and burdens of alliance with little improvement in its security" (Snyder, 1984: 462).

In the Indo-Pacific theatre, three key aspects of the security dynamic are prone to trigger security dilemmas for states: alliance, Indo-Pacific strategy, and technology. Reflecting on Jervis' (1978: 187) argument that "the security dilemma is at its most vicious when commitments, strategy, or technology dictate that the only route to security lies through expansion," the Indo-Pacific theater has all three that he mentioned.

First, US bilateral alliances and their networks are a key feature in the regional security dynamic. Since their formation, each alliance has been strengthened over the years, with some evolving further into a much more comprehensive partnership than what they were over 70 years ago. The US allies as well as the United States have a strong commitment to strengthen the alliance and abide by the rule of law; at the same time, China is also strongly committed to bringing about a new era for great China. The stronger the commitment of each side, the more severe the conflict—diplomatic and military—will become.

Second, states have announced their Indo-Pacific strategies and new national security/military strategies as they sense the need to adapt to the evolving security settings in the theater. The United States announced its Indo-Pacific strategy in 2018, and since then India, Australia, Japan—the Quad members, and South Korea also announced their Indo-Pacific strategy to show their support for shared strategic interest and commitment to the alliance. China is also asserting economic and military power through an all-of-nation, long-term strategy (DoD, 2018). China working with coalitions of its own like BRICS (Brazil, Russia, India, China, and South Africa) is expanding its sphere of influence and expanding its military, political, diplomatic, and economic capabilities according to its newly found national strategies.

Lastly, technology and the accompanying strategic edge over the adversary also dictates the current competition between the United States and China. Strategic sectors and industries like semiconductor and laser technology to other emerging technologies with dual usage of civilian and military applications are what heightens the competition. China has made it its goal to be the global leader in innovative technology by 2049 and embedded the operationalized segments of this plan in almost every aspect of its economy in great detail. The Military-Civil Fusion (MFC) Development Strategy of China established in 2007 integrates social, military, and economic governance for building a national strategic system for science and technology development. The United States following its third off-set strategy to the Indo-Pacific strategy is also recommitting to science, technology, engineering, and mathematics (STEM) initiatives aimed at securing an edge over China via long-term plans (DoD, 2021).

Under the deepening great-power competition and active military modernization in the Asian-Pacific, the balance between offense and defense becomes trickier. It will become more challenging for states to be completely free from an arms race dynamic, to managing inadvertent escalations that may trigger armed conflict, and maneuvering through security dilemmas in the Asia-Pacific theatre.

Case Study: Cross-Strait Conflict and Military Power in the Asia-Pacific Theater

In this section, the case of the cross-strait issue will be examined in light of military power and security concerns in the Asia-Pacific theater. The cross-strait crisis refers to near-conflict moments between the Republic of China (ROC), Taiwan, and the People's Republic of China (PRC), China.

The People's Liberation Army (PLA) of China has targeted 2027 for "developing [the] capabilities to be a more credible military tool for the CCP to wield as it pursues Taiwan unification" (DoD, 2022). To that end, the PRC has been actively training for a Taiwan contingency by conducting continuous military operations near Taiwan. On June 21, 2023, the Chinese Shandong Carrier Strike Group sailed through the Taiwan Strait, and basically transited the same route as the USCGC Stratton (WMSL-752), which conducted a passing exercise a day prior (LaGrone, 2023). China also had ten fighter jets cross the strait's median line on June 11, 2023 and had 37 military aircraft fly into Taiwan Air Defence Zone (TADIZ) a week earlier. The tension in the cross-strait area, especially the military aspect of the show of force is increasingly forcing the states in the Asia-Pacific theater to be on high alert and thereby providing an even stronger rationale for further military buildup.

As China has grown and developed into a global economic power, Beijing has become more assertive in pursuing its national interests at the expense of other states' security and regional stability. For this reason, many in the United States are calling for an upgraded deterrence strategy to prevent further deterioration of deterrence in the Asia-Pacific theater (Cancian et al., 2023; Gordon et al., 2023). As the report states "a conflict over Taiwan has thus far been avoided, but deterrence has dangerously eroded; under Xi Jinping's leadership, China is aggressively and consistently moving the status quo in its favor and increasing pressure on Taiwan" (Gordon et al., 2023: 9).

Under the One China policy, the PRC argues that "there is only one China in the world, and Taiwan is a part of China, ..." (PRC, 2022) where the PRC government is the only legitimate government that represents China. As Washington normalized its relations with Beijing, the US-ROC Mutual Defense Treaty was terminated on January 1, 1980. President Ronald Reagan, however, communicated "Six Assurances" to Taiwan in 1982 and the United States continues to maintain unofficial relations with Taiwan under the Taiwan Relations Act (TRA, P.L. 96–8; 22 U.S.C. §3301 et seq.). It also clearly states as follows (CRS Report, 2023):

- The United States "will make available to Taiwan such defense articles and defense services in such quantity as may be necessary to enable Taiwan to maintain a sufficient self-defense capability."
- It is U.S. policy "to maintain the capacity of the United States to resist any resort to force or other forms of coercion that would jeopardize the security, or the social or economic system, of the people on Taiwan" (Taiwan Relations Act, H.R. 2479, 96th Cong., 1979).

Led by the American Institute in Taiwan (AIT), the Relations Act include US defensive arms sales to Taiwan, supporting peaceful resolution of cross-strait issues, and opposing any unilateral changes to the status quo (CRS Report, 2023).

Three Crises and Counting

Taiwan initiated its de facto separation from mainland China in 1949 at the conclusion of the Chinese Civil War and became a self-ruled economy. Over the course of six decades, the Taiwan Strait has been a geopolitical flashpoint where multiple escalations have taken place between Beijing and Taipei. The first cross-strait crisis broke out in 1954 when the Nationalists claimed the two islands of Kinmen and Matsu just off the coast of mainland China. The PRC responded with heavy bombardment on the islands. The second crisis took place in 1958 when Beijing again bombarded the two islands to push off the Taiwanese troops. In both instances, the United States and China were led to near-direct conflict with the possibility of an escalation to a nuclear exchange. China announced a cease-fire failing to take the islands or bring the Nationalists into submission (AFP-JIJI, 2023).

The third cross-strait crisis was ignited by the United States' granting of a visa to Taiwanese President Lee Teng-hui for his speech at Cornell University in 1995. Lee being favorable to Taiwanese independence had fed into Chinese calculation. China responded with missile tests and Washington countered by dispatching two aircraft carriers to de-escalate the situation and force Beijing to stand down.

Cross-strait tension has been intensifying with the election of President Tsai Ing-wen in 2016. House Speaker Nancy Pelosi's visit to Taiwan on August 2,

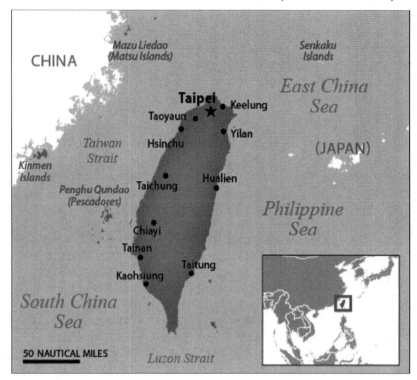

Figure 3.1 The Republic of China (Taiwan)
Source: CRS (2023).

2022 also triggered an aggressive response from China including air and sea military exercises of record scale, sending worships, missiles, and fighter jets near Taiwan. In 2020, President Tsai in her re-election victory speech reemphasized peace, parity, democracy, and dialogue for future positive cross-strait relations. The so-called Tsai Ing-wen's Consensus clearly delineated her vision for better relations between the two Chinas:

> These four words are also the only path to bringing together and benefiting both our two peoples. 'Peace' means that China must abandon threats of force against Taiwan. 'Parity' means that neither side of the Taiwan Strait should deny the fact of the other's existence. 'Democracy' means that the future of Taiwan must be decided by our country's 23 million people. 'Dialogue' means that we must be able to sit down and discuss the future development of cross-strait relations.
>
> (Tsai, 2020)

When President Tsai Ing-wen visited the United States to meet with newly elected House Speaker Kevin McCarthy in 2023 to thank the US for its support of Taiwan, Beijing condemned Tsai of such "Provocation" and responded with rounds of live-fire joint force training among its air force, navy, and ground forces and threatened to take further "countermeasures" (Ruwitch and Feng, 2023). The escalation of strained cross-strait relations seem to be on a steady, continuous, upward trajectory as stakeholders carefully calculate their next move.

Clash of Strategic Interests: the United States and China

The Taiwan Relations Act remains "remarkably modern for the strategic question" America faces (Burns, 2021); and the Assistant Secretary of State Kurt Campbell (2011) once referred to the TRA as one of the most important acts of "legislative leadership" and foreign policy in US history (HFAC, 2011). Since the last cross-strait crisis in 1995–1996, the theater witnessed the following changes: 1) the US–China strategic competition has been deepening, with the Chinese military continuing to upgrade and enhance its capabilities including counter-intervention capabilities (A2AD)[6]—capable of informationized warfare that increases the risk of escalation; 2) China experiencing a centralization of power with Xi being elected "President for life;" and 3) Taiwan experiencing a consolidation of democracy and declining interest in unification (Gunness and Saunders, 2022). China is currently so far removed from the once weak and inward-looking country of the 1970s, that it now is seeking to become the most powerful country of the world by destabilizing every dimension of power with predatory economic behavior and coercive efforts (Mendez, 2021; Zhang, 2019; Zhao, 2018).

For Washington, Taiwan holds strategic value that critically (and negatively) affects the US's preponderance in the theater if damaged. In addition to the core value of democracy and the rule-based order that is at the fundamental level, Taiwan is also an increasingly significant partner in trade, especially for semiconductors, and arms sales that totaled up to USD 21 billion since 2019 (Feng, 2023). In March 2023, the US State Department approved the Taipei Economic and Cultural Representative Office in the United States's (TECRO) request to buy AGM-88B High-Speed Anti-Radiation Missiles (HARM), AIM-120C-8 Advanced Medium Range Air-to-Air Missiles (AMRAAM), LAU-129 multi-purpose launchers, etc., leading to USD 619 million to US arms sales (DSCA, 2023).

Of most significance and importance, however, is the symbolic value Taiwan carries for the US's partners and allies in the region. Especially when its allies, such as Australia, are under Chinese intimidation and Japan and South Korea are under increasing threats posed by an emboldened and active Chinese military, how Washington treats its pseudo-ally, Taiwan, and deals with Chinese potential aggression will be put to the test. The alliance and the network of strategic partners are the key elements for the successful implementation of the US Asia-Pacific strategy; thus, successful deterrence or successful resolution of potential cross-strait conflict is directly connected to the future of the US's status in the theater.

China is currently set to 1) build a world-class military by 2049 under its thirteenth Five-Year Plan and Military-Civil Fusion Technology Development Strategy (DoD, 2021); 2) establish a "great modern socialist country" by 2035; and 3) launch "the great rejuvenation of the Chinese nation" by 2049 as Xi stated in 2019 (PRC, 2019). As China closely monitors the ongoing Russia–Ukraine war, the threat of isolation, the power of a rival coalition and alliance, and how the United States is working with these "tools" in Washington's diplomatic, military, and economic war chest provide a critical lesson. As much as China wants to physically suppress Taiwan and press on with its One China policy, US strategic interest in the region and its preponderance has turned the cross-strait relations into a strategic struggle, a regional and a global issue well beyond domestic political disagreement. Its relations with Taiwan, which China considers as its territory that is being governed democratically by Taipei (Reuters, 2023), is a localized flash point that may trigger a full-scale explosion to war with the United States.

Be on the Lookout for More Military Action in the Asian-Pacific?

According to the Center for Strategic and International Studies (CSIS) wargaming models on a Chinese amphibious invasion of Taiwan, the United States—with Taiwan and Japan—would defeat a conventional Chinese invasion and secure Taiwanese autonomy (Cancian et al., 2023). The wargaming scenarios were run in 24 iterations, and revealed that victory comes at a high price: the United States Navy and Air Force, lost between 169 and 372 aircrafts and the Navy lost 2 aircraft carriers and 7 to 20 destroyers and cruisers, while the Japanese lost around 122 aircrafts, in addition to tens of thousands of servicemembers (Cancian et al., 2023: 87–88). Furthermore, the results indicated that the cross-strait conflict will have a long-term effect on regional economic security to recover to the level previous to the invasion felt by every country in the world.

The conflict in the Taiwan Strait, however, is a simpler case compared to the potential crisis in the South China Sea. The territorial dispute of the South China Sea involves China, the Philippines, Brunei, Vietnam, Malaysia, and Taiwan who all have claims over different parts of the area. In the South China Sea, there are Chinese fighter jets and airborne early warning and control (AEW&C) aircraft operating and supported by 10,000-foot runways that Beijing has built on Woody Island, Fiery Cross Reef, Mischief Reef, and Subi Reef (AMTI, 2023). The disputed area is where the Chinese military is stationed and actively constructing infrastructure for a stronger Chinese presence and strategic military advantages. China's aggressive pursuit of territorial rights in the South China Sea is rooted in Chinese military strategy that is closely linked to its overall national development goals.

As China becomes more assertive in protecting its national interest, it is increasingly displaying its willingness to bend established international rules and norms (Vuković and Fechner, 2023). Thus, with the growing Chinese military presence in the region, the United States and its allies are placing greater importance on partnerships with Southeast Asian countries including the member states of the Association of Southeast Asian Nations (ASEAN) to expand the strategic network for deterring Chinese threat against regional peace and stability. Moreover, Southeast Asian countries are also keenly following cross-strait relations and participating in regional arms build-up.

Conclusion and Future Prospects

The Indo-Pacific theatre is rising as a priority theater for great power competition and potential adjustment of power configuration. The stakes are high for all the states since how they maneuver in this new era of great power competition, how they adapt to evolving security settings, and how the direction of their national security strategy and military posture will determine their fate in the long run. Amid the complex strategic calculations and multilayered security dynamics, military power and strategic deployment of military power sits at the center of national security of all nation-states in the theater.

As a revisionist power, China is challenging the US-led world order of the post-Cold War structure by expanding its military power. From the Chinese perspective, the US Indo-Pacific strategy or the relaunching of the Quadrilateral Security Dialogue (Quad) are instruments of a containment strategy against China, and thereby forcing Beijing's hand to increase its efforts to establish a new world order by boasting its military might and putting coercive pressure on its neighbors across various domains of nuclear, space, cyber, and maritime. Wielding its military power in coordination with its Belt and Road Initiative (BRI), and "wolf warrior" diplomacy, China is actively engaging in coercive measures to support its rise, "the rejuvenation of Chinese nation."

Due to the nature of the rising tension in the theater, the role of the United States in deterring threats against its allies in the region and promoting strategic partnerships between Washington and its allies becomes critical. As military power on all three levels of strategic, operational, and tactical acts is fundamental for states' security policy, the region will likely witness more events that test the US alliance system, more pressure on states' strategic power balancing, intensifying arms race and military buildups, and updates on states' deterrence posture. Despite the high stakes of the power competition in the Indo-Pacific era, the lessons from the Cold War, responsibility, and maturity in global policy making will guide us through the fog of war.

Notes

1 Scholars have different ideas on the concept of power. Hard power and soft power discussions see Joseph Nye's article (1990), and also see Richard Armitage's (2007) report on Smart Power. Freedman on power psychological and physical power (2008).

2 This often is called "security dilemma" in the realist literature. See Jervis (1978).
3 https://www.bbc.com/news/technology-49488614
4 https://www.nato.int/cps/en/natohq/topics_110496.htm#:~:text=Article%205%20provides%20that%20if,to%20assist%20the%20Ally%20attacked.
5 Hub-and-Spokes system is a unique security architecture found in Asia. It is a regional security architecture wherein the United States acts as a hub and its allies including Japan, South Korea, Australia, among others, are positioned as spokes via bilateral security agreements. Different from a multilateral setting like in the case of NATO, hub-and-spokes system is a collection of bilateral security ties centered around Washington. The United States offer security guarantee to these spokes with forward deployment/station of its armed forces. For more see Cha, V. D. (2009). Powerplay: Origins of the U.S. Alliance System in Asia. *International Security,* 34(3), 158–196. http://www.jstor.org/stable/40389236
6 "Counter-intervention capabilities" is Chinese wording equivalent to Anti Access Area Denial (A2AD) in the United States.

References

AFP-JIJI. April 9, 2023. "The Taiwan Strait: A History of Crises," *The Japan Times.* https://www.japantimes.co.jp/news/2023/04/09/asia-pacific/china-taiwan-strait-crises-history/.

Alagappa, Muthiah. 2001. *Coercion and Governance: The Declining Political Role of the Military in Asia.* Palo Alto: Stanford University Press.

Armitage, Richard and Nye, Joseph. 2007. "Smart Power and the US Strategy for Security in a Post-9/11 World." Testimony before the Subcommittee on National Security and Foreign Affairs, House Committee on Oversight and Government Reform, November 7.

Asia Maritime Transparency Initiative (AMTI). n.d. https://amti.csis.org.

Booth, Kenneth. 1991. "Security and Emancipation." *Review of International Studies* 17 (4): 313–326. http://www.jstor.org/stable/20097269.

Bracken, Paul. 2012. *The Second Nuclear Age: Strategy, Danger, and the New Power Politics.* New York: Henry Holt & Company LLC.

Brodie, Barnard and Frederick Dunn. 1946. *The Absolute Weapon: Atomic Power and World Order.* New Haven, CT: Yale Institute of International Studies.

Burns, Nicholas. 2021. "Senate Committee, Ambassadorship Confirming Hearing," https://www.c-span.org/video/?515354-1/ambassadorship-confirmation-hearing.

Buzan, Barry and Eric Herring. 2011. "Arms Races", in Barry Buzan and Eric Herring, C. Hughes and L. Meng. eds. *Strategic Studies.* New York and London: Routledge, pp. 213–231.

Buzan, Barry and Eric Herring. 1998. *The Arms Dynamic in World Politics.* Lynne Rienner Publishers.

Campbell, Kurt. October 2011. "House of Foreign Affairs Committee Hearing." Accessed June 26, 2023. https://www.govinfo.gov/content/pkg/CHRG-106shrg60900/html/CHRG-106shrg60900.htm.

Cancian, Mark, Matthew Cancian, and Eric Heginbotham. 2023. "The First Battle of the Next War: Wargaming a Chinese Invasion of Taiwan." Center for Strategic and International Studies (CSIS). https://www.csis.org/analysis/first-battle-next-war-wargaming-chinese-invasion-taiwan.

Cha, V.D. 2009. "Powerplay: Origins of the U.S. Alliance System in Asia." *International Security* 34 (3): 158–196. http://www.jstor.org/stable/40389236

Cottey, Andrew, Timothy Edmunds, and Anthony Forster. 2002. *Democratic Control of the Military in Postcommunist Europe: Guarding the Guards.* United Kingdom: Palgrave Macmillan.

CRS Report. 2023. "Taiwan: Political and Security Issues," June 13, 2023. https://crsreports.congress.gov/product/pdf/IF/IF10275.

Delpech, Thérèse, 2012. *Nuclear deterrence in the 21st Century: Lessons from the Cold War for a New Era of Strategic Piracy.* Santa Monica, CA: Rand Corporation.

DSCA (Defense Security Cooperation Agency), 2023. "Taipei Economic and Cultural Representative Office in the United States-F-16 Munitions." Accessed June 26, 2023. https://www.dsca.mil/press-media/major-arms-sales/taipei-economic-and-cultural-representative-office-united-states-f-16.

Fearon, James. 1998. "Bargaining, Enforcement, and International Cooperation." *International Organization* 52 (2): 269–305.

Feng, John. April 14, 2023. "Americans Warm to U.S. Defense of Taiwan if China Invades." *Newsweek.* Accessed June 26, 2023. https://www.newsweek.com/americans-warm-us-defense-taiwan-china-invades-1793738.

Finkelstein, M. David. 2007. "China's National Military Strategy: An Overview of the Military Strategic Guidelines." *Asia Policy* 4.

Freedman, Lawrence. 2004. *Deterrence.* Cambridge: Polity.

Freedman, Lawrence. 2014. "Strategic Studies and the Problem of Power." *Strategic Studies: A Reader*, pp. 22–33. London and New York: Routledge.

Glaser, Charles L. 1997. "The Security Dilemma Revisited." *World Politics* 50 (1): 171–201.

Glaser, Charles. 2000. "The Causes and Consequences of Arms Races." *Annual Review of Political Science* 3 (1): 251–276.

Gordon, Susan M., Michael G.Mullen, and David Sacks. 2023. *U.S.-Taiwan Relations in a New Era: Responding to a More Assertive China.* Independent Task Force Report No. 81., Council on Foreign Relations (CFR). Accessed June 29, 2023. https://live-tfr-cdn.cfr.org/sites/default/files/2023-06/TFR81_U.S.-TaiwanRelationsNewEra_SinglePages_2023-06-05_Online.pdf.

Gray, Colin. 1971. "The Arms Race Phenomenon." *World Politics* 24 (1): 39–79.

Gray, Colin. 1974. "The Urge to Compete: Rationales for Arms Racing." *World Politics* 26 (2): 207–233.

Gunness, Kristen and Phillip Saunders. 2022. "Averting Escalation and Avoiding War: Lessons from the 1995–1996 Taiwan Strait Crisis," National Defense University Press. https://ndupress.ndu.edu/Media/News/Article/3253814/averting-escalation-and-avoiding-war-lessons-from-the-19951996-taiwan-strait-cr/.

Hammond, Grant T. 1993. *Plowshares into Swords: Arms Races in International Politics.* Columbia: University of South Carolina Press.

House Foreign Affairs Committee (HFAC). 2011. "Why Taiwan Matters." October 4, 2011, https://democrats-foreignaffairs.house.gov/2011/10/why-taiwan-matters-part-ii

Huntington, Samuel P. 1958. "Arms Races-Prerequisites and Results." *Public Policy* 8: 41–86.

Huminski, Joshua. 2022. "Hard Power and Conventional Deterrence Still Matter, Just Ask Putin." *Breaking Defense*, January 5, 2022. https://breakingdefense.com/2022/01/hard-power-and-conventional-deterrence-still-matter-just-ask-putin/.

Jervis, Robert. 1978. "Cooperation Under the Security Dilemma." *World Politics* 30 (2): 167–214.

Jervis, Robert. 1976. "Perception and Misperception in International Politics." In *Perception and Misperception in International Politics*. Princeton University Press.

Kydd, Andrew. 1997. "Game Theory and the Spiral Model." *World Politics* 49 (3): 371–400.

Knopf, Jeffrey. 2010. "The Fourth Wave in Deterrence Research." *Contemporary Security Policy* 31 (1): 1–33, doi:10.1080/13523261003640819

LaGrone, Sam. June 21, 2023. "Carrier Sails Through Taiwan Strait One Day After U.S. Coast Guard Cutter" *USNI News*. https://news.usni.org/2023/06/21/china-sends-carrier-strike-group-through-taiwan-strait.

Lebow, Richard and Janice Stein. 1989. "Rational Deterrence Theory: I Think, Therefore I Deter." *World Politics*, 41 (2): 208–224.

Mahnken, Thomas. 2014. "Weapons: The Growth and Spread of the Precision-strike Regime" in Hughes, C. and Meng, L., eds. (2011). *Strategic Studies*. New York and London: Routledge, pp. 353–364.

Mendez, Robert. 2021. "Senate Committee, Ambassadorship Confirming Hearing." Accessed June 27, 2023. https://www.c-span.org/video/?515354-1/ambassadorship-confirmation-hearing.

Mietzner, Marcus. 2009. *Military Politics, Islam, and the State in Indonesia: From Turbulent Transition to Democratic Consolidation*. Institute of Southeast Asian Studies.

Morgan, Patrick. 1997. *Deterrence: A Conceptual Analysis*. Beverly Hills, CA: Sage Publication.

Nye, Joseph. 1990. "Soft Power." *Foreign Policy* (80): 153–171.

Paul, T.V., Patrick Morgan, and James Wirtz eds 2009. *Complex Deterrence: Strategy in the Global Age*. Chicago: University of Chicago Press.

Reuters. June 11, 2023. "Taiwan Sends Up Fighters as Chinese Warplanes Cross Strait's Median Line." Accessed June 26, 2023. https://www.reuters.com/world/asia-pacific/taiwan-says-10-chinese-warplanes-cross-straits-median-line-2023-06-11/.

Rider, Toby, Michael Findley, and Philip Diehl. 2011. "Just Part of the Game? Arms Races, Rivalry, and War." *Journal of Peace Research* 48 (1): 85–100.

Rim, Hyun Ji. 2023. "The US-China Strategic Competition and Emerging Technologies in the Indo-Pacific Region: Strategies for Building, Dominating, and Managing Networks." *Asian Perspective*, 47(1): 1–25.

Roberts, Brad. 2021. *Emerging and Disruptive Technologies, Multi-Domain Complexity, and Strategic Stability: A Review and Assessment of the Literature*. Center for Global Security Research, Lawrence Livermore National Laboratory.

Ruwitch, John and Emily Feng. 2023. "Taiwan President Tsai meets Kevin McCarthy despite Chines Warnings." April 5, 2023. *NPR*. Accessed June 26, 2023. https://www.npr.org/2023/04/05/1167872114/kevin-mccarthy-taiwan-president-tsai-meeting-california-china.

Sample, Susan. 1998. "Furthering the Investigation into the Effects of Arms Buildups." *Journal of Peace Research* 35 (1): 122–126.

Singer, J. David. 1958. "Threat-perception and the Armament-tension Dilemma." *Journal of Conflict Resolution* 2 (1): 90–105.

Snyder, Glenn. 1959. *Deterrence by Denial and Punishment*. Princeton: University of Princeton.

Snyder, Glenn. 1984. "The Security Dilemma in Alliance Politics." *World Politics*, 36 (4): 461–495.

The State Council The People's Republic of China (PRC). 2019. *China's National Defense in the New Era*. Accessed June 20, 2022. https://english.www.gov.cn/archive/whitepaper/201907/24/content_WS5d3941ddc6d08408f502283d.html.

The State Council Information Office of the People's Republic of China (PRC). August, 2022. "The Taiwan Question and China's Reunification in the New Era." Accessed June 20, 2023. http://english.scio.gov.cn/node_8032175.html.

The White House. 2022. *Indo-Pacific Strategy of the United States*. The White House.

Tian, Nan and Fei Su, 2021. *A New Estimate of China's Military Expenditure*. Stockholm International Peace Research Institute (SIPRI), Stockholm.

Tsai, Ing-wen. 2020. *President Tsai's Acceptance Speech*. Accessed June 10, 2023. https://www.taiwanembassy.org/kw_en/post/1360.html.

US Department of Defense (DoD). 2018. "National Defense Strategy: Sharpening the American Military Competitive Edge." Washington, DC. https://dod.defense.gov/Portals/1/Documents/pubs/2018-National-Defense-Strategy-Summary.pdf.

US Department of Defense (DoD). 2021. "Military and Security Developments Involving the People's Republic of China 2021." Washington, DC. https://media.defense.gov/2021/Nov/03/2002885874/-1/-1/0/2021-cmpr-final.pdf.

US Department of Defense (DoD). 2022. "2022 China Military Power Report." Washington, DC. https://media.defense.gov/2022/Nov/29/2003122280/-1/-1/1/2022-CHINA-MILITARY-POWER-REPORT.PDF.

US Department of Defense. 2023. "National Defense Science & Technology Strategy 2023." Available at: https://media.defense.gov/2023/May/09/2003218877/-1/-1/0/NDSTS-FINAL-WEB-VERSION.PDF

US Department of Defense. 2023. "DoD Releases National Defense Science and Technology Strategy". May 9, 2023. Washington, DC. https://www.defense.gov/News/Releases/Release/Article/3389118/dod-releases-national-defense-science-and-technology-strategy/.

Von Clausewitz, Carl. 1950. *On War*. Jazzybee Verlag.

Vuković, Sinisia and Paul Fechner. 2023. "China's Behavior and Ambitions to Become a Norm-maker in the South China Sea Dispute." *Asian Perspective* 47 (2): 247–265.

Zhang, Ketian. 2019. "Cautious Bully: Reputation, Resolve, and Beijing's Use of Coercion in the South China Sea." *International Security* 44 (1): 117–159.

Zhao, Suisheng. 2018. "China and the South China Sea Arbitration: Geopolitics Versus International Law." *Journal of Contemporary China* 27 (109): 1–15.

4 Terrorists Threats to Security

Maria Ortuoste and Cameron Olson

Introduction and Overview

Political violence is neither new, unique nor the sole preserve of any one country, ideology, religion, or culture. In world history, violence is "intimately intertwined" with the creation of, and perpetuation of, the contemporary Westphalian state. Colonial and contemporary states' practices of exclusion, intimidation, and cultural cleansing have led to armed challenges. Terrorism, including "transnational terrorism," is just one more iteration of this political violence.

This chapter discusses terrorism in South and Southeast Asia within the context of the globalized acceptance, but problematic nature, of the post-colonial state. That is, the organizational form of the state is sustained not only through force or compliance but, also by international and regional environments that privilege this political organization over all others, thereby rendering other polities as non-entities or subpar entities in the international arena. This leads to militancy and subsequent militarized responses by the government. The first section examines the following questions: Who has the legitimate right to survive and whose grievances are worthy of being addressed? To put it in contemporary security parlance, should the political survival of the state override human security? The second and third sections examine terrorism in South and Southeast Asia in a comparative and chronological manner. It begins with the wave of independence in the 1950s up to the end of the Cold War, and from *al Qaeda* to the Global War on Terror (GWoT) to the current time. The final section assesses different measures to prevent and counter terrorism in terms of their protection of, or harm to, human security.

The Use Of Political Violence By State And Non-State Actors

Global Acceptance of the State's Monopoly of Violence

To understand transnational terrorism, it is not enough to discuss how current technology diffused ideas more quickly or made attacks deadlier; rather, one has to take note of the globalized acceptance of the contemporary nation-state

DOI: 10.4324/9781003473206-4

"as the principal representative of a cohesive socio-political-cultural collective is entrenched in postcolonial societies" (Parashar, 2018: 113). Scholars of critical terrorism studies argue that because of this, there is a need to understand the "legacy of colonial control and marginalization which legitimizes territorial nation-states and challenges alternative ways of collective political and cultural existence" (Parashar, 2018: 111).

Colonial powers forcibly unified disparate polities into a few political entities. Co-optation, cooperation, and collusion were also part of this state-building process; however, the continued existence of these polities meant that their relations with the central government were tenuous at best, and conflictual at worst. These "competing referents for political community within states" involved not only the control of territory but also legitimacy of leadership. This is one of the reasons why Alagappa argues that any discussion of Asian security should include the "problematic nature of states" (1998: 679).

In this milieu, the colony's successor state seeks to prove its legitimacy through discourse and force. Discursively, it adopts the rhetoric of unified peoples under one nation-state that is sovereign and independent. Physically, the agents of the state seek to monopolize the legitimate use of violence within its territory. In the case of successor states, the military is primarily turned inward against challenges to the political survival of the new state rather than outward to external enemies. This brings to mind the *regime de la terreur* in late eighteenth-century France and, later, the fear and violence perpetrated in Nazi Germany, Stalin's USSR, and Mao Zedong's China.

Asian policy-makers' conception of national security revolves around the political survival of the state, notwithstanding discussions about "comprehensive security" at the end of the Cold War (Alagappa, 1998). Up to the current time, state practices and institutions privilege political survival over issues of human security. As such, successor states create more challengers who, at various points in time, were or continue to be labeled as terrorists, in the same manner as colonists labeled independence movements as terrorists.

Terror and Counter-Terror

Terrorism is a form of political violence that "has within its ambit most forms of politically motivated violent attacks targeted at unarmed civilians or security actors outside a regular war" (Parashar, 2018: 111). As it is used in contemporary legal contexts, the term "terrorists" refers to non-state or subnational actors that use lethal force against civilian actors or non-combatants located in "soft targets" (e.g. malls, hotels, places of worship).

In broad terms, militant groups seek to recast the states' territorial boundaries and the scope of their authority, while simultaneously trying to open up political space and economic opportunities for their groups. The motivations of militant groups can be a mix of ethno-nationalism or counter-nationalism, secular political ideologies, or religion. Moreover, militant groups do not rely solely on violence. Some of them have engaged in other activities which can include politics, local governance, charity, and education.

"By killing one and scaring a thousand," terrorism is a cost-effective way to garner compliance, at least in the short term. To be effective, political violence should not only "violate the taboos of the prevailing order but [it] also has to give the impression of an attempt not just to nudge, but to *overwhelm* some persons or objects symbolic of that order" (from Peter Merkl, 1986 in Parashar, 2018: 111). It is also meant to provoke governments into a militarized response, and to limit civil and political rights via extraordinary measures such as profiling, surveillance, warrantless arrests, extrajudicial killings, or limiting the movement and rights of suspected communities. Governments have also deputized some of these tasks to paramilitary groups that have no public accountability.

But this concern over political survival, defined within a Westphalian state system, also prevents negotiated settlements that could shrink the new states' territory, or limit its sovereignty. Identifying people as terrorists is, therefore, a "deeply political act" with the term applied by "state authorities to persons they deem may be legitimately killed or tortured" (Peoples and Vaugh-Williams, 2021: 233 and 243). Why then would governments want to give credence to their grievances no matter how real they are? Governments also contend that this appeasement will only embolden other militants to take up arms and will eventually lead to the state's downfall. These considerations make untangling the roots of discontent more difficult, which then prolongs conflict. And because no settlement will ever obtain unanimous approval, it is possible that some government or militant actors may withdraw from the process and become spoilers to any peace deal achieved.

Regional and Global Connections

States and militant groups have benefited from globalization. States are the only recognized legitimate entity in international law and are the only ones allowed to be members of the United Nations. Reinforcing statehood has been one of the aims of the United Nations, and other regional organizations such as the Association of Southeast Asian Nations (ASEAN). States and their citizens do benefit from international trade, but inequity persists. External assistance provided by allies and international financial institutions gave states access to finances, weapons, and other resources to solidify their institutions. Interstate competition and territorial disputes have also exacerbated domestic political violence either by the state or non-state actors. Over time, globalized processes and technologies have facilitated economic growth, and the spread of ideas and ideologies, but they also broadened the market for weapons, illegal drugs, and human trafficking. The linkages that made economic development possible have enabled the funding, arming, and recruitment of militant groups.[1] As a result, states do not necessarily have a monopoly over violence, or at least a monopoly over the means of violence anymore.

Governments have preferred to deal with militancy and terrorism unilaterally because they do not want to compromise their sovereignty, or they prefer solutions that are fine-tuned to their unique socio-cultural environment, or they may want to appear in control for other reasons such as to attract foreign investments. The second preference is bilateral cooperation, especially with formal allies, like the U.S. and USSR, which provide military and economic assistance. International cooperation was not pursued in earnest until after the September 11th attacks.

Terrorisms In South and Southeast Asia (1950s to Mid-1990s)

Political Survival of States versus Human Security[2]

Since independence, the primary concern of Asian policy-makers has been the political survival of their states (Alagappa, 1998: 679). In post-World War II conferences, Asian leaders understood that their multi-ethnic and multi-religious states were at risk for internal conflict, which former colonists could take advantage of to return to power. India, for example, has over 4,636 communities divided by caste, tribes, and different languages, and they adhere to various religions or sects thereof. There are around 135 different ethnic groups in Myanmar but only eight national races are officially recognized. Indonesia consists of 1,300 ethnic groups who speak over 300 languages and practice Islam, Catholicism, Protestantism, Confucianism, Buddhism, and Hinduism.[3]

To prevent re-colonization, the new leaders adopted discourses and practices that were similar to, if not the same as, those of the former rulers. Discursively, newly independent states argued that their political survival was a bulwark against external intervention. The call for Asian solidarity and national unity, however, was based on preconditions such as the assimilation of "non-indigenous groups" (primarily Indians and Chinese residing in other countries) into the new states, and on assumptions about the civilizational superiority of dominant ethnic groups over tribal populations (Thakur, 2019). It is therefore not surprising that some countries like Indonesia rescinded previous laws on regional autonomy, or that India withdrew support from similar promises made before independence. Discriminatory policies and heavy-handed tactics fueled militancy, many of which continue to this time. In India, for example, anti-Sikh riots in the 1970s led to the creation of the *Babbar Khalsa International* (BKI)* whose objective is to form an independent Sikh state of Khalistan in the Punjab region. In other cases, like in the southern Philippines and in Aceh, the locals continued their long history of resisting outsiders. Some groups like the *Liberation Tigers of Tamil Eelam* (LTTE) in Sri Lanka and the different Malay Muslim groups in southern Thailand were/are motivated by ethno-nationalism in the face of assimilationist policies from the center.[4] Prior to their independence, the Bangladeshis characterized West Pakistan's centralization of authority as "internal colonization" (Lionel, 2008).

But some newly independent countries annexed other territories for purported strategic or historic reasons. Indonesia took West Irian and occupied East Timor, while India formally incorporated Manipur. Although Timor-Leste eventually won its independence in 2002, the Free Papua Movement (OPM)* continues to clash with Indonesian forces while ethnic clashes among Meiteis, Kukis, and Nagas in India erupted in 2023.

Other militant groups fighting against inequitable social and economic structures do not seek to create separate states and are organized around secular political ideologies. *Janatha Vimukthi Peramuna* (JVP) sought to foment a communist revolution in Sri Lanka, while the New People's Army (NPA)* in the Philippines still wants to establish a socialist state even after more than 50 years. The Maoist Communist Party of India (CPI)* has a similar goal and has engaged in "competitive state-building" against the Indian state; but the CPI opposes Taliban threats to India's territorial integrity (Parashar, 2018: 118–119).

To enforce national unity over fragmented societies, colonial laws were adopted. Malaysia, Singapore, and Indonesia for instance retained Britain's Internal Security Act and the Dutch penal, civil, and criminal codes. These laws allowed individuals to be arrested without warrants and indefinitely detained even if they are merely suspected of sedition, secession, communism, or terrorism. Concomitantly, military establishments gained more power, especially in Pakistan, Myanmar, Indonesia, Thailand, and the Philippines. And they committed some of the most egregious human rights violations such as West Pakistan's Operation Searchlight, which resulted in the deaths of between 500,000 to three million people in East Pakistan and millions of refugees (Boissoneault, 2016), and Indonesia's massacre of between 500,000 to one million alleged communists, their sympathizers, and their families between 1965 to 1966.

Thus, while competing narratives existed within the newly independent states, the state narrative was backed up with a greater amount of force and was enabled by an international political order that privileged the nation-state.

Religion as Narrative and Counter-Narrative

Religions, such as Christianity or Islam, have been used to justify foreign occupation, and it is not surprising that many independence movements also evinced a range of religious beliefs. In the Philippines, the Muslims in southern Mindanao had been fighting for their homeland against the Spanish Catholic colonists and, later, the American Protestant colonists. With 60% of Muslims in the world living in Asia, it is also not surprising that different variants of Islamic thought would be part of competing narratives, but they manifested differently due to unique historic circumstances.

South and Southeast Asia underwent different patterns of Islamization (Mutalib, 1998). Traders brought Islam to Southeast Asia where the religion "overlaid on animist, Hindu, and Buddhist traditions in Indonesia," in contrast to the Middle East and South Asia where Islam spread by military conquest (CRS, 2005). Upon independence, religious extremism was just one of many counter-narratives against statist narratives in both sub-regions. In the 1960s, the original members of ASEAN coincidentally adopted policies to temper extreme versions of Islam. Thus, Islamic parties did not dominate politics in Indonesia or Malaysia despite their substantial Muslim populations (MacDonald and Lemco, 2002: 388). The "radical Islamic fringe" in Indonesian society and politics, which had called for the imposition of Sharia Law beginning 1945, was effectively "depoliticized and circumscribed" by the Suharto regime. The government imprisoned people like Abu Bakar Ba'asyir and Abdullah Sungkar who later became leaders of *Jemaah Islamiyah*,* one of the deadliest militant groups in Indonesia. But Southeast Asian governments also went after suspected communists, pro-democracy activists, indigenous groups, and other perceived competitors to the state. These actions were enabled by ASEAN principles of "unity in diversity" and non-interference in each other's internal affairs; thereby giving regional endorsement for forceful measures to quash dissent.

In South Asia, "competing conceptualizations of national identity" between the Congress Party and the Muslim League pre-dated independence. But beliefs in Hindutva and Islamism intensified during and after the traumatic 1947 partition when around 15 million people migrated across thousands of miles to newly created India and Pakistan (AFP, 2017). Not only did this arrangement ignore the sentiments of people who may have wanted to stay in their country irrespective of their religious affiliation, but it also unleashed widespread brutality that drive ethnic and religious narratives up to the current time. State enforcement of national unity did not help; for example, it was not uncommon for Muslims in India to be required to show their loyalty to the new state (PTI, 2016). Further demographic changes increased separatist sentiments in areas like the Indian Punjab after 1947 (Talbot, 2019: 13).

India declared itself a democratic secular republic upon independence; however, some of its state governments enacted laws that were more akin to Hindu nationalism. Pakistan became a military authoritarian regime, but, over time, conservative Islam played a greater role in its political, economic, and social life. Zia ul-Haq introduced "Islamic reforms in Pakistan's legal, educational, and economic system" to obtain support from major religious political parties, and to prevent the "political rehabilitation of secular and socialist elements" in other parties (Ahmad, 1996: 376). By delegitimizing secular political forces, the Pakistani government could credibly say that they were a, if not, the, "defender of Islam."

These ideologies also colored other regional flashpoints such as the occupation of Jammu and Kashmir. India and Pakistan accused each other of supporting militant groups against their respective governments, especially after the 1971 India–Pakistan War when the former supported East Pakistan's independence from West Pakistan.

Geopolitics

Cold War geopolitics reinforced the different trajectories of South and Southeast Asia. The anti-communist interests of the original ASEAN members coincided with those of the U.S. Asia-Pacific states also saw the U.S. as a stabilizing presence so ASEAN states focused on economic development. The U.S. supported the counter-insurgency operations of the Philippines and Thailand and also turned a blind eye to the 1965–1966 mass killings in Indonesia.

Pakistan similarly benefited from its anti-communist stance and India's close relationship with the USSR. The U.S. provided Pakistan with intermittent material support, which became more consistent when the USSR invaded Afghanistan in 1979. The U.S. had previously ignored calls from its own diplomats to prevent the 1971 Bangladeshi massacre.[5] The US, in effect, buttressed the legitimacy and capabilities of these new states against militant groups that had legitimate demands and grievances against the central government.

Pakistan became the conduit for U.S. and Saudi Arabian aid to the anti-Soviet *mujahideen* forces, as well as a sanctuary for organized military operations, and a host of Afghan refugees.[6] U.S. provided economic and military assistance, but Pakistan's Inter-Services Intelligence (ISI) was in charge of distributing this aid to the various *mujahideen* groups. ISI, however, favored the Islamist groups linked to Gulbuddin Hekmatyar who was motivated by jihadist ideology and was the mastermind of acid attacks against women, according to historian Ali A. Olomi (Stewart, 2021). They shared similar ideologies and opposed Afghan president Daoud's efforts to create *Pashtunistan*, which would have resulted in the loss of Pakistan's northwestern territories (Galster, 2001). Because there was a constant need to replenish people at the battlefront, external funding was also used to recruit foreign fighters into the *mujahideen*. This became the seeds for the transnationalization of terrorist activities under *al Qaeda*.

Global Processes and Violence (Mid-1990s to the Current Time)

States' Narratives

During this period, Southeast Asian states supplemented their narrative of national unity with a mantra of economic growth, which they saw as "a critical resource for political legitimation" and "a critical element of national power" (Alagappa, 1998: 685–686). Coupled with neoliberal economic policies on open domestic markets to global trade and investments, Southeast Asian states benefited from the spread of technology and the development of global supply (value-added) chains. From 1975 to the 1990s, several ASEAN countries experienced annual GDP growth rates that ranged from 3.4% to 12.2% – Singapore, Malaysia, Thailand, and Indonesia were considered as newly (or almost) industrializing countries. The states attributed this growth to "Asian Values" which argued that human rights should be implemented in sequential order, i.e. ensure people's rights to "prosperity" first before civil and political rights. To put it bluntly, authoritarianism is justified as long as people get rich.

In stark contrast, South Asia was "wracked by terrorist, insurgent, and separatist violence in a manner unmatched in the world" (Chellaney, 2001: 96). Statist narratives remained the same although racist and religious overtones were becoming more noticeable. During this period, several South Asian states were fighting militants whose attacks were bolder such as the one perpetrated by the LTTE against Rajiv Gandhi in 1991. India was also dealing with militants fighting against its occupation of Kashmir, for separatism, or for the overhaul of its economic system. Some of these militant organizations – the United Liberation Front of Assam*, the Nationalist Socialist Council of Nagaland-Isak-Muivah (NSCN-IM)*, the National Liberation Front of Tripura*, and the Communist Party of India* – are still active to this day.

Southeast Asia, however, was not immune from non-state political violence. Underneath the façade of stability and prosperity, "there was huge change, social ferment, competing interests, and few lawful outlets for public debate and public disagreement" in Suharto's Indonesia and in Malaysia (Taylor, 2003: 373). In newly democratic Thailand, the economic disparities between urban and rural populations resulted in serious political crises, while in democratic Philippines, agrarian reform was stalled and the establishment of the Autonomous Region of Muslim Mindanao in 1989 did not dampen the fight for secession by other Muslim militants like the Moro Islamic Liberation Front (MILF) separatists. More importantly, regional economic growth did not alleviate old grievances such as those of ethnic minorities in Myanmar, the separatists in Aceh and southern Thailand, and pro-democracy activists in these countries precisely because of state-led political violence. Popular disaffection facilitated the recruitment and indoctrination of new people into radical ideologies (Abuza, 2003 and Gunaratna, 2002).

Thus, the call for a global *jihad* against communism was attractive to many Indonesian, Malaysian, and Filipino Muslim militants. The money, munitions, and other supplies provided by the U.S. and Saudi Arabia were used to recruit and to equip these foreign fighters.[7] They received weapons and explosives training in the *mujahideen* camps, gained actual combat experience, and they began to support the creation of an Islamic caliphate across countries. When the USSR was defeated in 1989, Southeast Asian militants who joined the *mujahideen* returned home, bringing with them combat training and radical ideologies that permeated their organizations. The leaders of *Jemaah Islamiyah* (Abdullah Sungkar and Abu Bakar Bashir), the *Moro Islamic Liberation Front* (Hashim Salamat), and the *Abu Sayyaf Group* or ASG* (Abdurajak Janjalani) all fought in this war.[8] More importantly, they formed strong fraternal bonds and operational relationships among themselves and with other fighters in the *mujahideen*. The extent and depth of these connections were unearthed only after the 9/11 attacks – an operation that took years of planning involving Saudis, Yemenis, Pakistanis, and Filipinos who were located in various cells in Afghanistan, the Philippines, and Germany.[9]

In Afghanistan, the withdrawal of Soviet troops in 1989 led to civil war, which the Taliban would win in 1996. They created an Islamist state that effectively terrorized their own citizens. The *mujahideen* training camps were not dismantled. Combined with the lucrative poppy trade, the availability of loose firearms and an active black market for weapons, and the organizational savvy of Osama bin Laden, Afghanistan became the central headquarters of *al Qaeda* whose goal was to wage a worldwide *jihad* against the West.

In effect, *al Qaeda* embodied the rejection of a Westphalian system of state territoriality in favor of an imagined transnational Caliphate. By the end of this period, states found that they did not have a monopoly over resources and the use of force; neither were they able to control the spread of counter-narratives (religious or otherwise) that were transmitted via the web and social media. However, it should be noted that other militant groups continued to commit acts of terrorism only within their own countries even if they were, in one way or another, linked to global processes like financial transfers, the smuggling of illegal arms, and drug trafficking.

Global War on Terror

In less than one month after 9/11, the US bombed and invaded Afghanistan targeting *al Qaeda* strongholds. This massive military operation drove out *al Qaeda* and led to the Taliban's fall from power, and the start of their own terrorist attacks on the new Afghan government and occupying military forces. In 2003, the US invaded Iraq and inadvertently opened a new front for self-proclaimed jihadists worldwide, leading to the creation of the *Islamic State (IS)*.

Bush's GWoT offered a justification for the states to continue narratives about national unity; and much like the Cold War, the U.S. offered material resources to enforce that national unity. Sri Lanka supported GWoT and received international assistance to stop foreign funding for the LTTE, and the U.S.-trained Sri Lankan counter-terrorist mobile forces routed LTTE leaders and members, leading to their ultimate defeat in 2009. The Philippines was another recipient of U.S. aid and training to fight the *al-Qaeda*-allied ASG that had been kidnapping and killing many foreigners.

India also realized narrative and geostrategic victories. First, Pakistan was weakened with less U.S. aid and stricter monitoring. And when Pakistan was subjected to around 430 confirmed U.S. drone strikes between 2004 to 2018 (Khudadad, 2022), India felt vindicated in its accusations of Pakistan as a state-sponsor of terror. Four years after 9/11, India reaped another geopolitical advantage: it signed a bilateral agreement with the U.S. for a Civil Nuclear Agreement which *de facto* recognized India's nuclear-weapon status without having been a party to the Nuclear Non-Proliferation Treaty. Third, India gained material support from the U.S. after the 2008 Mumbai attacks by the Pakistan-based terrorist group *Lashkar-e-Taiba** whose aim is to liberate Kashmir from Indian control. In a way, this appeared to support India's legitimate claims for coercive tactics in Kashmir. Finally, the Pakistani government was suspected of being complicit in U.S. drone strikes that killed approximately 2,500 4,026 individuals – 424 to 959 were civilians and included children. This severely undermined the legitimacy of the Pakistani government to its people, especially in the Federally Administered Tribal Areas (FATA) where an alliance of militant groups formed the *Terik-e-Taliban** to fight the Pakistani army.

Countries with Muslim majorities, specifically Indonesia and Malaysia, were more hesitant and less vocal in supporting the U.S. But the bombing of resorts in Bali by *Jemaah Islamiyah* (JI) in 2002, as well as the discovery of JI sympathizers in Malaysia, led to more active efforts. Malaysia began to quietly cooperate with the U.S., while Indonesia set up its anti-terrorist force, *Densus 88*, with funding from the U.S. State Department (Dayley, 2017). In the ensuing years, more groups would pledge loyalty to *al Qaeda* and, later, to *Islamic State* (IS) in Southeast Asia, even though the attraction of these ideologies differed in each country.[10] Some of the worst terrorist attacks over the next 20 years occurred in India, Pakistan, Afghanistan, Iraq, Syria, Indonesia, and the Philippines.

Problematic Solutions

From 2000 to 2018, the worldwide economic costs of terrorist attacks were $855 billion with 51% due to deaths, 43% from GDP losses; and the rest from property damages and injuries (Bardwell and Iqbal, 2021). Counter-terrorist measures have helped decrease global deaths due to terrorist attacks from 10,699 in 2015 to 7,142 in 2022 – a 33.5% decrease – but terrorist attacks have become deadlier with 26% more people likely to die in those attacks in 2022 than in 2015 (IEP, 2023).[11]

By 2016, attacks on civilians were declining and by 2018, more attacks on police, military, and infrastructure were recorded (IEP, 2023). Militant groups have different primary targets. In Kashmir, "Islamist threat groups" targeted minorities and migrant workers (mostly Indian). In southern Thailand, secessionist groups targeted the "economic bases of the Thai state" such as stores and gas stations. In Afghanistan, *Islamic State-Khorasan Province* (ISK)* targeted mosques, schools, and workplaces possibly to ensure that extremist views persist. In Myanmar, the military and the police have been the targets of bombings, shootings, and knife attacks by militants fighting against the junta.

Unfortunately, the costs of terrorism are borne disproportionately – Middle East and Africa (MENA), South Asia, and sub-Saharan Africa accounted for 91% of all deaths from terrorism and have experienced the largest economic impact in terms of GDP (Bardwell and Iqbal, 2021). Looming environmental disasters are expected to compound the reasons for violence. Six out of ten countries most impacted by terrorism have "the worst ecological threats and lowest resilience" according to the 2022 *Ecological Threat Report*, and around 58% of the world's 830 million food insecure live in the 20 countries most affected by terrorism (IEP, 2023). States, therefore, need to calibrate a range and combination of responses that will help solve the causes, and not merely the symptoms, of terrorism.

Kinetic Measures

Military or militarized responses are the default modes for governments in order to neutralize the threat. Their objectives are to "decapitate" or kill the leaders of the groups, to eliminate or imprison followers and sympathizers, and to deny them access to possible support from the civilian population. These can be effective in the short-term but there are negative long-term effects.

First, the militant groups can simply re-group and return. The U.S. bombing of Afghanistan destroyed much of *al Qaeda*'s sites and even killed several leaders, but its cells regrouped in Yemen, Iraq, and the Islamic Maghreb (Cragin, 2014). Similarly, after being driven from their stronghold and some leaders killed, the members of ASG returned several months after the U.S. and Philippine forces left Basilan. ASG resumed kidnap-for-ransom activities, bombings, and attacks on towns in the islands of Visayas and Mindanao.

Second, the conduct of war can lead to greater or new resistance. As previously mentioned, the drone attacks in the Federally Administered Tribal Areas (FATA) led to further distrust of the Pakistani government and is probably one reason for the creation of *Tehrik e-Taliban* (Khan et al., 2021: 28–30). The U.S. invasion of Iraq in 2003 led to widespread chaos which made it fertile ground for radicalization and provided combat training for fighters that would form the *Islamic State* (IS).

Third, turning the war into a "nation-building" enterprise was extremely challenging – the U.S. and allied forces stayed for more than 20 years in Afghanistan. During that time a new government was formed, security forces were trained, and reforms such as the education of girls were undertaken. There was widespread mistrust of the Afghan governments and the Taliban's terrorist attacks were relentless. The war claimed around 243,000 lives, of which almost 70,000 were civilians at the Afghan/Pakistani front from both Taliban and allied forces actions. Eventually, the U.S. and Taliban negotiated the *Doha Agreement* which included the withdrawal of foreign forces from Afghanistan. In August 2021, the Taliban defeated the Afghan security and the U.S. completed its troop withdrawal.

Issues in International Cooperation

The transnational linkages among militant groups pushed countries to embark on cooperative arrangements to disrupt financial links, which was always a sensitive issue. The Financial Action Task Force (FATF) is the international watchdog for money laundering and terrorist financing. They set standards for financial systems and provide advice for national governments. Other groups seek to improve capacities, such as the Southeast Asian Regional Center for Counter-Terrorism's (SEARCCT) goal is similarly training, capacity-building, and research on various aspects of terrorism which includes aviation, maritime, and transportation security, as well as crisis management and CBRNE (chemical, biological, radioactive, nuclear, and explosive) weapons. The Proliferation Security Initiative (PSI), which was launched by the U.S. in 2003, is supposed to prevent the spread of WMDs, their delivery systems, and their materials. Around 106 countries have endorsed the PSI and they receive training on developing interdiction capacities. It is, however, difficult to assess the PSI's success rate because "it uses shared intelligence" and interdictions are conducted in separate operations (Davenport, 2022).

Other arrangements are operational in nature. In 2017, Indonesia, Malaysia, and the Philippines concluded their Trilateral Cooperation Agreement to jointly police their shared seas where militants have been known to cross and perpetrate terrorist attacks. The ASEAN members are also trying to improve the exchange of strategic intelligence through the Our Eyes Initiative they finalized in 2018. Yet concrete cooperation among ASEAN countries is extremely slow and hampered by concerns about their respective sovereignties.

Unfortunately, some countries have malign intentions for cooperating. China and Russia enthusiastically supported the GWoT if only to lessen international scrutiny and criticism over their treatment of minorities like the Uighurs and the Chechens, respectively. The political motives in defining terrorists is also a danger with national anti-terror laws.[12]

Anti-Terror or Anti-Human Rights?

Over the past two decades, several anti-terrorism/counter-terrorism legislation were passed in Asian countries that are similar in three ways.[13] First, the definition of "terrorist" and "terrorism" can be overly broad so that almost anyone can be labeled a terrorist for defying the government. Second, due process and human rights are not the priorities of these laws. Third, these laws typically grant governments sweeping powers without effective safeguards and oversight, the denial of due process, and the "exercise of excessive powers by law enforcement agencies." The United Nations has found that these legislations and policies breed a "climate of impunity and has undermined the effectiveness of counter-terrorism measures."[14] Unfortunately, many governments had already been employing such repressive practices before 2001. The GWoT simply provided many governments with another narrative to justify taking extraordinary means to ensure state security and survival.

These laws are more dangerous when paired with populist rhetoric. India's prime minister Narendra Modi revived Hindu nationalism, ushering in a new wave of Islamophobia. Under India's UAPA, police have arrested activists, government critics, student protesters, persons from rural and tribal communities, political opponents, and minorities, especially Muslims. In addition, many protesters and journalists who happen to be Muslim Kashmiris have been detained as terrorists under the Public Safety Act (Tayler, 2022). "The fear [of Muslims to practice their religion] is linked to zealous vigilantism, but also amended citizenship laws that prohibit Muslim immigrants from becoming naturalized and seek to strip bona fide Muslim citizens of their status" (Beydoun, 2020: 98). That is, to be a citizen of India, one has to be Hindu – a form of identity and association that reminds one of post-partition politics.[15]

In Southeast Asia, there is a similar toughening of laws and increasing the capabilities of these agencies. Indonesia's premier counter-terrorism force, *Densus 88*, has been extremely successful in neutralizing *Jemaah Islamiyah*. However, *Densus 88* reports to "Brimob, the paramilitary corps of the Indonesian police force" and in 2015 the government created "a new anti-terrorist unit under the control of the Indonesian army, the Joint Special Operations Command" (Facal, 2020: 134–135). The militarization of these responses harkens back to the colonial period of turning the military inward to control the country's citizens. And in South Asia, there are around 62 paramilitary police units (PPUs) with four distinct characteristics – they carry offensive weapons and technologies; they adopt "military-style appearances, beliefs, and cultures;" they prefer battle-sized formations, and they take "an offensive posture in gathering intelligence and handling high-risk operations" (Ashraf, 2019).

Negotiated Peace and Structural Violence

According to the Institute of Economics and Peace, terrorism is highly correlated with "political terror" or state-directed violence and "group grievances." That is, governments that commit human rights violations such as "extra-judicial killings, torture, and imprisonment without trial," coupled with a long history of conflict due to structural socio-politico-economic problems tend to be the site of terrorist attacks. It is necessary for lasting solutions to address these structural problems, but there are few examples of such.

In Sri Lanka, the government "won" the war with a mix of strategies that eventually limited the number of LTTE fighters, and dried up their funding sources. The government also engaged in addressing poverty in order to gain public support (Layton, 2015). Slowly, the country grew, economically, but its recent crises led to protests and the government used the old anti-terror law against the peaceful protesters (HRW, 2022).

In the Philippines, the government's negotiations with MILF led to breakaway groups such as the *Bangsamoro Islamic Freedom Fighters*,* the *Rajah Solaiman Movement*,* and the *Maute Group*, which are more brutal and reportedly had ties with *Jemaah Islamiyah*. Nevertheless, a peace agreement was finalized and the *Bangsamoro Autonomous Region in Muslim Mindanao* (BARMM) was finally established in 2019 following two referendums. BARMM still needs assistance to become more self-sufficient, but in May 2023, BARMM reported a decrease in inflation rates, which has helped reduce costs for food, transport, housing, water, electricity, and gas (BIO, 2023). In addition, it is reported that the government's combatant surrender program has successfully led the surrender of 1,600 IS-linked militants but there are concerns about its "fiscal sustainability" (Tangging and Yeo, 2023). In Marawi province, a five-month siege involving the *Maute Group*, the Philippine military and special forces, and U.S. assistance, ended with the destruction of the province. More than 900 local and foreign militants, 150 security forces, and 45 civilians were killed. The conflict displaced 98% of the population, or 350,000 individuals, and rebuilding will cost more than $1 billion. During the martial law period imposed in the area, "thirty-seven mosques, forty-four madrasas, and twenty-two schools" were destroyed (Facal, 2020: 136). Several environmental defenders, farmers, and local officials were killed during that time by the armed forces who claimed that they were members of the communist New People's Army (Ortuoste, 2022). It took more than five years for displaced persons to return to their homes.[16] Moreover, the plan to rebuild with Marawi has been criticized for corruption and lack of interest for the residents' interests (Aben, 2020).

Resilience

Militant groups have also demonstrated remarkable resilience. *Islamic State* lost control of its territories, but it continues to spread its propaganda and recruit people via the web and social media platforms. Scholars have called this decentralized community of supporters a "digital Caliphate" or a "virtual Caliphate" the aim of which is to "create, connect, and deceive" (Criezis, 2022). Militants are also quick to use emerging technologies. The *Maute Group* used off-the-shelf UAVs for reconnaissance during the 2017 Marawi siege, while civilian drones rigged with explosives were used to attack military bases, police stations, and checkpoints in Myanmar (Ramakrishna, 2023). Moreover, it is expected that artificial intelligence (AI) will "enhance cyber-attacks and digital disinformation campaigns" and might even provide launch-and-forget capabilities for crafts (Schori Liang, 2023: 74).

Jemaah Islamiyah has also changed tactics from violent attacks to "infiltration" of political parties, mass organizations and government agencies (Chew, 2023). And in Malaysia and Singapore, which have very strong anti-terror laws, lone-actor attacks are common. Hybrid militants, described as "civilians with no known links to militant groups" but who were "'radicalized online, carry out an attack … [and] slip back to civilian life,'" also operate in Kashmir (Ramakrishna, 2023).

Conclusion and Future Prospects: Political Survival and Human Security

The United Nations recognizes that terrorism requires comprehensive solutions that go beyond "law enforcement, military or security measures to address development, good governance, human rights, and humanitarian concern."[17] To do this, the notion of political survival needs to be re-imagined so that states move away from: Should political survival outweigh human security? To answer that question, it is necessary to re-imagine the concept of political survival, specifically the bases of the political survival of the state. And that reconceptualization requires moving away from colonialist practices and to consider structural problems – inequity, distrust, hate – as a nationwide problem and not limited to certain areas. That is, calls for autonomy by minority groups are not simply about "threatening the country's territorial integrity"; rather they are symptoms of deep societal and political problems that affect everyone, including the majority population, albeit in differing degrees. Thus, we need to look at political survival and human security as an integrated system where even minute changes can have widespread effects.

In the final irony, once the Taliban took over the government in Afghanistan, it was removed from the "designated terrorist organization" list. So, technically, as a representative of the state, the Taliban can claim (non-interference and respect for sovereignty). Yet the Taliban government is now facing its own terrorist challenge from ISK which conducted some of the deadliest attacks in 2022 (IEP, 2023). The question that faces the international community now is: Should they or should they not help the Taliban deal with its own transnational terrorist problem?

Notes

1 Funding can come from governments, transnational organized criminal groups, and unfortunately from some diaspora communities and charitable organizations.
2 The groups marked with an asterisk are currently "designated terrorist organizations" by one or more of the following: the United Nations, South and Southeast Asian states, and the US State Department.
3 IWGIA (2023); Pritzker (2021); Borualogo and Van DeVijver (2023).
4 In southern Thailand, Malay Muslims want the liberation of Patani, which is seen to be a colony of Thailand, and where the identity of Patani-Malays was being eroded by "Siamification" (ICG, 2017). This is a similar grievance of the Bangladeshis prior to their independence.
5 Declassified U.S. documents published by the *National Security Archive* show that the U.S. government was aware of these operations.
6 The *mujahideen* actually included different (very diverse) groups with diversity within each group as well: Islamists led by jihadist Gulbuddin Hekmatyai, moderates led by Ahmad Shah Mahmoud who wanted a more egalitarian Islamic republic, Maoists and leftists, and ordinary people (Stewart, 2021).
7 It should be noted that the militants in southern Thailand did not adhere to jihadist ideology at the time.
8 Other notables; JUMB and HUJIB in Bangladesh, and JeM in Pakistan.
9 The Federal Bureau of Investigation reported that al-Qaeda had cells in Sudan, Egypt, Saudi Arabia, Yemen, Somalia, Eritrea, Djibouti, Afghanistan, Pakistan, Bosnia, Croatia, Albania, Algeria, Tunisia, Lebanon, the Philippines, Tajikistan, Azerbaijan, the Kashmiri region of India, and the Chechen region of Russia (Caruso, 2001).

10 The appeal of ISIS differs per Southeast Asian country ranging from its "eschatological ideology" to the involvement of "kinship networks" or simply for criminal purposes (Liow, 2016).
11 It should also be noted that terrorist acts are responsible for a small percentage of global deaths, e.g. 0.05% in 2017 (Ritchie et al., 2013; last revised October 2022).
12 According to Sean Roberts, China claimed that the East Turkistan Islamic Movement (ETIM), which was a minor Afghan-based Uighur insurgency group, was affiliated with al Qaeda (Kine, 2021). According to Matthew Evangelista, Russia wanted to change the West's mind about Chechen as being freedom fighters (Wheeler, 2003).
13 Among the laws or draft laws are: Sri Lanka's new counterterrorism bill; Bangladesh's 2019 Anti-Terrorism Act; Thailand's Internal Security Act of 2007; India's Unlawful Activities Prevention Act; Indonesia's Anti-Terrorism Law; and the Philippines' Human Security Act of 2020.
14 "Negative effects of terrorism on the enjoyment of all human rights and fundamental freedoms." Report of the UN High Commissioner for Human Rights, 2017. A/HRC/34/30.
15 In addition, the terrorist attacks were also reactions to Indian PM Narendra Modi's actions that "scrapped the region's limited autonomy, imposed a months-long security clampdown, arrested hundreds of Kashmiris, and introduced laws that threaten to alter the demography of the country's only Muslim-majority region" (Fareed, 2021).
16 During which time they lived in temporary shelters that lacked adequate sanitation and basic utilities.
17 "Plan of Action to Prevent Violent Extremism," Report of the Secretary-General, 2016. https://www.un.org/sites/www.un.org.counterterrorism/files/plan_action.pdf

References

Aben, Ellie. October 20, 2020. "Homesick Marawi Residents Yearn to Rebuild Lives as Philippines Rebuilds City." *Arab News.* https://arab.news/capy7.

Abuza, Zachary. 2003. "The War on Terrorism in Southeast Asia." In Richard J. Ellings, Aaron L. Friedberg, and Michael Willis eds. *Strategic Asia 2003–04: Fragility and Crisis.* Seattle: The National Bureau of Asian Research, 321–364.

Agence France-Presse (AFP). 2017. "Partition at 70: The Numbers That Divided India and Pakistan." *Hindustan Times.* https://www.hindustantimes.com/india-news/partition-at-70-the-numbers-that-divided-india-and-pakistan/story-KvuFkeJlqNBky3JT5ZaZuK.html (May 12, 2023).

Ahmad, Mumtaz. 1996. "The Crescent and the Sword: Islam, the Military, and Political Legitimacy in Pakistan, 1977–1985." *Middle East Journal* 50 (3): 372–386.

Alagappa, Muthiah. 1998. *Asian Security Practice: Material and Ideational Influences.* Stanford, California: Stanford University Press.

Ashraf, ASM Ali. "The Global War on Terrorism, Domestic Imperatives, and Paramilitary Police Units: Lessons from South Asia." *International Centre for Counter-Terrorism - ICCT.* https://www.icct.nl/publication/global-war-terrorism-domestic-imperatives-and-paramilitary-police-units-lessons-south (May 19, 2023).

Bangsamoro Information Office (BIO). 2023. "BARMM's Inflation Rate Drops to 6.7% in April, Marking Stable Economic Situation." *BARMM Official Website.* https://bangsamoro.gov.ph/news/latest-news/barmms-inflation-rate-drops-to-6-7-in-april-marking-stable-economic-situation/ (May 15, 2023).

Bardwell, Harrison, and Mohib Iqbal. 2021. "The Economic Impact of Terrorism from 2000 to 2018." *Peace Economics, Peace Science and Public Policy* 27 (2): 227–261.

Beydoun, Khaled A. 2020. "Exporting Islamophobia in the Global 'War on Terror.'" *New York University Law Review Online* 95 (81): 81–100.

Boissoneault, Lorraine. December 16, 2016. "The Genocide the U.S. Can't Remember, But Bangladesh Can't Forget." *Smithsonian Magazine*. https://www.smithsonianmag.com/history/genocide-us-cant-remember-bangladesh-cant-forget-180961490/.

Borualogo, I., and Fons van de Vijver. 2016. "Values and Migration Motives in Three Ethnic Groups in Indonesia." In Unity, Diversity and Culture: Research and Scholarship Selected from the 22nd Congress of the International Association for Cross-Cultural Psychology, International Association for Cross-Cultural Psychology, 253–260.

Caruso, J.T. 2001. "Testimony about Al-Qaeda International." *FBI*. https://www.fbi.gov/news/testimony/al-qaeda-international (May 14, 2023).

Chellaney, Brahma. 2001. "Fighting Terrorism in Southern Asia: The Lessons of History." *International Security* 26 (3): 94–116.

Chew, Amy. 2023. "JI's Infiltration of state Institutions in Change of Tactics." *Counter Terrorist Trends and Analyses* 15 (3): 10–14.

Cragin, R. Kim. 2014. "A Recent History of Al-Qa'Ida." *Historical journal (Cambridge, England)* 57 (3): 803–824. http://dx.doi.org/10.1017/s0018246x14000065.

Criezis, Meili. 2022. *Create, Connect, and Deceive: Islamic State Supporters' Maintenance of the Virtual Caliphate through Adaptation and Innovation*. Washington, D.C.: George Washington University.

Congressional Research Service (CRS). 2005. *Islam in South and Southeast Asia*. Washington, D.C.: Congressional Research Service. https://www.everycrsreport.com/reports/RS21903.html.

Davenport, Kelsey. 2022."The Proliferation Security Initiative (PSI) at a Glance." Arms Control Association. https://www.armscontrol.org/factsheets/PSI

Dayley, Robert. 2017. *Southeast Asia in the New International Era*. 7th ed. Boulder, Colorado: Westview Press.

Facal, Gabriel. 2020. "The Geopolitics of Islamist Terrorism in Southeast Asia: Between Long-Established Networks and Deterritorialized Cells." *Hérodote* 176 (1): 125–138.

Fareed, Rifat. 2021. "Kashmir Migrant Workers Flee amid Rise in Suspected Rebel Attacks." *Al Jazeera*. https://www.aljazeera.com/news/2021/10/19/india-kashmir-attacks-non-locals-migrant-workers-exodus-civilians (May 19, 2023).

Galster, Steve. 2001. "Afghanistan: Lessons from the Last War." https://nsarchive2.gwu.edu/NSAEBB/NSAEBB57/essay.html (June 11, 2023).

Gunaratna, Rohan. 2002. *Inside Al Qaeda: Global Network of Terror*. New York: Berkley Books.

Human Rights Watch (HRW). 2022. "Sri Lanka: End Use of Terrorism Law Against Protesters." *Human Rights Watch*. https://www.hrw.org/news/2022/08/31/sri-lanka-end-use-terrorism-law-against-protesters (June 13, 2023).

"India - IWGIA - International Work Group for Indigenous Affairs." Iwgia.org (IWGIA). (2023) https://www.iwgia.org/en/india.html (May 11, 2023).

Institute for Economics and Peace (IEP). 2023. *Global Terrorism Index 2023: Measuring the Impact of Terrorism*. Sydney: Institute for Economics and Peace. http://visionofhumanity.org/resources.

International Crisis Group (ICG). 2017. "Thailand: Malay-Muslim Insurgency and the Dangers of Intractability." *International Crisis Group.* July 20, 2017. https://www.crisisgroup.org/asia/south-east-asia/thailand/thailand-malay-muslim-insurgency-and-dangers-intractability.

Khan, Sobia, Umar Sohail, and Syed Taimoor Shah. 2021. "The Violent Toll of Kinetic Counterterrorism: Revitalizing Non-Kinetic Counterterrorism Model." *ISSRA Papers* 13: 27–40.

Khudadad, Aqdas. 2022. "Secret War: U.S. Drone Strikes in Pakistan." *Immigration and Human Rights Law Review.* https://lawblogs.uc.edu/ihrlr/2022/11/29/secret-war-u-s-drone-strikes-in-pakistan/ (May 19, 2023).

Kine, Phelim. 2021. "How China Hijacked the War on Terror." *POLITICO.* https://www.politico.com/news/2021/09/09/china-hijacked-war-on-terror-511032 (June 12, 2023).

Layton, Peter. 2015. "How Sri Lanka Won the War." *The Diplomat.* https://thediplomat.com/2015/04/how-sri-lanka-won-the-war/

Lionel, Baixas. 2008. "Thematic Chronology of Mass Violence in Pakistan, 1947–2007." *Sciences Po.* https://www.sciencespo.fr/mass-violence-war-massacre-resistance/en/document/thematic-chronology-mass-violence-pakistan-1947-2007.html (May 12, 2023).

Liow, Joseph Chinyong. 2016. "ISIS in the Pacific: Assessing Terrorism in Southeast Asia and the Threat to the Homeland." Testimony before the Subcommittee on Counterterrorism and Intelligence Committee on Homeland Security, Washington D.C.

MacDonald, Scott B. and Jonathan Lemco. 2002. "Political Islam in Southeast Asia." *Current History* 101 (658): 388–392.

Mutalib, Hussin. 1998. "Islam in Southeast Asia and the 21st Century: Managing the Inevitable Challenges, Dilemmas and Tensions." *Islamic Studies* 37 (2): 201–227.

Ortuoste, Maria. 2022. "The Pandemic and Other Ills: The Philippines in 2020." In *2020 Asia Pacific Anuario* from el Centro de Estudios de Asia y África de El Colegio de México. Available at: https://anuarioasiapacifico.colmex.mx/index.php/aap/article/view/328.

Parashar, Swati. 2018. "Terrorism and the Postcolonial 'State.'" In Olivia U. Rutabzibwa and Robbie Shilliam eds. *Routledge Handbook of Postcolonial Politics.* New York: Routledge.

Peoples, Columba, and Nick Vaughan-Williams. 2021. *Critical Security Studies: An Introduction.* Oxford and New York: Routledge.

PTI. 2016. "Aiyar Raises the Matter of Muslims Subjected to Loyalty Test." *The Times of India.* https://timesofindia.indiatimes.com/city/delhi/aiyar-raises-the-matter-of-muslims-subjected-to-loyalty-test/articleshow/51672011.cms (May 12, 2023).

Pritzker Legal Research Center: Myanmar: Center for International Human Rights: Population, Ethnic Groups, and Languages (Pritzker). 2021. https://library.law.northwestern.edu/myanmar/population (May 11, 2023).

Ramakrishna, Kumar. 2023. "Global Threat Assessment 2022." *Counter Terrorist Trends and Analyses* 15 (1): 1–11.

Schori Liang, Christina. 2023. "Terrorist Digitalis: Preventing Terrorists from Using Emerging Technologies." In *Global Terrorism Index 2023*, Sydney: IEP, 72–74.

Stewart, Emily. 2021. "The History of US Intervention in Afghanistan, from the Cold War to 9/11." *Vox.* https://www.vox.com/world/22634008/us-troops-afghanistan-cold-war-bush-bin-laden.

Talbot, Ian. 2019. "Legacies of the Partition of India and Pakistan." *Politeja* 59 (2): 7–25.

Tangging, Nurhati and Kenneth Yeo. "Reintegrating Former Terrorist Combatants in Mindanao." *Counter Terrorist Trends and Analyses* 15 (3): 31–38.
Tayler, Letta. 2022. "India's Abuses at Home Raise Concerns About Its Global Counterterrorism Role." *Human Rights Watch*. https://www.hrw.org/news/2022/10/28/indias-abuses-home-raise-concerns-about-its-counterterrorism-role (May 16, 2023).
Taylor, Jean Gelman. 2003. *Indonesia: Peoples and Histories*. New Haven and London: Yale University Press.
Thakur, Vineet. 2019. "An Asian Drama: The Asian Relations Conference, 1947." *The International History Review* 41 (3): 673–695.
Wheeler, Nicholas. 2003. "Chechnya: Anti-Terrorist Operation or Human Rights Disaster?" *Wilson Center*. https://www.wilsoncenter.org/publication/chechnya-anti-terrorist-operation-or-human-rights-disaster (June 11, 2023).

5 Economic Threats to Security

Shu Fukuya and Zongyuan Zoe Liu

Introduction and Overview

The trend towards regionalism in East Asia has become pronounced since the end of the Cold War. The Asia-Pacific Economic Cooperation (APEC) forum serves as a framework for cooperation in the broader Asia-Pacific region spanning from China, Japan, Korea, members of ASEAN (Association of Southeast Asian Nations), to the U.S., Russia, and beyond. The framework aims to avoid the drawbacks of expansive multilateralism (Beeson, 2014), steering clear of the establishment of vertical power relations in a region with varying political systems and vast economic disparities to prevent the formation of a closed-off world. However, given differences in political systems, religious beliefs, and economic size among participating members, APEC has focused on coordinated and voluntary actions by its participants. In contrast to the capitalist economic system of many Western economies, most East Asian economies are not purely market-based capitalism. Even countries that embrace American values and ideals do not necessarily fully adopt the liberal, market-based approach to economic development.

An East Asian regional security community needs social institutions and recognition of shared geographic and ecological characteristics (Beeson, 2014). Different priorities in bilateral relations among major East Asian powers, such as Japan's prioritizing the importance of the U.S. and China's growing assertiveness, have suggested the possibility of insurmountable structural constraints (Emmers and Tan, 2011; Beeson, 2014, 10). Despite these challenges, East Asia has enjoyed a period of peace and stability since the end of the Cold War, thanks, partially, to the multifaceted involvement of the U.S. through its political, military, economic, and social engagements with the region. The U.S. has employed a hard bilateral security relationship and a soft multilateral economic relationship towards East Asia (Brands, 2016; Ikenberry and Moon, 2008), which suggests that the U.S. is unlikely to tolerate any situation that could disrupt the bilateral alliance or the U.S.-led security regime in East Asia, such as the Taiwan contingency.

The remainder of this chapter is organized as follows: Section 1 discusses the unchallenged U.S. hegemony that underpinned the East Asian order in

DOI: 10.4324/9781003473206-5

the immediate post-Cold War era. Sections 2 and 3 analyze the impact of the rise of China on regional and international trade relations and the U.S. reaction to its perceived challenge presented by China's growing influence. Section 4 reviews East Asian economic cooperation. Section 5 surveys U.S. economic policy towards Asia. Section 6 examines economic security in the context of globalization. The chapter concludes with a discussion of the impact of U.S. policy on East Asian regional order.

Section 1: East Asian Regionalism in the 1990s

Although the U.S. has strengthened ties with allies against the growing threat of North Korea's nuclear capacity since the end of the Cold War, it has never fully committed to shaping the rules and institutions in East Asia (佐橋亮, 2020). While Japan sought to leverage its economic advantages in East Asia to advance economic cooperation in the Asia-Pacific region, it viewed U.S. participation in Asian regional institutions as a prerequisite under the hub-and-spoke system. When APEC was established in 1989, Japan strongly insisted that the U.S. should be included (Terada, 1999). As a result, the U.S. joined APEC, and open regionalism became the U.S. standard for East Asia.

With the end of the Cold War, U.S. domestic perceptions shifted away from security threats and reoriented toward its domestic economy. In this context, Japan's insufficient market opening became a major concern for U.S. policymakers. During the Clinton administration, trade with Japan was a top priority, and economic nationalists had a strong influence at the Office of the U.S. Trade Representative (USTR). At the April 1993 U.S.–Japan summit, President Clinton declared that the Cold War partnership between the two countries had become obsolete and urged Japan to open its markets and reduce its trade surplus (Government Publishing Office, 1993). During this period, the U.S. also intensified its confrontation with China and Southeast Asia, and the pursuit of U.S. economic interests upset the countries of East Asia.

An example of the U.S. deterring against initiatives that may pose a threat to its interests in the 1990s was Washington's destruction of the East Asian Economic Caucus (EAEC) concept proposed by Malaysian Prime Minister Mahathir. Malaysia reportedly intended for the EAEC to become a regional trading bloc that systematically exclude the U.S. from East Asia (Higgott and Stubbs, 1995). The Bush administration believed that the EAEC would divide the Asia-Pacific region and hinder U.S. economic interests in Asia (Baker and DeFrank, 1995). Japan and many other Asian countries exhibited obvious unease about forming a trading bloc that would place them at odds with the U.S., ultimately leading them to gravitate towards a deeper involvement in APEC. After President Clinton took office in 1993, the U.S. government tried to use APEC to shape the rules of trade and investment liberalization in Asia to favor the U.S. While this attempt was unsuccessful, it shed light on America's wariness regarding the emergence of regional structures in East Asia that would threaten America's interests.

When many Asian countries turned to the U.S. and the IMF for assistance at the time of the Asian currency crisis in 1997, Japan attributed the cause of this crisis to the U.S.-led liberalization drive and launched the concept of the Asian Monetary Fund (AMF) in light of the urgency to secure financial liquidity (Lee, 2008; Lipscy, 2003). Sakakibara Eisuke, Japan's Vice Minister for International Affairs at the Ministry of Finance, acknowledgment of Lawrence Summers', U.S. Deputy Secretary of the Treasury, strong opposition to the AMF proposal (日本経済新聞, 2016a), provided further evidence of how shaky the U.S.–Japan economic relationship had become. The Clinton administration was thoroughly against the idea of an AMF as it could be a harmful outcome-based institution. Some scholars have argued that despite the U.S. government's opportunistic attempt to use the Asian currency crisis to achieve its political goals, the Clinton administration did not intend to create a new regional order. Neither would the U.S. tolerate an East Asian dynamic that could threaten its interests (佐橋亮, 2020).

Section 2: Growing U.S. Concerns Regarding China's Expanding Influence

China's influence in East Asia has greatly expanded since the late 1990s, especially following the Asian currency crisis (高原 明生, 2003). The U.S. government increasingly views China's rise in East Asia and globally as challenging the U.S.-led regional order and the international system. Concerns about China have increased as China shifted from a multilateralist path, which had previously focused on WTO accession, to a regionalist path. More specifically, in October 2000, China embarked on Free Trade Agreement (FTA) negotiations with ASEAN and began to take a serious approach to regional economic diplomacy. The U.S. started to feel challenged by China's growing influence over ASEAN+3 (ASEAN plus China, Japan, South Korea) initiatives and the perception that China aimed to avoid U.S. pressure by cooperating with other regional members (Liao, 2012). In addition, some other regional members, including Japan, believed that the ASEAN+3 members feared China would reshape the regional order. Such fear also contributed to the growing prospect of an emerging East Asian Community.

Under Prime Minister Koizumi, Japan focused on strengthening the Japan-U.S. alliance and invited Australia, New Zealand, and India to the first East Asia Summit held in Kuala Lumpur in December 2005 to address the U.S. concerns about China (Ministry of Foreign Affairs of Japan, 2005). Furthermore, to counter China's rise, Prime Minister Abe proposed the formation of a quadripolar grouping of Japan, the U.S., Australia, and India when he met with Vice President Cheney in February 2007 to involve the U.S. in East Asian regionalism (Ministry of Foreign Affairs of Japan, 2007). Abe focused on showing China that he would build a security structure with a quadripolar grouping that upholds democracy. When an informal meeting of representatives of the four countries took place on the sidelines of the ASEAN Regional

Forum (ARF) in May 2007, China expressed opposition and launched diplomatic protests against Japan, Australia, and India, as it was deeply concerned that these regional players could form an anti-China security alliance with the U.S. (Chanlett-Avery and Vaughn, 2008). Thus, by the late 2000s, the U.S. and Japan had already perceived China's rise in East Asia and beyond as a potential political and economic threat.

Since 2000, the movement toward bilateral trade agreements has accelerated in East Asia. In October 2000 and January 2002, China and Japan respectively proposed an FTA with ASEAN. Subsequently, in 2004 China proposed the East Asia Free Trade Agreement (EAFTA) among the ASEAN+3 countries, followed by, in 2006, by Japan's proposal for the Comprehensive Economic Partnership for East Asia (CEPEA), an FTA among ASEAN+6 (ASEAN plus Australia, China, India, Japan, South Korea, New Zealand) countries. The EAFTA primarily aims to integrate ASEAN with China, Japan, and South Korea. In contrast, the CEPEA aimed at economic cooperation and sustainable development, emphasizing institutional design in East Asia (Borthwick and Yamamoto, 2011). While Japan and China have been competing for the initiative of these two broad FTAs in East Asia, none of these discussions of East Asian regional integration has included the U.S. In August 2011, Japan and China jointly proposed an initiative to accelerate the construction of an EAFTA and CEPEA, which gained support from ASEAN to establish a comprehensive economic partnership with other countries and laid down the foundation for the Regional Comprehensive Economic Partnership (RCEP).

In response to EAFTA and CEPEA, the U.S. government has used the APEC framework to deter unilateral, Asian-based regionalist moves in East Asia. The exclusion of American firms from legally binding East Asian FTAs, which could have caused significant economic disadvantages and trade diversion effects for U.S. companies competing with firms based in East Asia, prompted the Free Trade Area of the Asia-Pacific (FTAAP) to establish rules-based, mutually beneficial integration norms. However, after the 9/11 terrorist attacks, the U.S. government began to use APEC as a forum for consensus-building on counter-terrorism measures, suggesting the U.S. government shifted to prioritize security rather than economic interests. As a result, some countries indicated they would be willing to pursue economic goals in a framework that excludes the U.S. Against this backdrop, the APEC Business Advisory Committee recommended the FTAAP concept to APEC Leaders in 2004, calling for trade liberalization in the Asia-Pacific region while maintaining consistency with WTO rules, as bilateral trade agreements were in flux in the mid-2000s. At the APEC Leader's Meeting in Hanoi in November 2006, American officials proposed to conduct a study on the ways and means to promote regional integration, including the FTAAP. Regional countries viewed this proposal as APEC's official endorsement of the FTAAP as an agenda item.

When regionalism began to emerge in East Asia, the U.S. government was preoccupied with rethinking its bilateral trade policy. The U.S. concluded bilateral trade agreements with Singapore, Australia, and South Korea that required significant political resources for congressional ratification (Solís, 2022). In particular, the U.S.–Korea FTA was delayed five years beyond the original schedule, partly due to political headwinds. These circumstances on the U.S. side led the U.S. to push for the FTAAP.

Although the U.S. supported the FTAAP concept, many were skeptical about its feasibility. Among the skeptics were concerns about the difficulty of reconciling the differing preferences of APEC members and the large trade deficit. The U.S. government, keenly mindful of American business groups' concerns about being excluded from East Asia due to the rise of regionalism in the region, sought to counter-act these developments by launching the FTAAP concept. A major stimulator that propelled this move was the "Nikai Shock," a proposal made by Nikai Toshihiro, Japanese Minister of Economy, Trade and Industry, at the ASEAN+3 Economic Ministerial Meeting in Kuala Lumpur in August 2006. Minister Nikai Toshihiro proposed the promotion of an FTA and CEPEA by the ASEAN+6, excluding the U.S. (三浦秀之, 2020). In response to the Nikai Shock, American officials increased their visits to East Asian countries. Furthermore, in November 2006, the Bush Administration announced the FTAAP initiative.

The 2007 subprime mortgage crisis in the U.S. did not immediately accelerate the materialization of the FTAAP concept. However, in September 2008, economic ministers from five countries, including the U.S., collectively decided to begin the Trans-Pacific Partnership Agreement (TPP) negotiations. The joint statement of this meeting noted that the TPP would strengthen APEC's goal of promoting regional economic integration and could be a future pathway to creating an FTAAP (United States Trade Representative, 2008), suggesting that the U.S. government at that time viewed the TPP as a building block for the FTAAP.

America's decision to join the TPP was driven by a strong desire to avoid being pushed out of the East Asian trade framework as U.S.–China competition intensifies (Solís, 2013). President Obama stated, "if the U.S. doesn't write the rules, China will write the rules" (Reuters, 2015). This suggests that President Obama's push for the TPP was to apply U.S. norms and rules in shaping order in the East Asian region. Moreover, the U.S. joined the TPP mainly because of its quality. The TPP was promoted for its high level of trade liberalization, contributing to the formation of a new trade order in East Asia. It also aimed to establish new international standards, including broad provisions such as cooperation on intellectual property protection, regulation of anti-competitive practices, and government procurement rules. This had an affinity with the U.S. vision in that it included an ambitious agenda for the introduction of WTO+ rules, which would impose greater tariff reductions and regulations than the WTO. The introduction of WTO+ rules took shape at the TPP Ministerial in Atlanta in October 2015. In addition, unlike other trade agreements, the TPP introduced a new membership provision that allows APEC members and others to join the TPP if TPP member countries agree.

Against this backdrop, APEC members began to express interest in the TPP, while the momentum of ASEAN+3 and ASEAN+6 had begun to wane. The U.S. had tried to make APEC the center of East Asian integration by joining the TPP. From the perspective of the U.S., which has been trying to shape the norms of East Asian regional integration in the APEC process, the realization of the FTAAP is a result-oriented liberalization of trade and investment, which can be seen as a diplomatic success for the U.S. The U.S. has been trying to shape the norms of East Asian regional integration in the APEC process.

The Obama administration also strengthened America's engagement policy towards East Asia. For example, the Accession to ASEAN's Treaty of Amity and Cooperation (TAC) signed in July 2009 fulfilled the requirement for formal participation in the East Asia Summit (EAS). In November 2009, President Obama visited Japan and emphasized U.S. interest in the EAS. He then met with Southeast Asian leaders at the U.S.–ASEAN Summit in Singapore. Previous U.S. administrations have reportedly refused to sign the TAC based on the principle of non-interference in internal affairs as demanded by ASEAN. This was because political pressure on military regimes, such as Myanmar, was believed to be eliminated (Manyin, Garcia, and Morrison, 2009). However, the U.S. decided that signing the TAC would not cause diplomatic problems because U.S. allies, Japan and Australia, had signed it. The U.S. decision to join the TAC was seen as an opportunity to increase the U.S. presence in East Asia in the face of China's growing influence in the region.

Section 3: U.S. East Asia Policy Swings Since 2010

Around 2010, as Beijing began to take a more intransigent stance, there was a shift in U.S. policy toward China. The Obama administration, referring to the pivot to Asia, made clear its stance to expand and strengthen its engagement in the Asia-Pacific region (Clinton, 2011). The Obama administration's pivot to an Asia strategy was to engage in regional agreements in the Asia-Pacific region and work with allies and partners to counter China's rise in the face of increasing U.S.–China competition (He, 2019). ASEAN was also eager to engage the U.S. in the region, partly because Japan was underpowered. In President Obama's speech to the Australian Parliament on November 2011, he noted that the U.S. is and will be a Pacific nation that maintains and develops a free, fair, and open international economic system and engages in regional cooperation mechanisms for peace and stability in the Asia-Pacific (The White House, 2011). In this sense, the TPP was clearly at the heart of the Obama administration's policy of re-balancing to Asia (Solís, 2022).

Negotiations for the TPP began in March 2010 with eight countries (the four original members – Brunei, Chile, New Zealand, Singapore – plus Australia, Peru, Vietnam, and the U.S.), and by the 18th round (2013), a total of 12 countries (i.e., Canada, Japan, Malaysia, Mexico) were negotiating the agreement. Japan, which took on the role of promoting the TPP, decided to participate after PM Abe was re-elected in December 2012, and the Prime Minister's Office has taken the political lead in making policy decisions. In March 2013, PM Abe announced his decision to join the TPP negotiations, which led to significant progress (首相官邸, 2013). The decision was made shortly after his first meeting with President Obama in February 2013. According to PM Abe, there were conflicting opinions within his government before his trip to the U.S. in February 2013. While half of the governing Liberal Democratic Party (LDP) and agricultural cooperatives were against the TPP, some believed Japan should wait until after the Upper House election in July 2013 to announce its participation in the negotiations. However, PM Abe believed that by joining the negotiations immediately, Japan would have a stronger bargaining position among the participating countries (安倍晋三, 2023: 98). At the U.S.–Japan summit, two countries reportedly confirmed that they would not seek unilateral commitments to eliminate all tariffs in the TPP negotiations while recognizing sensitivities of agricultural products for Japan and industrial products for the U.S. Although PM Abe opposed the "tariff elimination without safeguard," he also recognized the need to reform the organization of the agricultural lobby. At the U.S.–Japan summit, President Obama agreed with Prime Minister Abe's statements, saying, "I am comfortable with what the Prime Minister has said" (安倍晋三, 2023: 100). Japan and the U.S.'s shared vision of strengthening the Japan-U.S. alliance structure through the TPP agreement and recognized the need to continue efforts to conclude the TPP negotiations (日本経済新聞, 2015; Froman, 2014; 安倍晋三, 2023: 99–100).

In addition to eliminating tariffs on goods, liberalizing trade in services, and establishing rules in areas such as investment, competition, intellectual property, and government procurement, the TPP negotiations included discussions on the environment and labor. The TPP negotiations were difficult, but in April 2015, in a speech to the U.S. Congress, PM Abe emphasized the strategic importance of the TPP, saying, "The TPP goes far beyond just economic benefits. It is also about our security. Long-term, its strategic value is awesome. We should never forget that" (Ministry of Foreign Affairs of Japan, 2015). Moreover, President Obama made every effort to quickly pass the Trade Promotion Authority Act (TPA), which gives the president authority to negotiate trade agreements. TPA was seen as essential to completing the TPP negotiations, and Congress passed the 2015 TPA bill in June 2015. On February 2016, the TPP agreement was signed by 12 countries in Auckland, New Zealand.

The inauguration of President Donald Trump on January 2017 brought major changes to U.S. trade policy. One of the first acts of his presidency was to withdraw from participation in the TPP: on January 23, President Trump told the Office of the United States Trade Representative (USTR) that he supported permanently withdrawing from the TPP (The Washington Post, 2017). The U.S. then officially withdrew from the TPP on January 30, 2017 (United States Trade Representative, 2017).

The U.S. withdrawal is a major structural change that has forced Japan to shift its trade policy. After the U.S. withdrawal, Japan could not seriously consider the TPP without the U.S. as a realistic policy option. PM Abe denounced that there was no point in pursuing entry into the TPP without the U.S. and publicly stated that he would continue to emphasize the importance of the TPP to the U.S. (日本経済新聞, 2016b). Later in March 2017, however, at a ministerial-level meeting of the TPP-11, the three Latin American countries – Mexico, Chile, and Peru – notified their intention to abandon the TPP and focus on the Pacific Alliance if Japan was not willing to pursue the TPP-11. Japan had no choice but to commit to the TPP-11 after PM Abe reaffirmed President Trump's determination to withdraw from the TPP at the first official Japan–U.S. summit in February 2017.

President Trump shifted from David Ricardo's "comparative advantage" theory to the economic security argument, rejecting multilateralism and expressing concerns about trade deficits. He emphasized bilateral trade deals with America's major trading partners to reduce the trade deficit. As a result, the Trump administration imposed tariffs on China and its allies and friends. For China, it launched investigations into intellectual property and technology practices, and by 2019, the U.S. had applied tariffs to more than $350 billion in Chinese imports. In addition, the U.S. has begun reviewing foreign direct investment and tightening export controls on dual technology, concerned about the national security risks posed by the outflow of key technologies and the overseas expansion of Chinese telecommunications and other companies. China also responded by imposing $110 billion worth of counter-tariffs, strengthening its Export Control Law in December 2020 and its Foreign Economic Sanctions Law in June 2021. On the other hand, the U.S. invoked Section 232 of the Trade Expansion Act of 1962, imposing increased import tariffs on steel and aluminum for allied and friendly nations.

A hallmark of the "America First" trade policy is the use of unilateral tariff measures to review the terms of existing trade agreements (Solís, 2022). The U.S. withdrawal from the TPP and its indiscriminate tariffs are believed to have undermined the trust that East Asian partners had in the U.S. (Solís, 2022).

The deteriorating trust between the U.S. and China has led to an expansion of animosity. While the WTO rules GATT (General Agreement on Tariffs and Trade) establish tariffs and trade regulations, Article 21 of GATT includes provisions for security exceptions. Since the Trump administration implemented export restrictions, it has become evident that this particular provision represents a significant loophole in free trade. The negative chain reaction resulting from the US–China confrontation has shattered the ideals of globalization, ushering in an era where power clashes with power.

Section 4: East Asian Economic Cooperation – RCEP and CPTPP

As the concept of an FTA in the Asia-Pacific region became a reality in the late 2000s, ASEAN, which had been committed to ASEAN-centrality, felt the greatest sense of urgency. Accordingly, at the ASEAN Summit in November

2011, ASEAN countries put forward the concept of the RCEP (Regional Comprehensive Economic Partnership), and in parallel with the progress of the TPP negotiations, the 16-member (Australia, Brunei, Cambodia, China, India, Indonesia, Japan, Laos, Malaysia, Myanmar, New Zealand, the Philippines, Singapore, South Korea, Thailand, Vietnam) RCEP negotiations were officially launched in November 2012.

Unlike the TPP, the RCEP was smoothly signed by 15 countries in November 2020 and entered into force in January 2022, even after India's withdrawal in 2019. India's decision to withdraw from the RCEP, due to concerns about its growing trade deficit with China and other issues, was a major blow to the other 15 countries. India feared that reducing or eliminating tariffs under the RCEP would result in a massive influx of cheap imports, hurting its own manufacturing, agriculture, and livestock industries as well as employment. The Modi government has been trying to reduce its dependence on imports and promote exports and has been under constant pressure from domestic industry groups. However, even with India's withdrawal, the RCEP remains the world's largest trade agreement, accounting for about 30% of global GDP, population, and total trade.

Significant differences exist between the TPP and the RCEP regarding rules and degree of liberalization. While the TPP has a 99% tariff elimination rate for all member countries, the RCEP has only 91%, and agricultural liberalization has been carved out. In addition, the RCEP covers a shallower area of rules than the TPP. For example, the provisions on cross-border data flows allow parties discretion to impose restrictions on international data flows to protect public policy needs or vital national security interests; the TPP has provisions prohibiting arbitrary or unjustifiable means of discrimination and prohibiting the transfer of more information than necessary, while the RCEP is left entirely to the judgment of the signatory countries.

Thus, the RCEP is a framework with a strong focus on developing countries, and it will be highly significant for ASEAN-centrality to take root in the world's largest trading bloc. Before the RCEP, East Asia had only had the AEC and the ASEAN+1 FTA. While the RCEP may not be strong enough to spur economic reforms in member countries, it will promote trade in goods and services and investment in East Asia and contribute to economic development. The RCEP has also led to the elimination of many tariffs between China, Japan, and South Korea. There is still significant room for improvement in tariff liberalization among the three Northeast Asian countries (Solís, 2022). However, the use of RCEP has been growing rapidly in Japan since January 2022, making the RCEP the most used EPA in Japan (Shimizu, 2022). On the other hand, among the three Northeast Asian countries, China is the one benefiting the most from tariff reductions. Tariff reductions on Chinese exports to Japan and Korea totaled $5.6 billion, tariff reductions on Japanese exports to China and Korea amounted to $4.7 billion, and tariff reductions on Korean exports to Japan and China stood at $2.8 billion (高橋俊樹, 2022). In addition, China has stepped up its efforts to promote cooperation with the BRICs and other emerging economies in response to U.S. friend-shoring. A case in point is that 13 emerging economies that are candidates for BRIC Plus, including Indonesia, Malaysia, and Thailand, participated in an online BRICS summit in June 2022. However, many of the BRICS Plus countries do not prefer China's expanding influence or a two-sided strategy with the IPEF. These factors suggest that China may further liberalize the RCEP and strengthen its supply chain by expanding its membership to include India and Pacific Island countries.

The TPP and the RCEP have led to the formation of new trade rules in East Asia, and the TPP's provisions on intellectual property protection, labor standards, environmental standards, digital trade, and state-owned enterprises are groundbreaking. The RCEP, on the other hand, does not include labor- or environment-related provisions. The RCEP's provisions on cross-border data distribution are also inferior to those in the TPP. The goal of U.S. foreign economic policy is to formulate and disseminate trade rules that also serve its own interests, but the reality is that U.S.-style trade rules are not being disseminated to East Asian countries. While both Republicans and Democrats in the U.S. have undoubtedly placed the highest priority on Asia since the 2010s, it must be said that the U.S. foreign economic policy has stalled; with the completion of the RCEP, it is hoped that the U.S. will renew its commitment to East Asia, which will lead to its future rejoining the TPP.

With the withdrawal of the United States from the TPP, the 11 remaining members (Australia, Brunie, Canada, Chile, Japan, Malaysia, Mexico, New Zealand, Peru, Singapore, and Vietnam) reformulated the free trade agreement into the Comprehensive and Progressive Agreement for Trans-Pacific Partnership (CPTPP).

The United Kingdom formally joined in 2023. As of December 2022, China (September 2021), Taiwan (September 2021), Ecuador (December 2021), Costa Rica (August 2022), Uruguay (December 2022), and Ukraine (May 2023) have applied for membership while the Philippines, South Korea, and Thailand have expressed in joining the organization.

Among these countries, China is uncertain whether it will be able to meet the high-quality standards of the CPTPP. This is because, unlike the RCEP, to which China is a signatory, the CPTTP contains provisions that could transform China's state-led model. Examples of CPTPP rules include: prohibition of technology transfers and other requirements for investment enterprises in the host country; prohibition of the free flow of information across borders and the imposition of tariffs on digital content; prohibition of non-commercial assistance that adversely affects the interests of other parties; and strict rules against counterfeit and counterfeit goods, etc. (Solís 2022).

China's accession to the CPTTP will either 1) provide an opportunity for China to undertake deep structural reforms, or 2) allow for a significant extension of the implementation period for tariff reductions and elimination, with many provisions of the CPTTP being treated as exceptions (Solís, 2022). China continues to favor state-owned enterprises in sectors such as petrochemicals, finance, and steel. In contrast, Japan, Australia, and other countries that led the CPTPP insist that the quality of the CPTPP should not be compromised and that the current rules should be respected. China's Ministry of Commerce announced at the end of October 2022, that, to actively promote the process of joining the CPTPP, it has conducted a comprehensive and detailed study and evaluation of the CPTPP provisions and has compiled a list of reform measures and laws and regulations that it believes are necessary for joining the CPTTP. It has also stated that it will continue to strive to meet the standards of the CPTTP rules fully and achieve a higher level of openness in market access than China currently has under its existing treaties and other agreements. Although the timing of China's accession to the CPTTP has not yet been determined, it is clear that China is steadily preparing to join the CPTTP. The U.S. has not been particularly enthusiastic about China joining the CPTTP because the intended effect of the TPP on China was to raise the standard of liberalization and put pressure on China to further reform its economic system; the TPP is often seen as a system of economic rejection of China, but in fact, it was intended to develop a process of economic engagement (佐橋 亮, 2020: 84).

Section 5: U.S. Foreign Economic Policy

Despite RCEP and CPTPP increasing the risk of marginalizing the United States, the Biden administration decided not to return to the CPTPP, but instead to engage East Asian countries in the four-pillar Indo-Pacific Economic Framework (IPEF) to develop a digital economic framework, supply chains, and more in the Indo-Pacific region independent of China. As this is not a trade agreement, the main focus is on strengthening contingency preparedness through closer economic ties among the 14 participating countries – Australia, Brunei, Fiji, India, Indonesia, Japan, Malaysia, New Zealand, Singapore, South Korea, the Philippines, Thailand, the U.S., and Vietnam. In September 2022, the 14 countries held a ministerial-level meeting in Los Angeles and set negotiating goals in four areas: (1) trade, (2) supply chain, (3) clean economy, and (4) fair economy (U.S. Department of Commerce, 2022). The first round of negotiations was held in Brisbane, Australia, in December 2022, bringing together a total of 450 officials from various countries. The USTR held detailed discussions on the environment, labor, the digital economy, competition policy, and inclusiveness, emphasizing the ambitious scope of the negotiations (United States Trade Representative, 2022). The Commerce Department also shared concept papers on supply chain, clean economy, and fair economy with participating countries, and claimed to have had productive discussions. The IPEF is a soft framework that differs in character from the CPTPP and RCEP because it does not call for tariff reduction or elimination. Given the U.S. focus on a results-oriented approach, a soft approach such as the IPEF can be seen as a departure from its past foreign economic policy. Since East Asian countries are comfortable with binding trade and investment liberalization and rule-making such as

CPTPP and RCEP (Solís, 2022), it is not certain that IPEF can work well in East Asia. Nevertheless, in November 2022, USTR Deputy U.S. Trade Representative Sarah Bianchi stated that "negotiations are proceeding at a faster pace than expected" and she expressed her desire to achieve a positive outcome by the end of next year (朝日新聞, 2022). Commerce Secretary Gina Raymond is also enthusiastic about asserting U.S. economic leadership in the Indo-Pacific region through the IPEF (日本貿易振興機構, 2022).

The Biden administration, with an eye on the 2024 presidential election, demonstrated its commitment to achieving tangible results at the APEC summit in San Francisco in November 2023. However, upon closer inspection, there was growing resistance within the U.S. to the trade pillar, which led to the postponement of the negotiations (Cutler, 2023). This led to dissatisfaction among the partner countries, especially the Southeast Asian countries.

Nevertheless, the main benefit of the IPEF lies in the U.S. commitment to East Asia to ensure stable supply of critical items, the most vulnerable links in the supply chain. Market access in the form of tariff reduction or elimination, which is outside the scope of the negotiations, is expected to have an immediate impact.

On the other hand, it is important to note that the impact of the IPEF is uncertain and it is difficult to predict its economic impact. Regarding the fair economy pillar, while the IPEF advocates greater transparency in taxation, the unclear scope of meaningfulness without legal binding and enforcement capabilities raises concerns.

The IPEF, seemingly led by the United States, does not appear to be making significant progress on the trade front during the 2024 presidential election cycle. As a result, partner countries fear a loss of U.S. commitment to East Asia.

Section 6: Economic Security and Globalization

As seen so far, the US–China confrontation has highlighted China's strengths in maintaining a robust industrial base that is capable of mass production within the framework of globalization. It also reveals its vulnerability in semiconductor-related items, where it relies heavily on exports to Europe and the U.S. as well as a direct challenge from the American semiconductor industry for market share.

China has been promoting high-level external openness through the conclusion of FTAs as part of its efforts to restructure supply chains. Examples include its signing of the RCEP, and its application for membership in the CPTPP.

While the U.S. deploys delay tactics through export restrictions, China has been pushing forward relevant legislative measures as countermeasures due to the time required to maintain technological advantages and diversify supply chains. Particularly since 2020, China has implemented regulations such as the Entity List registration provisions targeting foreign companies that violate the principles of fair market transactions. It has also established export control laws restricting transactions that may harm national security and interests. In January 2021, China enacted the Blocking Statute to prevent the extraterritorial application of foreign laws and measures, which specifies necessary countermeasures against the extraterritorial application of U.S. export control rules (Atlantic Council, 2021). In June of the same year, China implemented the Anti-Foreign Sanctions Law, which lays out countermeasures against sanctions imposed by foreign countries (Merics, 2021).

In the U.S., the CHIPS Act passed in August 2022, allocated substantial subsidies for domestic semiconductor development and production, intensifying government support for the semiconductor industry (The White House, 2022). Companies with semiconductor manufacturing divisions in the U.S., such as Intel, IBM, GlobalFoundries, and Micron Technology, have announced investment plans one after another. As companies that previously handled everything from design to production under the wave of globalization faced growth challenges, the shift towards industrial policies involving active government intervention in businesses and markets revealed how globalization has affected national security. U.S. export regulations not only aim to contain China, but also serve as a means of protecting the domestic industry. The export control strengthening announced by the U.S. Department of Commerce's Bureau of Industry and Security in October 2022 primarily focuses on strengthening export controls for semiconductor manufacturing equipment (Department of Commerce, 2022). Both the CHIPS Act and export regulations share a common goal of reviving domestic manufacturing capabilities, not just design capabilities (Japan Center for Economic Research, 2023: 16). In the past, U.S. companies had refrained from significant capital investments and relocated production to cost-effective regions in East Asia. Now, with the help of subsidies, the trend is being reversed as they strive to regain an understanding of the industrial sector.

The most potent tool of U.S. export regulation is said to be the application of Section 301 of the Trade Act, which the Clinton administration used extensively as a legal basis for trade management during the trade frictions in the 1990s (Japan Center for Economic Research, 2023: 10). Additionally, during the Trump administration, Section 232 of the Trade Expansion Act of 1962 (Department of Commerce, n.d.)was misused to impose high tariffs on steel and aluminum imports, a memory still fresh in people's minds. The Biden administration did not completely revoke Section 232 but, more importantly, the strengthening of export regulations concerning semiconductor-related items since August 2022 indicates the U.S.'s efforts to construct a trade order for the leading-edge semiconductor industry under its leadership. While U.S. companies have been involved in the international division of labor, delegating a significant portion of the manufacturing process to their factories in China or Chinese companies, the era of reviewing global supply chains under government direction, aligning with national security policies, has arrived.

Conclusion and Future Prospects

This chapter has examined the evolution of the East Asian regional order, focusing primarily on U.S. involvement in East Asian regionalism in the post-Cold War era. The regional order in East Asia has been a major focus of the U.S. During and after the end of the Cold War, the U.S. sought to maintain the stability of its alliance network and U.S.–China relations through its overwhelming power. The basis of U.S. economic policy in East Asia was "hard bilateral security relations and soft multilateral economic relations" (Ikenberry and Moon, 2008). Therefore, when process-oriented regional integration such as ASEAN+3 and ASEAN+6 was promoted in East Asia from the 1990s to around the 2000s, the U.S., which aimed to shape East Asian rules and institutions in the APEC process, did not feel threatened. Because of the overwhelming power of the U.S., as long as relations with its allies and U.S.–China relations remained stable, no one saw China's rise as a threat.

In the 2010s, China's rise was increasingly seen as a threat, and the U.S. advocated a pivot to Asia and made a major shift in its foreign economic policy by deciding to participate in the TPP negotiations. The U.S. commitment to the TPP as an economic factor can be seen as the birth of a new model, reflecting the rethinking of the postwar hub-and-spoke system and building strong relationships among the spokes.

However, when the Trump administration came to power in 2017, the shift to a U.S.–China-first policy was made as U.S.–China competition intensified, and divisions in East Asia also worsened. In the 2020s, an increasingly complex regional order is being formed, with the US-led IPEF, the Japan-led CPTPP, and the China–ASEAN-led RCEP, all giant economic blocs in disarray. Amidst the loss of inclusivity in the East Asian order and the wavering of US-led rules and institutions, there seems to be a fervent effort to maintain dominance by emphasizing economic security and security arguments. We must recognize that we are now at a major turning point where there is a possibility of a transition of the East Asian order.

References

Atlantic Council. February 8, 2021. "The 'Blocking Statute': China's New Attempt to Subvert US Sanctions." *Atlantic Council* (blog). https://www.atlanticcouncil.org/blogs/new-atlanticist/the-blocking-statute-chinas-new-attempt-to-subvert-us-sanctions/.

Baker, James Addison, and Thomas M. DeFrank. 1995. *The Politics of Diplomacy: Revolution, War, and Peace, 1989–1992*. New York: Putnam. http://www.booknotes.org/Watch/68174-1/James+Baker.aspx.

Beeson, Mark. 2014. *Regionalism and Globalization in East Asia: Politics, Security and Economic Development*. Palgrave.

Borthwick, Mark, and Tadashi Yamamoto, eds. 2011. *A Pacific Nation: Perspectives on the US Role in an East Asia Community*. Japan Center Intl Exchange. https://www.jcie.org/analysis/books-reports/pacificnation/.

Brands, Hal. 2016. "American Grand Strategy and the Liberal Order: Continuity, Change, and Options for the Future." RAND Corporation. https://www.rand.org/pubs/perspectives/PE209.html.

Chanlett-Avery, Emma, and Bruce Vaughn. 2008. "Emerging Trends in the Security Architecture in Asia: Bilateral and Multilateral Ties Among the United States, Japan, Australia, and India." https://apps.dtic.mil/sti/citations/ADA478343.

Clinton, Hillary. 2011. "America's Pacific Century." *Foreign Policy* (blog). October 2011. https://foreignpolicy.com/2011/10/11/americas-pacific-century/.

Cutler, Wendy. 2023. "U.S. Made the Most of APEC given What It Had to Work With." *Nikkei Asia*, November 27, https://asia.nikkei.com/Opinion/U.S.-made-the-most-of-APEC-given-what-it-had-to-work-with.

Department of Commerce. 2022. "Public Information on Export Controls Imposed on Advanced Computing and Semiconductor Manufacturing Items to the People's Republic of China (PRC)." October 7, 2022. https://www.bis.doc.gov/index.php/about-bis/newsroom/2082.

Department of Commerce. n.d. "Section 232 Investigation on the Effect of Imports of Steel on U.S. National Security." U.S. Department of Commerce. Accessed August 6, 2023. https://www.commerce.gov/issues/trade-enforcement/section-232-steel.

Emmers, Ralf, and See Seng Tan. 2011. "The ASEAN Regional Forum and Preventive Diplomacy: Built to Fail?" *Asian Security* 7 (1): 44–60. https://doi.org/10.1080/14799855.2011.548211.

Froman, Michael B. 2014. "The Strategic Logic of Trade." *Foreign Affairs*. https://www.foreignaffairs.com/articles/americas/2014-11-13/strategic-logic-trade.

He, Kai. 2019. "Contested Multilateralism 2.0 and Regional Order Transition: Causes and Implications." *The Pacific Review* 32 (2): 210–220. https://doi.org/10.1080/09512748.2018.1465455.

Higgott, Richard, and Richard Stubbs. 1995. "Competing Conceptions of Economic Regionalism: APEC versus EAEC in the Asia Pacific." *Review of International Political Economy* 2 (3): 516–535.

Ikenberry, G. John, and Chung-in Moon, eds. 2008. *The United States and Northeast Asia: Debates, Issues, and New Order. Asia in World Politics.* Lanham, Md: Rowman & Littlefield Publishers.

Japan Center for Economic Research. 2023. *Asia no keizai anzen hosho [Economic Security in Asia]*. Nikkei BP and Nikkei Shimbun. https://www.jcer.or.jp/publications/2023068.html.

Lee, Yong Wook. 2008. *The Japanese Challenge to the American Neoliberal World Order: Identity, Meaning, and Foreign Policy.* 1st ed. Stanford University Press. https://doi.org/10.2307/j.ctvr33bbh.

Liao, Ning. 2012. "China's Regional Diplomacy toward Southeast Asia: Calculations and Constraints of Beijing's Engagement in Security Multilateralism." *American Journal of Chinese Studies* 19 (1): 29–46.

Lipscy, Phillip Y. 2003. "Japan's Asian Monetary Fund Proposal." *Journal of East Asian Affairs* 3 (1).

Manyin, Mark E., Michael John Garcia, and Wayne M. Morrison. 2009. "U.S. Accession to ASEAN's Treaty of Amity and Cooperation (TAC)." https://apps.dtic.mil/sti/citations/ADA501031.

Merics. 2021. "China's Anti-Foreign Sanctions Law: A Warning to the World." June 24, 2021. https://merics.org/de/kommentar/chinas-anti-foreign-sanctions-law-warning-world.

Ministry of Foreign Affairs of Japan. 2005. "小泉総理の東アジア首脳会議等への出席（概要と取りあえずの評価）." December 2005. https://www.mofa.go.jp/mofaj/kaidan/s_koi/asean05/gh.html.
Ministry of Foreign Affairs of Japan. 2007. "Visit to Japan of the Honorable Dick Cheney, Vice President of the United States of America (Summary)." February 22, 2007. https://www.mofa.go.jp/region/n-america/us/vpv0702.html.
Ministry of Foreign Affairs of Japan. 2015. "Address by Prime Minister Shinzo Abe to a Joint Meeting of the U.S. Congress." Ministry of Foreign Affairs of Japan. April 30, 2015. https://www.mofa.go.jp/na/na1/us/page4e_000241.html.
Reuters. 2015. "Obama Says U.S., Not China, Must Write Trade Rules." *Reuters*, January 21, 2015, sec. Emerging Markets. https://www.reuters.com/article/us-usa-obama-trade-idUSKBN0KU0BE20150121.
Shimizu, Kazushi. 2022. "RCEP's Great Impact on Japan and East Asian Economies." August 2, 2022. https://www.jiia.or.jp/en/ajiss_commentary/rceps-great-impact-on-japan-and-east-asian-economies.html.
Solís, Mireya. 2013. "Endgame: Challenges for the United States in Finalizing the TPP Negotiations." *International Affairs* 622, June 2013: 1–15.
Solís, Mireya. 2022. "Heyday of Asian Regionalism? The Implications of the Regional Comprehensive Economic Partnership for the United States." Economic Research Institute for ASEAN and East Asia - ERIA. 2022. http://www.eria.org/publications/heyday-of-asian-regionalism-the-implications-of-the-regional-comprehensive-economic-partnership-for-the-united-states/.
Terada, Takashi. 1999. "The Genesis of APEC: Australia-Japan Political Initiatives." Asia Pacific Economic Papers, Asia Pacific Economic Papers, December. https://ideas.repec.org//p/csg/ajrcau/298.html.
The Government Publishing Office. 1993. "Weekly Compilation of Presidential Documents" Volume 29 Issue 15. Weekly Compilation of Presidential Documents, April 19, 1993.
The Washington Post. 2017. "President Trump Signs Order to Withdraw from Trans-Pacific Partnership." January 23, 2017. https://www.washingtonpost.com/news/wonk/wp/2017/01/23/president-trump-signs-order-to-withdraw-from-transpacific-partnership/.
The White House. 2011. "Remarks By President Obama to the Australian Parliament." *Whitehouse.Gov*. November 17, 2011. https://obamawhitehouse.archives.gov/the-press-office/2011/11/17/remarks-president-obama-australian-parliament.
The White House. 2022. "CHIPS and Science Act Will Lower Costs, Create Jobs, Strengthen Supply Chains, and Counter China." *The White House*. August 9, 2022. https://www.whitehouse.gov/briefing-room/statements-releases/2022/08/09/fact-sheet-chips-and-science-act-will-lower-costs-create-jobs-strengthen-supply-chains-and-counter-china/.
United States Trade Representative. 2008. "Trans-Pacific Partners and United States Launch FTA Negotiations." United States Trade Representative. September 2008. http://ustr.gov/trans-pacific-partners-and-united-states-launch-fta-negotiations.
United States Trade Representative. 2017. "The United States Officially Withdraws from the Trans-Pacific Partnership." United States Trade Representative. January 30, 2017. http://ustr.gov/about-us/policy-offices/press-office/press-releases/2017/january/US-Withdraws-From-TPP.
United States Trade Representative. 2022. "Joint USTR and Department of Commerce Readout of the First Indo-Pacific Economic Framework Negotiating Round." United States Trade Representative. December 15, 2022. http://ustr.gov/about-us/policy-offi

ces/press-office/press-releases/2022/december/joint-ustr-and-department-commerce-rea
dout-first-indo-pacific-economic-framework-negotiating-round.

U.S. Department of Commerce. 2022. "United States and Indo-Pacific Economic Framework Partners Announce Negotiation Objectives." U.S. Department of Commerce. September 9, 2022. https://www.commerce.gov/news/press-releases/2022/09/united-states-and-indo-pacific-economic-framework-partners-announce.

三浦秀之. 2020. "アジア太平洋地域における地域経済統合と日本." 杏林社会科学研究 = *Kyorin University, Journal of Social Sciences* / 杏林大学社会科学学会 編 3: 93–115.

佐橋亮, ed. 2020. 冷戦後の東アジア秩序：秩序形成をめぐる各国の構想. 勁草書房. https://www.amazon.co.jp/%E5%86%B7%E6%88%A6%E5%BE%8C%E3%81%AE%E6%9D%B1%E3%82%A2%E3%82%B8%E3%82%A2%E7%A7%A9%E5%BA%8F-%E7%A7%A9%E5%BA%8F%E5%BD%A2%E6%88%90%E3%82%92%E3%82%81%E3%81%90%E3%82%8B%E5%90%84%E5%9B%BD%E3%81%AE%E6%A7%8B%E6%83%B3-%E4%BD%90%E6%A9%8B-%E4%BA%AE/dp/4326302887.

安倍晋三. 2023. 安倍晋三 回顧録. Edited by 橋本五郎 and 尾山宏. Translated by 北村滋. 中央公論新社.

日本経済新聞. 2015. "TPP交渉、我々がルールをつくる (ルポ迫真) (写真=共同)." 日本経済新聞. October 14, 2015. https://www.nikkei.com/article/DGXLZO92786800U5A011C1EA1000/.

日本経済新聞. 2016a. "日本の基金構想 米中が阻む." 日本経済新聞. July 3, 2016. https://www.nikkei.com/article/DGKKZO04395260T00C16A7TZG000/.

日本経済新聞. 2016b. "首相「TPP 米抜きでは意味ない」." 日本経済新聞. November 22, 2016. https://www.nikkei.com/article/DGKKASFS22H1F_S6A121C1MM0000/.

日本貿易振興機構. 2022. "レモンド米商務長官、対中競争で国内投資の重要性強調も中国とのデカップリングは「追求せず」（中国、米国） | ビジネス短信 ―ジエトロの海外ニュース." ジエトロ. December 2022. https://www.jetro.go.jp/biznews/2022/12/1dd3bd4fb2a3b1e0.html.

朝日新聞. 2022. "IPEF、来年にも「前向きな成果」 米次席通商代表インタビュー." November 1, 2022. https://www.asahi.com/articles/ASQB05QL0QBPULFA01F.html.

首相官邸. 2013. "TPP (環太平洋パートナーシップ) 協定交渉への参加." 首相官邸ホームページ. March 15, 2013. https://www.kantei.go.jp/jp/headline/tpp2013.html.

高原明生. 2003. "東アジアの多国間主義-日本と中国の地域主義政策-." 国際政治 2003 (133): 58–75, L9. https://doi.org/10.11375/kokusaiseiji1957.133_58.

高橋俊樹. 2022. "中国のドイツやRCEPを重視したサプライチェーン戦略の可能性と日本の対応～低くはない中国のRCEPによる関税削減メリット～ - 一般財団法人国際貿易投資研究所(ITI)." December 14, 2022. https://iti.or.jp/column/107.

6 Criminal Threats to Security

Joel R. Campbell

Introduction and Overview: Images of Organized Crime in Asian Films and TV

Organized crime has often been figured as a prop device in movies set in Asia. Films present East Asian countries as inherently dangerous and violent societies in which organized crime lords dominate local communities, prostitution and drug dealing are rampant, and gangsters enact retribution on those who have crossed them. Hong Kong, Korean, and Japanese mobster movies have been the most common. Martial arts movies by Bruce Lee set the tone, with Lee's characters going after crime bosses who have wronged him, especially in *Enter the Dragon* (1973). South Korea's *Nameless Gangster* (2012) takes on issues of corruption and drug dealing, Takeshi Kitano of Japan gives us American-style police action movie tropes in *Violent Cop* (1989), and Hong Kong's *Election* (2005) presents a conflict for control of a Triad organization (Jake D, 2022:1–5; Yogesh-Odyssey-Opera, 2014:1–12).

The realities of organized crime (hereafter referred to as OC) in East Asia are very different from the celluloid versions. East Asian societies are among the safest in the world, with low levels of both violent crime and gun violence. Effective policing has reduced mob activity, and gang organizations have been marginalized in several Asian societies (Campbell, 2022: 30). Traditional gang organizations, such as the Japanese Yakuza or the Hong Kong Triads, restrict their local activities to areas that are less likely to attract police attention, such as illegal gambling for the Yakuza and drugs trade outside Hong Kong for the Triads. Most people in Northeast Asia do not pay much attention to gangsters in their midst, who do not receive extensive news media coverage. To be sure, North Korea operates as a kind of gangster state, as it raises funds for its missile and nuclear programs by producing illegal goods such as amphetamines and counterfeit U.S. dollars. However, this is perceived as a problem of interstate relations.

Urbanites in Southeast Asia similarly often do not encounter the mob. Even so, organized crime since the 1990s is more present in much of the region, especially in Southeast Asia, and more attention has been paid to illegal businesses, such as illegal arms sales, maritime piracy, and human

DOI: 10.4324/9781003473206-6

trafficking. Strong economic growth and the effects of globalization throughout the region have increased opportunities for gangsters to make money off legitimate businesses and to use recently built-up infrastructure and transportation and communications systems to move illegal products and services from one region to another. For instance, it was once an arduous task to transport heroin and other illegally produced drugs out of Southeast Asia, but they now can use airports and ground transportation hubs throughout continental and insular Southeast Asia.

This chapter explores the security challenges resulting from increased OC activities in the East Asian region in the past three decades. The first section presents organized crime in theoretical terms and sketches the most salient organized crime issues in the region: military and societal security, drugs and illegal arms sales, as well as organized crime organizations emanating from China and Burma/Myanmar, and piracy in Indonesia, an island nation whose geography is almost tailor-made for piracy operations. Section two analyzes security concerns of OC activities in terms of globalization, transportation, the changing nature of crime organizations, the weakness of states, and challenges facing law enforcement agencies. The final section suggests policies that may allow East and Southeast Asian states to better contain organized crime in light of evolving state capabilities.

The Nature of the Problem of Asian Organized Crime

Organized crime is usually defined as a group of criminals who "work together on a continuous basis in illegal enterprises" (Potter, 2007: 7). They usually contain core groups and various others associated with them that carry out assigned tasks. Their activities may include both legitimate and illegal activities. Traditional OC tended toward hierarchical and nationally focused organizations, such as the Sicilian and American Mafia families, the Japanese Yakuza, and the Chinese Triads. Many experts used a corporate analogy to describe organized criminal organizations, but more recent analysis suggests that both traditional and post-modern gangs are "loose networks of entrepreneurs" who operate transnationally within the globalized economy. Instead of generating a "global Mafia," we see small and flexible organizations that are more profitable, better able to regulate production, and safer from police action against them (Potter, 2007:6–9).

Major activities performed by most organized criminals include providing illegal services, especially gambling, prostitution, protection rackets, and loansharking; along with transport and sales of illegal goods, most notably illegal drugs or narcotics, pornography, unregistered guns and other weapons, unlicensed liquor or tobacco products, fake goods, and protected animals or animal products. OC as an organization commits various crimes on a daily basis, but it also controls, operates, or influences legitimate businesses, to create a cloak of legitimacy or launder money. The American Mafia long has been associated with restaurants/nightclubs, construction contracting, and waste management businesses. Organized criminals resort to extortion, e.g., threats of violence if legitimate businesses do not use their services, such as linen services for restaurants. Finally, gangsters often engage in corruption. By assisting or paying off public officials, such as politicians, judges, prosecutors, and police, along with professionals such as lawyers, bankers and accountants, criminals can gain protection for their operations from legal sanctions (Potter, 2007:17–18).

Antonio Maria Costa, Executive Director of the U.N. Office on Drugs and Crime sketched out the seriousness of the global OC problem in 2010. For the first time in history, OC has globalized and now spans most countries. Illegal flows of money, goods, and people now affect most countries, especially geographically large countries, and major powers. He noted that there are now over 140,000 human trafficking victims annually, earning their traffickers over $3 billion a year, and the biggest flows are from Africa to Europe and Latin America to the U.S. Recent U.N. figures peg trafficking victims at forty million internationally, with twenty-five million of them in Asia. Europe now has the largest heroin market, at over $20 billion, but Russia became the largest heroin-consuming country. Meanwhile, the market for previously popular drugs such as cocaine has significantly shrunk. While news media attention is given to sources of drugs, especially Afghanistan for heroin and Colombia for cocaine, most profits are made by drug distributors in rich countries (UNODC, 2010:1–5; Seefar, 2022:1–9).

The U.S. National Security Council under President Joe Biden states that "transnational organized crime" (or TOC) has become a serious security threat, as it now penetrates key national institutions, promotes corruption, and undermines effective governance. It also amounts to a serious threat to economic development. As has been the case since the 1990s, the "crime-terror nexus" is still a major problem in several countries in Latin America and Asia. Meanwhile, expanded drug trafficking, human smuggling, illegal weapons trade, and intellectual property theft have become more serious. The world is now experiencing more cybercrime than ever before. The Asia Pacific is unique in experiencing nearly all these problems, though the cooperation between terrorists and organized criminals is less extensive in Asia than in Latin America (NSC, The White House, 2016:1–12).

The transformation of OC and TOC in Southeast Asia has been dramatic. First, many criminals have moved out of China to establish criminal franchises in the region. Second, policing methods and government capacities often are more suited to the conditions in the 1960s to 1980s, when most criminal activity was local. Third, pirates have taken advantage of the unique insular geography of the region, and their success has undermined the economies of the region. Over 120 piracy incidents occur in the Singapore Strait per year, and piracy has also grown off the coast of Sri Lanka and Vietnam. Fourth, purveyors of illegal goods have expanded by taking advantage of the expanding trade networks. Transnational illicit trade boosts economic development, even as they present clear security challenges. Trade in wildlife and illegal wood amounts to over $24 billion per year, and as much as 40 percent of Southeast Asian timber exports are illegal. Fifth, increasing ease of travel means that TOC operations can more easily find labor and traffic workers for their operations. Sixth, the number of fake products and medicines traded has exploded, most of which come from China and exploits flexible trade routes, by which suppliers can be easily replaced, if necessary (Southeast, 2023:1–10).

Lo insists that China has become a central locus of Asian OC and TOC. Complex relations among state capacity, state autonomy, and state legitimacy have meant increasing "penetration" of OC groups into government at local and provincial levels. Problems of corruption tend to demonstrate internal difficulties more than any external "challenges." Several weak Asian states are noted for their corrupt police, which tends to delegitimize the state. All the Sinocentric states or entities (the PRC, Taiwan, Hong Kong, and Macau) have increased state capacity, even as the "three poisons" (prostitution, gambling, and narcotics trade), have returned with a vengeance, along with money laundering and heavy-duty corruption (Lo, Siegel and Kwok, 2021:1–7).

Societies considered "safe" also can face major obstacles in eliminating OC or TOC. Chin illustrates the difficulty that the Taiwanese government has had stamping out OC, even though overall crime rates on the island are low and Taiwan is known for social stability and generally effective governance. This "black" underworld is an embarrassment to most Taiwanese people. Despite three high-profile anti-OC campaigns in the 1980s and 1990s, gangs continued to flourish by finding ways to legitimate their businesses, thus entering the "Upperworld" of ordinary business, and they forged corrupt and protective ties with politicians. Some of them found that the best way to avoid prosecution was to become politicians themselves. This is like the actions of the urban American Mafia mentioned above, which has run legitimate businesses and once maintained relations with corrupt police and judges (Chin, 2015:3–20).

Even a fully developed economy like Japan harbors resilient gangsters. The Yakuza were once among the most important Asian criminal organizations. Their heyday was the 1950s to 1980s when they focused on gambling, prostitution, and illicit goods trade. Yakuza members could often be seen cruising Tokyo's Shinjuku district in Cadillacs or riding the subways in gaudy clothes. Since then, they have been restricted to a few large cities, such as Tokyo, Yokohama, Osaka, and Kobe. The Yakuza are known for their strict rituals and complicated organization, based on traditional Japanese oyabun-kobun paternalistic relations. Due to a strong anti-gang law passed in 1992, Yakuza membership began to decline at the turn of the twenty-first century.

Like the American Mafia, Yakuza invest in legitimate businesses and cultivate relations with the political world and news media. While they usually avoid drug trafficking, they deal in other illegal substances and participate in human trafficking, especially of Asian and Eastern European women into Japan to work as prostitutes, strippers, and entertainers. Since 2011, a yakuza exclusion law has extended financial crimes regulation and has led to an even steeper decline in membership, yet the organization's core remains intact (Chacko, 2022:129–135).

Theoretical Approaches to Asian Gangsters

Various criminal justice theories have attempted to explain the origins of organized crime. Each approaches a different aspect of organized crime activities. Deterrence theory posits that general or specific punishments may deter individuals from participating in certain kinds of crime. This may not be effective in stopping OC, since gangs operate as collectives that provide a multitude of benefits and services for members. Other theories consider why individuals join gangs, such as rational choice theories that consider gangs as ways for members and leaders to maximize gains; and theories of psychological traits and criminality, which examine anti-social personalities and dependent personalities that thrive in gang milieus. Social disorganization theories look at the social needs fulfilled by gangs, including overcoming relative deprivation of members, the establishment of a warped form of social mobility, lack of opportunities available to various ethnic groups, and blocked opportunities. Still other theories look at the actual operations of gangs, such as community social organizations that dispense various services and form a layer of governance in many communities (Potter, 2007:61–81).

Schulte-Bockholt categorizes political theories that have been applied to OC. First, some scholars study organized criminals as organizations and institutions. This approach has been particularly popular in the U.S. since the 1960s, with its focus on the tightly knit Mafia "families." Second, are patron–clientelist studies, which look at the informality of OC operations. These arrangements work well because the self-interest of all parties is served. Third are enterprise theories, which derive from the economics of supply and demand. These can help explain why many criminal organizations keep functioning though their top leaders are sent to prison. Fourth, social network theory combines both patron–client and enterprise approaches and spells out various actors' roles in criminal activities. Fifth, succession theories look at the passing of criminal activities from one ethnic group to another, e.g., the eclipsing of Irish gangsters by Jewish and Italian mobsters, the exit of Jewish gangsters, and eventually the decline of the Mafia and replacement by Asian, Latin American, and Russian gangsters (Schulte-Bockholt, 2006:5–7).

Marxist OC theories receive less attention in America. These include critiques of "pathologies" of capitalism that give rise to criminality, Gramscian studies that look at OC variously as expressions of the structure of capitalism or actors that help provide stability to the system, and mobsters as supporters of capitalism since they benefit from its continued success. Socioeconomic elites often benefit from the existence of OC because it provides services that legitimate providers do not want to touch (Schulte-Bockholt, 2006:7–9).

While intriguing, each of these theories contains limitations that prevent comprehensive explanations of OC activities. Gangster organizations may have structure, but they do not mirror corporations or government organs. OC operations do not operate as enterprises, as they do not require profits and so function like rent-seekers in authoritarian states. Patron–clientelism may operate at the local level, but mobsters dispense favors on a very limited basis. Network theory fails for the same reasons that enterprise theory lacks explanatory power. Succession theory makes sense and may show how twentieth-century American OC worked, but it cannot explain the complex, multi-level organizations that have arisen in much of the world in the past forty years.

Among international relations theories, constructivism provides unique insights into the phenomenon of organized crime, how gangs interact with society, and the ways that gangs fit into governance. Constructivism usually focuses on norms, values, identities, and institutions that are socially constructed and subject to constant change. The evolution of attitudes toward Asian organized crime illustrates how this works. OC arises to address the employment and capital accumulation needs of marginal communities, such as the mountain people of the Golden Triangle. Working for organized crime groups allows a selection of each group to gain an economic foothold in their society. OC groups function with an unofficial code that, however, warped it may be to outsiders, provides prescribed behavior and allows them to operate relatively freely. Gangsters become popular because they provide goods and services demanded within their societies. Ordinary people are not directly affected by gangster activities, such as gambling, prostitution, and maritime piracy. Though by turns repelled and fascinated by the mob, Asians do not prioritize round-ups and prosecution of gangsters.

As in IR, three levels of analysis can be applied to Asian OC: global, national, and individual, as Asian OC functions at all three levels (Keo, 2017:2–10). TOC in East and Southeast Asia tends to be decentralized and partially networked, and so all three levels are at work. Most gangsters begin as individual operators working within local groups. These local groups may extend their operations nationally. The products that TOC networks then sell abroad go regionally and globally.

Asian Organized Crime, Globalization, and National Security

The most serious threats by OC and TOC to national security are both insidious and undermine political and social cohesion. Corruption of local and national politicians, the military, and local police make it difficult for states to control their territory and extend the rule of law to all citizens. OC organizations, flush with cash, possess resources to pay off poorly paid local and national officials. Government officials and police then come to depend on relationships with OC leaders and protect them from arrest and prosecution. This is particularly true in countries with endemic poverty or chronically poor regions, ruled by weak or underdeveloped states, most notably Burma/Myanmar, Laos, Cambodia, and Indonesia. Governments often are unable to upgrade or adequately train personnel, and corruption worsens over time. Military leaders and small units develop relations with local gangsters and drug traffickers and benefit from their illicit activities. Instead of defending the nation, the military becomes a patronage system in which both officers and enlisted personnel depend on illegal rent-seeking for livelihoods.

The U.S. National Security Council (NSC) considers international organized crime organizations a "significant and growing threat" to both national and international security, and it notes "dire implications for such policy areas as public health, democratic governance, and economic management." The NSC made particular note of "penetration" of governmental institutions, especially where states possess weak rule of law, growing ties between TOC groups and state units, and politicians or bureaucrats looking the other way and allowing criminal activities. TOC organizations subvert governance in various ways, including direct bribes, the establishment of "shadow economies," forging close ties with financial and security sectors, and criminal organizations becoming "alternative providers" of governance, local security, local services, and jobs. Through bribery and corruption, they also undermine the operations of free markets, and these frequent bribes increase the costs of doing business in many counties (NSC, The White House, 2016:1–12).

Lo, Siegel, and Kwok assert that the most serious problem attending Asian OC is cross-border corruption. Corruption used to be an ad hoc local phenomenon but is now "syndicated" throughout the region. Countries are increasingly concerned about the export of corruption across borders, as well as the increasingly transnational nature of Asian crime. The fast development of East and Southeast Asia, with attendant progress in both transportation and communications, means that Asian TOC has many more resources to use to corrupt local and national police and government officials. Several Southeast Asian countries have become "addicted" to "Chinese sweeteners" in terms of foreign direct investment, the extension of Chinese state-owned enterprise operations, and increased overseas sourcing of resources and components. The Chinese Open Door policy since 1978 has encouraged various illegal activities, especially prostitution, abductions, drug smuggling, organized robberies, illegal firearms trafficking, and various economic crimes. Illegal trade in antiquities and wildlife has also grown apace. (Lo, Siegel, and Kwok, 2020:4–11).

Globalization of criminal activities is the most potent issue For East and Southeast Asian OC. Globalization is most often defined as the erasure of barriers to trade in goods and services, financial transactions, and labor flows or migration. Production and distribution are usually undertaken via transnational commodity or production chains. Communication and transportation services become vital to globalized economic activity and increasing reliance on technology drives much recent economic exchange. As the region consists of eighteen nation-states and territories, no single organized crime group controls illegal activities, regionally. While the Yakuza and Triads are important in Japan and Hong Kong, they have limited influence regionally. Accordingly, Asian organized crime must operate transnationally through trade and cooperative networks.

Globalization has brought new opportunities to previously declining organizations and Northeast Asian outfits have been able to link with TOC organizations throughout East Asia or other regions. The very economic growth that has brought prosperity to China has meant greater opportunities for mobsters as illicit activity has proliferated. Deng Xiaoping once said that when you open a window flies come in, meaning that unwanted influences enter a country when it opens to the world.

A major U.N. Report discusses OC globalization since 2000, addressing members' concerns about the extent of international illicit fund flows. The report noted several key international problems that have worsened in recent years. It paid special attention to human trafficking, in the form of both smuggling of migrant labor and female sex workers. Heroin and cocaine remain major issues, but many Asian producers have shifted to methamphetamines and other synthetic drugs. The firearms market ballooned in the post-Cold War era as ethno-nationalist conflicts and insurgencies increased throughout the developing world. Criminals also traffic natural resources, such as timber, along with counterfeit goods, in greater volumes than ever. Finally, identity theft has become a major concern of the global economy (UNODC, 2010:1–7).

Asian organized crime got a major boost from the COVID-19 pandemic, especially in Southeast Asia. The pandemic and the shutdown of the region's entertainment industry meant that organized crime could not make money off traditional gambling, illegal drug distribution, and prostitution. Specialized criminal zones arose in Burma, Cambodia, Laos, and elsewhere in Southeast Asia. As China encouraged its expatriates to come home, criminals needed new workers. In Cambodia, over 50,000 foreigners were lured with promises of high-paying jobs to run online computer scams and were held as virtual slaves. Casinos were set up to attract Chinese gambling money, and local governments benefited from the crime-controlled sites in Cambodia and Laos. The Cambodian government was only able to take occasional action and the net result was to undermine the state (Clapp and Tower, 2022:1–6).

Burma saw a big increase in criminal activities in border areas. The Shwe Kokko Yatai New City project was a large, sophisticated operation, and the operators applied for funds from China's Belt and Road Initiative. The democratic government led by the National League for Democracy (NLD) tried to shut down the town, China backed away from supporting it, and the Thai government cut off electric power and telecommunications services. However, after the military coup d'etat in early 2021, as many as fifteen new enclaves were set up, especially along the Moei River. The local Karen militia provides security for the towns, and they receive payments in return. These newer zones operate like penal colonies, as trafficked workers are confined in dorms and threatened if they do not produce sufficient revenue for their bosses. One of the towns houses 10,000 enslaved workers. An enclave kingpin, She Zhi, was arrested in 2020, but his associates remained at large (Clapp and Tower, 2022:1–6).

The "crime-terror-insurgency nexus" allows TOC organizations and armed political opposition groups to support each other. Almost half of all groups on a U.S. Justice Department priority list show such connections. These have included the Taliban before they took over Afghanistan's government in 2021, the Revolutionary Armed Forces of Colombia (known by its Spanish acronym FARC), and Al Qaeda in the Arab Maghreb. Such tie-ups have aided the expansion of illegal drug networks. In Asia, the most notable such drug-terror trafficking connections are via Afghan and Burmese organizations (NSC, The White House, 2016:1–12).

East Asia became an important locus for TOC activity because of global economic ties throughout the region. Unlike some other regions of the world, state or quasi-state organizations play key roles in illegal activities. The NSC notes that the most notable activities are intellectual property theft in China and Southeast Asia, human trafficking from China and Southeast Asia to Western countries (one Chinese trafficker, Cheng Chui Peng, smuggled over 1,000 people into the U.S.), and North Korea's production of illegal drugs and counterfeit U.S. currency (NSC, The White House, 2016:1–12).

Southeast Asian organized criminal activity also has been fueled by external actors. Chinese criminals moved out of their homeland to avoid government crackdowns. Maritime Southeast Asia, especially in Indonesia and the Philippines, has traditionally been an effective arena for illegal activities, as there are thousands of unpoliced islands where criminals can hide their operations. There is a long tradition of illegal cross-border trade, and the region's speedy economic integration has stimulated both legal and illegal trade. Greater social and political connections across the region make cross-border contacts easier, and this aids the transfer of not only drugs, but natural resources such as wildlife and timber (U.N. Meetings, 2022:1–20).

China and Hong Kong also loom large in any discussions of Asian organized crime. Chinese organized crime has a long history going back to before the Green Gang which controlled parts of Shanghai and other cities in the 1920s and developed close ties with the Guomindang leaders of the country. The Hong Kong Triads have been active in the illegal drug trade and other illicit activities for over a century. The Communist government stamped out organized crime activities during the 1950s, but corruption was never absent from China. Informal criminal organizations began to take advantage of the Reform and Opening policies during the 1980s, and the openness of China's liberalized economy created myriad opportunities for money-making in counterfeit or sub-standard goods sold abroad. China's shady businesses venture abroad to other Asian countries, and Chinese human trafficking networks extend to North America and Europe (GF Integrity, 2022:1–4).

China is unique not only in being a source of illicit goods, as well as a source of demand and a transit site. Unlike most key economies, Chinese organizations engage in various illegal activities, such as the use of forced labor and the copying of intellectual property. Russian Mafia operations tend to be more decentralized and flexible than their American or European counterparts, but they have extensive connections with Asian criminal organizations, such as the Hong Kong Triads (GF Integrity, 2022:1–4).

North Korea (Democratic People's Republic of Korea – DPRK) is the closest thing to becoming a criminal state in East Asia. For much of the Cold War era, Pyongyang did not have to rely on internationally proscribed activities, as its trade with neighbors China, Russia, and Japan sustained mining, agriculture, and heavy industries, and it received significant foreign aid from both of its large Communist neighbors. Once the Cold War ended, most of the DPRK's trade dried up and both of its northern friends demanded hard currency payments for exports to the North. North Korea could have taken the Reform and Opening path followed by China and later Vietnam in the 1980s, but instead they doubled down on their Juche, or self-reliance, policies. As the DPRK launched extensive nuclear weapons and ballistic missile development programs, the U.N. Security Council imposed numerous sanctions on Pyongyang, and various countries imposed additional targeted sanctions, all of which made trade even more difficult. The sanctions in the late Obama and Trump administrations were designed to apply "maximum pressure" and so force Pyongyang to negotiate an end to its nuclear program, but the DPRK had devoted so much effort to nuclear weapons that it was unlikely to give them up.

North Korea has concentrated on producing items that it can quickly sell and make hard currency to fund both nuclear and missile development and its patron–clientelistic distribution system. Contraband items include methamphetamines and other synthetic drugs that it markets in Japan and other Asian countries, along with small arms and missiles that it sells to Middle Eastern and African countries. North Korea also produces very high-quality counterfeit U.S. $100 bills, which have the potential to undermine the real dollar, the key international exchange currency. North Korea also has trafficked endangered animal products and over-harvested sea products.

TOC Trafficking – Drugs, Illicit Goods, and People

A hallmark of OC globalization is the profusion of illegal sales of various goods. For instance, the illegal firearms market burgeoned in the early years of the century and accounts for $170 million to $320 million yearly. Illegal use of natural resources, especially wildlife and wildlife products, has become a major environmental issue in Africa, South Asia, and Southeast Asia and has accelerated environmental degradation. It increased ten-fold in the first decade of the century and accounts for $10 billion per year. Around the world, 1.5 million people suffer identity theft of some kind. Cybercrime hurts the economic security of both businesses and governments in many countries (UNODC, 2010:1–5).

Costa insists that the world community needs to "disrupt market forces," for anti-OC police operations to be successful. He notes that most national responses are inadequate, and the U.N. needs to come together to confront the differences between countries willing to fight OC and those unwilling to undertake serious efforts. He added that, as criminals are primarily motivated by the need for profits, "let's go after the money" (UNODC, 2010:1–5).

The Golden Triangle along the borders of Thailand, Myanmar, and Laos remains one of the most active regions for narcotics and other illegal drug production. In the popular imagination, three myths persist about the area: 1) that the name is an old one; 2) that it has produced opium for centuries; and 3) that the battle for control of the area is one between "good guys" and "bad guys." In truth, the area was not known as a producer of illicit drugs until the post-World War II era, and so it did not traditionally produce opium or heroin. The name only came about in the early 1970s, mostly in America. Thailand was trying to rebuild relations with the U.S. after the Vietnam War and Beijing was cooperating with America in the Cold War. The title seized the imagination of the American public and, over time, this small region bordering China came to symbolize the entire Southeast Asian drugs trade. The region has neither distinct borders nor a designated size. Early drug operations were fairly simple: harvesting of poppy plants occurred in Burma, whereas drug production mostly took place across the border in Thailand (Lintner, 2022:1–7).

After World War II and the end of the Chinese Revolution, Guomindang (KMT) units escaped China and set up operations across the Burmese border. They received some CIA assistance but needed a steady stream of funds, and opium production seemed the best way to support themselves. Due to Burmese complaints and an ensuing diplomatic row, the U.S. pressured Taipei to evacuate its forces and dependents. This was done in two waves: 1953–1954 when most forces were evacuated via northern Thailand and the 1960–1961 withdrawal of roughly 4,400 remaining troops. Some KMT troops settled in northern Thailand (Charoenwong, 2004:1–17). Those who control the area have included a variety of actors who exhibit shades of gray, including Burmese rebels resisting the government. The Burmese economic collapse since the coup d'etat in 2021 has only worsened the situation.

The end of Southeast Asian colonialism caused the opium trade to decline, though production greatly expanded. The Shan State's resistance to the Burmese state created another entity that, like the KMT, needed a revenue stream. The Burmese state permitted local army units to engage in opium production and trade, so both sides were doing it. As other countries, such as Afghanistan and Turkey, competed for world heroin markets, Golden Triangle drug lords began to produce more profitable and popular drugs, such as methamphetamines. They also shifted other illegal trades, such as human trafficking, wildlife smuggling, rare earth mining, and antiquities trade. Meanwhile, the Burmese government pursued its anti-insurgency efforts half-heartedly and both sides continued to benefit from the drug trade. Most outside parties, especially the Thais, Taiwanese, and Americans, were willing to work with the drug lords if it suited their self-interest (Charoenwong, 2004:1–17).

The U.S. Institute of Peace agrees that the biggest increase in organized crime activity in Asia has been in Burma. The 2021 coup seems to have "opened the floodgates" to organized criminal operations, and the country has become a "magnet" for criminals based in Southeast Asia. A witches' brew of increased corruption, the deleterious effects of the COVID-19 pandemic, the collapse of law and order in remote areas, and China's attempts to force its nationals living abroad to come home have given indigenous criminals more opportunities and allowed them to set up more enclaves. The pandemic especially hurt the government's efforts to extend law enforcement throughout the countryside. Though the government made a big splash about the arrest of a local "kingpin," the report suggests that Burmese operations are now hurting both overall regional security (Clapp and Tower, 2022:1–9).

Illicit trade and distribution of small arms also has become a serious problem in Southeast Asia. It worsens existing conflicts and organized crime in the region and hurts efforts to bring existing conflicts to an end. As most ongoing conflicts are in developing countries of South, Southeast, and Central Asia, the circulation of small arms makes these conflicts more violent and more difficult to resolve. While many of the region's states lack the political will to settle internal conflicts, non-state actors fuel these fights, and so they get involved in selling illegal drugs and contraband. The countries with the greatest consumption of small arms are Pakistan, Afghanistan, Myanmar, and the nations of the Golden Triangle (GlobalSecurity.org, 2023:1–6).

Human trafficking has become one of East Asia's most serious concerns. Unlike most regions, most trafficking here (up to 85 percent) takes place within the region. About 60 percent of that is for sex work. Major economic powers China and Japan are key magnets for trafficking, but Malaysia and Thailand also absorb much illegal labor. Child trafficking is often for use in child pornography or live streaming of children engaged in sexual acts. It accounts for between $3 and 20 billion per year. Forced labor occurs when adults seek jobs and are forced into manual labor in fishing, agriculture, construction, and domestic work. Endemic corruption facilitates the transfer of people across national boundaries and within countries (Caballero-Anthony, 2018:1–8).

Asian refugee and trafficking issues have become linked. Unlike in the West, 85 percent of Asian refugees stay within the region. Roughly 40 percent performed casual labor or bonded labor. The region's conflicts and natural disasters have helped fuel the movement of people, and traffickers take advantage of this. Though there are various international protocols against trafficking, widespread corruption throughout Asia makes it easier for traffickers and their allies to function within countries and across borders. As the realities of human trafficking become complex, issues are more difficult to solve (GF Integrity, 2022:1–5; Punnen, 2020:1–19).

Not all scholars find Asian human trafficking to be a major concern. Keo insists that his research does not affirm common images of traffickers' "prevalence," large profits being made by traffickers, or even their leading role in Asian OC activities. He did a pilot study of seventeen children who supposedly had been trafficked, and he noted that none of them saw themselves as victims, but instead thought that they were doing their duty to support their families. His subsequent work suggests that instead of a serious problem, a "moral panic" has been created by Western NGOs and governments, placing Asian countries on their human rights and security agendas. He notes that moral panics are created through the interaction of civil societies as expressed by NGOs, and political societies through the world of elected representatives and bureaucrats. This moral panic, based on neo-colonial images of backward Asian societies, leads to "wildly inflated statistics" and discounting of alternative explanations, with unsupported research and conflating of various crimes into the category of OC. Human trafficking becomes a socially constructed category to fit preconceived Western ideas. In truth, most Asian traffickers are small operators who feel that they are fulfilling an important social role and who usually are not profitable (Keo, 2017: 2–10).

Southeast Asian Maritime Piracy

Maritime piracy has been a major hindrance to trade by sea since the ancient world. The most active piracy theater since the 1990s has been the Horn of Africa, where desperate Somalis and their warlords jockeying for power prey on the busy shipping lanes that pass through the Red and Arabian Seas. Southeast Asia is the second most active venue for piracy. Traditional poverty, along with the thousands of available island hideouts in the Philippines and Indonesia provide incentives to take advantage of the multiple shipping lanes that cross the region, most notably the South China Sea and especially the Strait of Malacca, the world's busiest shipping channel. Additional roots of Asian piracy are in the hit-and-run tactics employed by modern pirates, overfishing (which puts fishermen out of work), and border disputes that have incentivized local gangs to engage in piracy. Maritime rules and regulations are ambiguous and often unenforced in the region, piracy has been a magnet for Southeast Asia's TOC organizations, and the recent terrorist–gangster nexus has created mutually supportive ties in both the Philippines and Indonesia. For instance, the Abu Sayaf group in the southern Philippines has specialized in hostage-taking for profit, often raiding boats near Mindanao (Interpol, n.d.:1–4; Ling and Cheng, 2020:1–10).

The linked Straits of Singapore and Malacca are the region's most dangerous bodies of water. According to one study, 41 percent of all Asian piracy attacks take place in and around the straits, accounting for $7–12 billion in losses per year. About 80 percent of all attacks in the region are on anchored ships and boats. Regional governments and the Association of Southeast Asian Nations (ASEAN)[1] have sought to improve cooperation to round up pirates, but they find that they do not have sufficient personnel or boats. These governments are "uncomfortable partners" that have found it difficult to work together because of clashing maritime interests. Outside major powers, especially the U.S. and Japan, have clear interests to police maritime piracy, and so have extended help to regional countries, but the problem remains largely intractable (Caballero-Anthony, 2018:1–8).

Conclusion and Future Prospects

Globalization has facilitated the development of Asian criminal organizations. Without the outsized intervention of economic development and foreign business in East Asia, the region could have never become the hotbed of economic growth that stimulated criminal activities of various kinds, and Asian OC would have remained atomized and small. Economic development, while promoting modernization and democratization, has facilitated cheating, illegal sales, and corruption on a vast scale. The post-1980 liberalization that has made economic maturation possible has also provided more opportunities for money-making in partially legal/partially illegal businesses. Businesses see the benefits of globalization, including increased production and decreased costs, the vast expansion of foreign travel through direct air connections to much of the world, and containerized shipping to major international markets. Opportunities open equally for both legal and illegal businesses.

This revolution in transportation has facilitated East Asian development. The building of modern infrastructure, including maritime ports, airports, and highways, has made the transport of goods easier than ever before. This started with Japan, which is well situated on the Pacific Ocean, spread to the Four Tigers and China, then all of Southeast Asia, and finally India. China has invested more in infrastructure than almost any country. Containerized shipping has regularized the mass transportation of manufactured goods and made sales to developed and developing markets uncomplicated. Better transport has also made the cross-border illicit transfer of goods and drugs both simpler and cheaper. Widespread use of air transport also allows criminals to easily transit international borders. People also can be trafficked easily by sea or air transport.

The advent of post-modern technology, especially the widespread use of computers, the internet, and social media allows Asian criminals to communicate relatively easily with potential partners and customers. They can trade information about obstacles to transport and policing methods in the countries through which they pass. These technologies also present many opportunities for such crimes as theft of intellectual property, stealing of identities and personal information, and luring vulnerable people into illegal labor or sex trafficking.

Due to these changes, criminal organizations have shifted away from traditional organizational structures. The old-line top-down Mafia-like criminal organizations have been replaced by more flexible and decentralized unitized groups within various countries, based on Russian Mafia models. Each local group cooperates with similar organizations that serve as their partners in other countries. Within countries, specialist units can deal with different kinds of economic activity, such as economic crimes, computerized theft, and human trafficking operations.

Corruption has always been a major political problem throughout the region but, with more widespread criminal activity, protection from politicians, bureaucrats, and police becomes ever more vital. The problem for criminal organizations is that, as governments have modernized their operations, they can crack down more extensively on corruption in their midst. Singapore was one of the first Southeast Asian countries to set up rigorous anti-corruption measures. While other Southeast Asian countries have been slower to upgrade their operations, they have been making progress at stamping out corrupt practices. Anti-corruption programs have been less successful in countries with endemic crime or cultures in which corruption is widely accepted as normal practice. This is especially true in China, in which efforts to stop corrupt practices often are linked to power struggles and punishment of Communist Party factions that lose those fights. Relatively poor countries such as Burma, Cambodia, and the Philippines do not have the resources to mount major anti-corruption campaigns, and local businesses often benefit from dishonest practices.

While the globalization and regionalization of Asia have created greater opportunities for OC and TOC operations, they have also provided more effective methods for combatting organized criminal organizations. First, the creation of ASEAN, ASEAN+3,[2] and other cooperative forums provides governments with mechanisms by which they can cooperate to control crime. This is especially true in Southeast Asia, though governments also have worked together in Northeast Asia. Expansion of such efforts will allow governments to limit crime operations across the region.

National governments can take cues from national governments about how to corral and hem in OC and TOC activities. Japan, South Korea, and Taiwan have been most effective in controlling their traditional OC organizations, and this has brought peace to the streets and stability to national economies. Chinese efforts have weakened since the start of the reform era, but its occasional anti-OC campaigns have resulted in curbing criminal operations in some local areas, and occasional crackdowns on intellectual property and identity theft could be expanded and made more consistent. National governments can also learn much from generally clean governments such as in Hong Kong, Taiwan, and Singapore about setting ethical standards and enforcing anti-corruption laws. Civil servants, military personnel, and police need to be paid adequate living wages so that they will not be tempted to accept bribes and gifts or engage in other corrupt behavior.

The most extensive action needs to be taken at the local level, where most of the Southeast Asian TOC enclaves have been operating in recent years. Stronger efforts to close forced labor operations and cut back human trafficking feeding them can dry up sources of human capital for computer scams and identity theft. International NGOs and national governments can do much more to beef up local government administrations and policing. Much more can be done to professionalize government, military, and police service, so the local government needs ready access to greater financial and educational resources.

Notes

1 The Association of Southeast Asian Nations (ASEAN) is regional intergovernmental organization that was established in 1967 to promote economic and security cooperation. Member states include: Brunei, Cambodia, East Timor, Indonesia, Laos, Malaysia, Myanmar, the Philippines, Singapore, Thailand, and Vietnam.
2 ASEAN+3 was established in 1997 and focuses primarily on greater economic cooperation between ASEAN and the three East Asian countries of China, Japan, and South Korea.

References

Caballero-Anthony, Mely. 2018. "A Hidden Scourge: Southeast Asia's Refugees and Displaced People are Victimized by Human Traffickers, but the Crime Usually Goes Unreported." *International Monetary Fund, FD Finance, and Development*. https://www.imf.org/en/Publications/fandd/issues/2018/09/human-trafficking-in-southeast-asia-caballero (retrieved 2/12/23).

Campbell, Joel R. 2022. *Politics Go to the Movies: International Relations and Politics in Genre Films and Television*. Lanham, MD: Lexington Books.

Chacko, Marlin. 2022. *Organized Crime in Asia*. Middletown, DE: Self-published.

Charoenwong, Kaemmanee, 2004. "The Evacuation of the Nationalist Chinese (Kuomintang/KMT) Troops in Northern Thailand from the 1950s to Today." *CORE*. https://core.ac.uk/download/pdf/234717468.pdf (retrieved 3/31/23).

Chin, Ko-lin. 2015. *Heijin: Organized Crime, Business, and Politics in Taiwan*. London: Routledge.

Clapp, Priscilla A. and Jason Tower. 2022, November 9. *Myanmar's Criminal Zones: A Growing Threat to Global Security: New forms of human trafficking, slavery, and international fraud are rife in lawless Myanmar*. United States Institute of Peace. https://www.usip.org/publications/2022/11/myanmars-criminal-zones-growing-threat-global-security (retrieved 2/6/23).

Jake D, "5 Films for Free: East Asian Crime Movies." *Richland Library*, June 24, 2022: 1–5. https://www.richlandlibrary.com/blog/2022-04-13/test-jake (retrieved 12/10/22).

GF Integrity. "Made in China: China's Role in Transnational Crime and Illicit Financial Flows," 2022. https://gfintegrity.org/report/made-in-china/ (retrieved 2/12/23).

GlobalSecurity.org. 2023. "Southeast Asia Organized Crime." *GlobalSecurity.org*. https://www.globalsecurity.org/military/world/para/organized-crime-sea.htm (retrieved 2/7/23).

Interpol, n.d. "How INTERPOL Supports China to Tackle International Crime: Fighting Organized Crime in China." https://www.interpol.int/en/Who-we-are/Member-countries/Asia-South-Pacific/CHINA (retrieved 2/12/23).

Keo, Chenda. 2017. *Human Trafficking in Cambodia*. London: Routledge.

Ling, Bonny and Isabelle Cheng. 2020. "Combatting Human Trafficking in East Asia and Beyond." *The Newsletter, International Institute for Asian Studies*, University of Leiden. 87 (Autumn). https://www.iias.asia/the-newsletter/article/combatting-human-trafficking-east-asia-and-beyond (retrieved 2/12/23).

Lintner, Bertil. 2022, November 28. "Guide to Investigating Organized Crime in the Golden Triangle — Introduction." *Global Investigative Journalism Network*. https://gijn.org/2022/11/28/guide-to-investigating-organized-crime-in-the-golden-triangle-introduction/ (retrieved 2/6/23).

Lo, T. Wing, Dana Siegel, and Sharon I. Kwok., eds., 2021. *Organized Crime and Corruption Across Borders: Exploring the Belt and Road Initiative.* London: Routledge.

National Security Council (NSC), The White House. 2016. *Transnational Organized Crime: A Growing Threat to National and International Security.* https://obamawhitehouse.archives.gov/administration/eop/nsc/transnational-crime/threat (retrieved 2/7/23).

UNODC. 2010."Organized Crime Has Globalized and Turned into a Security Threat." *Press Release*, United Nations Office on Drugs and Crime. https://www.unodc.org/unodc/en/press/releases/2010/June/organized-crime-has-globalized-and-turned-into-a-security-threat.htmlch (retrieved 2/6/23).

Potter, Lyman. 2007. *Organized Crime*, 4th ed. Upper Saddle River, NJ: Pearson Education, Inc.

Punnen, Joseph. 2020. "Small Arms Trafficking in South And South East Asia – Analysis." *Eurasia Review,* https://www.eurasiareview.com/03092020-small-arms-trafficking-in-south-and-south-east-asia-analysis/ (retrieved 2/12/23)

Schulte-Bockholt, Alfredo. 2006. *The Politics of Organized Crime and the Organized Crime of Politics.* Lanham, MD: Lexington Books.

Seefar. 2022. "Trafficking in Persons in Southeast Asia: Analysis of Data from the US Trafficking in Persons Report." *Seefar,* https://seefar.org/news/research/trafficking-in-persons-in-southeast-asia-analysis-of-data-from-the-us-trafficking-in-persons-report/ (retrieved 4/30/23).

United Nations, Meetings Coverage, and Press Releases (U.N. Meetings). 2022. "Organized Crime Perpetuating Instability, Violence, Poverty across West Africa, Sahel, Executive Director Tells Security Council": 1–9. https://press.un.org/en/2022/sc14761.doc.htm (retrieved 2/7/23)

United Nations Office on Drugs and Crime, Press Release (UNODC). 2010. "Organized Crime Has Globalized and Turned into a Security Threat." https://www.unodc.org/unodc/en/press/releases/2010/June/organized-crime-has-globalized-and-turned-into-a-security-threat.htmlch (retrieved 2/6/23).

Yogesh-Odyssey-Opera, "Best Asian Gangster Movies." *IMDb*, Sept. 1, 2014: 1–12. https://www.imdb.com/list/ls055090559/ (retrieved 12/10/22).

7 Environmental Threats to Security

Luba Levin-Banchik

Introduction and Overview

Each September, the leaders of nearly all countries in the world gather at the headquarters of the United Nations for high-level meetings to discuss the most pressing global issues, including environmental threats, from the perspective of their nation-states. While climate change affects all people and nation-states, the leaders of Asian countries commonly describe it as the gravest, even existential, threat. In 2022, during the 77th session of the United Nations General Assembly, for example, Ferdinand Romualdez Marcos, President of the Philippines, referred to climate change as "the greatest threat affecting our nations and peoples" and described it as the first of the primary challenges "to the continued survival of our global community" (United Nations, 2022). Vivian Balakrishnan, Minister for Foreign Affairs of Singapore, called the climate crisis "a clear and present threat" and "the most pressing challenge confronting humanity today." (Ministry of Foreign Affairs Singapore, 2022). Pham Binh Minh, Deputy Prime Minister of Vietnam, said that "climate crisis and other non-traditional security risks threaten our very existence" (UN Web TV, 2022).

Despite the broad meaning of the concept of "environmental security" and the increasing impact of the environment on Asian security, a study by Busby and Krishnan (2015:23) finds that the nexus of environment and security in the Asian region remains understudied, especially in academic literature. At the same time, official statements and policy reports by governments and international organizations typically focus on four major ways in which environmental threats affect security in Asia. These are food, water, energy, and military security. Alternatively, the discussion focuses on the impact and mitigation of natural disasters and extreme weather events, such as rising sea levels, tsunamis, and earthquakes. This chapter follows both approaches. The first section provides a theoretical framework for the discussion of environmental threats in Asia, followed by a survey of research and data analysis on the links between globalization and the environment in the second section. The third and fourth sections discuss food and water security, respectively, as examples of environmental threats to Asia. The fifth section focuses on the phenomena of rising

DOI: 10.4324/9781003473206-7

sea-level to illustrate how slow-onset events associated with climate change affect various aspects of security in Asia. The chapter concludes with a discussion of prospects for the management and containment of regional environmental threats in the increasingly globalization world.

Theoretical Orientation and Evolving Milieu

Climate change poses a particularly grave risk to Asian countries for several reasons. A report by the International Monetary Fund suggests that temperatures are rising two times faster in Asia than the global average and finds that in the past twenty years (2000 to 2019), the region experienced a greater number of weather-related disasters than any other region in the world (Dabla-Norris, Daniel, and Nozaki, 2021). Moreover, Asian countries face increased environmental threats due to regional and local processes, specifically industrialization and development, which also play a key role in contributing to climate change. According to Dabla-Norris, Daniel, and Nozaki (2021), the region produces about half of the world's carbon dioxide (CO_2) emissions and contains five of the largest greenhouse-gas emitting countries in the world. Moreover, Asian reliance on coal-based power generation and carbon-intensive manufacturing leads to dangerously high air pollution with the ten most polluted cities in the world located in the region (Dabla-Norris, Daniel, and Nozaki, 2021:50). Other studies reinforce these arguments and suggest an additional aspect that makes Asian countries especially vulnerable: The size and rate of population growth. According to Busby and Krishnan (2015:23), Asian countries have high population densities along rivers and low-elevation coastal zones, which increases the risk of massive exposure to and death from climate-related hazards. Similarly, according to Maddock (1995:25), it is the combination of large and fast-expanding populations and rapid economic development that makes the region especially vulnerable to the climate crisis.

Climate change occupies an increasingly central place in the policy, discourse, and actions of nation-states. Yet, scholars of international relations and comparative politics disagree on whether and under what conditions environmental threats should be considered security threats (Maddock, 1995:21–25). On the one hand, environmental threats, alone, rarely pose an immediate or grave threat to war and peace (Morton, 2008:53). Thus, the traditional understanding of security in military terms treats environmental threats as a low-tier issue. An alternative approach, however, follows an expanded definition of security that includes major threats to human well-being, including grave threats posed by the environment, as a security concern. According to this approach, environmental hazards, such as rising sea levels, earthquakes, tsunamis, wildfires, floodings, and other extreme weather events, pose security risks to military and civilian infrastructure and population. Hyun and Kim (2007:9) suggest that "Environmental security can be thought of in terms of the source of environmental problems, the scope and impact of those problems, and the level of threat perceived by states or nations in relation to the problems" (Hyun and Kim, 2007:9). As such, environmental threats affect multiple, oftentimes overlapping, aspects of security and can be linked to both "human security" and "traditional security." Indeed, according to Joshua Busby, climate hazards can be conceptualized as security threats if they "significantly diminish or challenge the country's way of life or the way of life of a sizable proportion of the country" (Busby 2019:57). This chapter follows this definition in the discussion of the environmental threats faced by countries in Asia.

Globalization and Threats to the Environment

Globalization involves increasing economic, political, cultural, and technological connectivity, openness, and interdependence across the globe (International Monetary Fund, 2008). Gygli et al. (2019:546) define globalization as "the process of creating networks of connections among actors at intra- or multi-continental distances, mediated through a variety of flows including people, information and ideas, capital, and goods." Globalization has a profound impact on the environment as it can both embolden the threats to the environment and facilitate the efforts to contain them. On the one hand, increased transport of goods and economic specialization, which are characteristic of globalization, have a negative environmental impact, such as increased emissions, habitat destruction, invasive species, deforestation, overfishing, and decreased biodiversity (Stobierski, 2021). Yet, globalization also enables and encourages a greater worldwide awareness of those threats, which can help to limit their negative effect.

A study by Wu et al. (2022) specifies numerous ways globalization can have both positive and negative influences on environmental quality, indicated by CO_2 emissions. They note that while the introduction of eco-friendly products and technologies as well as stricter environmental regulations decrease emissions, the open trade and foreign investment, extensive use of energy, and the relocation of industries to countries with weaker environmental regulations of the globalizing process also increases emissions. Panayotou (2000) reaches a similar conclusion on the complex ways globalization affects the environment. In the extensive survey of scholarships on globalization and environment, the study shows, for instance, how foreign direct investment can have a positive influence on a country's environment by increasing investment in clean energy and higher environmental standards, but may lead to environmental degradation through increased pollution and energy use when there is no environmental policy in place.

The complex relationship between globalization and the environment and the varied effects they have on each other is also demonstrated in the work of (Baek, Cho, and Koo, 2009). In their study of the linkages between globalization and the environment in twenty-four countries across different regions, they found that the causal relationship between globalization and the environment is largely conditioned by economic development. In developed countries, such as Japan, Korea, and Singapore, globalization, measured by an increased level of income and trade openness, leads to improved environmental quality, while in developing countries, such as Sri Lanka, globalization deteriorates environmental quality. A study by Wu et al. (2022) demonstrates, however, that both developed and developing countries can benefit from globalization. In their analysis of three major CO_2 emitting countries from 1970 to 2018, the scholars find that globalization is improving the environment in the United States and India but leading to environmental degradation in China. The case of India suggests that globalization can reduce pollution in developing countries when their national government support environmentally friendly rather than profit-oriented activities (Wu et al., 2022:7). The case of China demonstrates that strong reliance on energy for economic growth, as well as other factors, such as unbalanced urbanization, may distort the positive impacts of globalization. Interestingly, the authors recommend that the Chinese government enhances rather than limits globalization, as this can lead to increased attention to environmental threats and a more environmentally conscious policy.

While much of the existing research examines how globalization and the environment impact one another, numerous studies include environmental processes as part of a conceptual definition of globalization. One example of such environmental globalization approach is the Maastricht Globalization Index (MGI), which conceptualizes globalization as a multidimensional process that consists of five domains, including that of the environment (Figge and Martens, 2014). The MGI uses data from The Global Footprint Network, an international nonprofit organization that calculates the national Ecological Footprint of more than 200 countries, territories, and regions from 1961 to the present (Footprint Data Foundation, 2023).

An analysis of the most up-to-date data from the Global Footprint Network shows that since the early 1970s there have been continuous worldwide trends of decreasing biocapacity coupled with increasing ecological footprint of consumption and production. This means that the world's population has been using more resources than the Earth's ecosystem can regenerate. This phenomenon is called an ecological deficit (Footprint Data Foundation, 2023). The Global Footprint Network's (n.d.) data suggest that among ten countries with the highest estimated ecological deficit in the world in 2022, three are in Asia: Singapore, Bruneau Darussalam, and the Republic of Korea. A striking finding is that only two of the Asian countries in the data—Myanmar and Bhutan—had some ecological reserve, while all other nations in the region experienced an ecological deficit.[1] Interestingly, Myanmar and Bhutan are also among the least globalized countries in Asia and among the thirty least globalized countries in the world, as indicated by the KOF index of globalization discussed in the analysis that follows.

To further explore the link between globalization and the environment, a set of figures below graph the scores of KOF globalization and the greenhouse gas emissions for Asian countries in the period from 1990 to 2020. The KOF globalization index (Gygli et al., 2019; Dreher, 2006) is a widely used comprehensive measure of globalization that combines 46 variables on economic, social, and political aspects of globalization into a single score that ranges from 1 (a completely isolated country) to 100 (a completely globalized country). In 2020, the most recently available data, the globalization of the world received 61 points out of the 100. The least global countries were Eritrea and Somalia (each with a KOF score of 31), while the most globalized country, Switzerland, received a score of 91. How globalized are the countries in Asia? Is globalization rising or declining in the region? How do the globalization trends compare to the trends in environmental quality in Asia? The analysis below explores these questions based on the data on globalization from the KOF index and the World Bank's data on total greenhouse gas emissions, a common measure of environmental quality in the literature.[2]

Figure 7.1 ranks countries in Asia based on their globalization score in 2020. Noticeably, in most Asian countries, the globalization levels exceeded the average globalization of the world. Only seven countries—Bhutan, Laos, Myanmar, Nepal, Bangladesh, Pakistan, and Cambodia—scored below the world average indicating that they were the least integrated in the world. India's and China's globalization scores stood at 63 and 65 respectively, nearly the same as the world average, though still far below other Asian countries such as Thailand, Japan, South Korea, Malaysia, and Singapore, which were the five most globalized countries in the region.

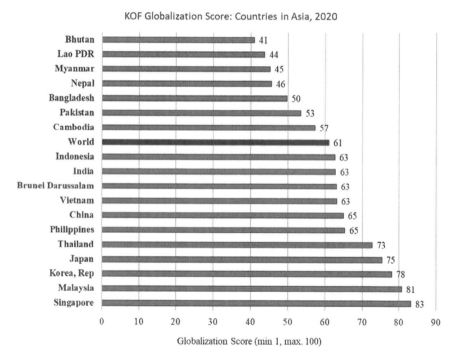

Figure 7.1 KOF Globalization Score for Countries in Asia
Source: KOF Globalization Index Website (2023).

Figure 7.2 ranks countries in Asia based on their environmental quality in 2020 as indicated by total greenhouse gas emissions (in CO_2 equivalent). Emissions are one of the major factors contributing to climate change and global warming. According to the World Bank, greenhouse gases, primarily carbon dioxide (CO_2), have a detrimental impact on the environment by leading to an increase in the earth's surface temperature and related effects on climate, sea level rise, and world agriculture (Climate Watch Historical GHG Emissions, 2023).[3]

India and most noticeably China took the lead in the total amount of greenhouse gas emissions in the region, followed by Japan, South Korea, and Indonesia. There was a major gap between the most and the least polluting Asian countries. Nine least polluting countries emitted less than 55 thousand kilotons of greenhouse gas each in 2020, while the five most polluting countries produced more than tenfold more each. The difference between countries such as Bhutan with 1,000 kilotons of emissions and China with nearly 11 million kilotons of emissions is striking. Figures 7.3 and 7.4 accentuate this difference by providing a comparative outlook on the relative share of the most polluting countries in Asia compared to the rest of the region (Figure 7.3) and the rest of the world (Figure 7.4).

China accounted for two-thirds of total greenhouse gas emissions in Asia in 2020, more than all other countries in the region combined (Figure 7.3). China also accounted for roughly one-third of the global emissions, more than any other single country in the world (Figure 7.4). Considering the previous finding that China's globalization level is lower than that of many other countries in Asia and just slightly above the world average, a reasonable initial conclusion is that globalization alone cannot account for the difference in environmental quality in the region.

While globalization may not be the only driver of environmental degradation, its detrimental effect does play an significant role in facilitating it. Figures 7.5 and 7.6–8 combine the data on globalization and greenhouse gas emissions to explore the association between them over time. The period of analysis is from 1990 to 2020 due to the availability of data on the emissions starting in 1990. Figure 7.5 demonstrates that over time, globalization, and emissions have both increased in all countries in Asia, apart from Japan. In the past three decades, Asian countries have become more globalized, on average, by 23 points, with Singapore (from 69 to 83 points) and Cambodia (from 43 to 65 points) having the lowest and highest increases in globalization scores, respectively. During the same period, Asian countries have also become increasingly greater polluters, releasing, on average, 728 thousand kilotons of greenhouse gases per year more in 2020 than in 1990.

The white circles in Figure 7.5 indicate the change in the total greenhouse gas emission for each country. Analysis of their distribution across countries shows that countries with the same magnitude of change in globalization experienced different levels of change in emissions. Bangladesh, Nepal, and Japan, for instance, had a similar change in the globalization score but the

110 *Luba Levin-Banchik*

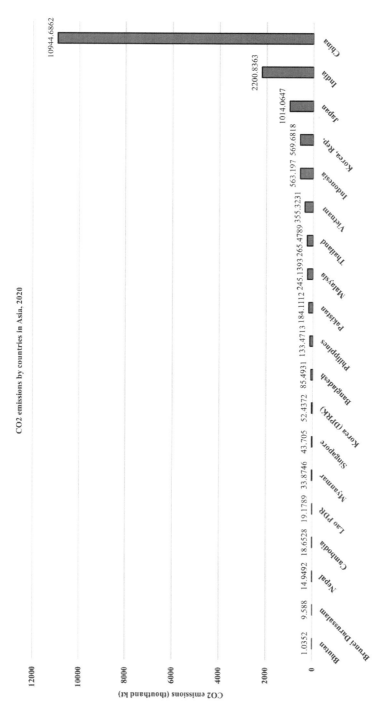

Figure 7.2 Total greenhouse gas emissions by countries in Asia in 2020
Source: Climate Watch Historical GHG Emissions (1990–2020) (2023). Washington, DC: World Resources Institute.

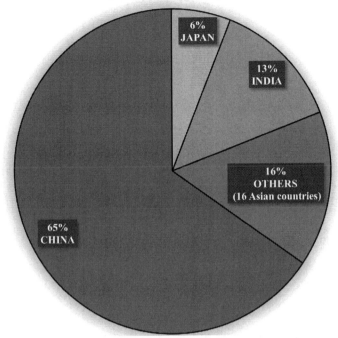

Figure 7.3 The Share of Most Polluting Countries in Asia Compared with the Rest of the Region
Source: Climate Watch Historical GHG Emissions (1990–2020) (2023). Washington, DC: World Resources Institute.

increase in emissions was considerably lower in Nepal than in Bangladesh, while Japan was the only country in the region that decreased its emissions. Similarly, South Korea, Vietnam, and India had a similar increase in globalization score, but India's increase in emissions was nearly five times greater than that of South Korea and Vietnam. The difference between China and Thailand is difficult to ignore. Both countries became more globalized by 29 points, but China's increase in greenhouse gas emissions over the same period was 50 times greater than that of Thailand. These findings reinforce the conclusion in the existing research that it is not globalization per se, but policies concerning globalization that shape environmental threats of globalization (Wu et al., 2022:7).

Analysis of change in globalization score and emissions should also consider the possibility that some countries that experience the same change in globalization score may have a different starting point. Pakistan and Singapore, for instance, had a similar increase in globalization, but Pakistan's globalization score in 1990 was considerably lower than that of Singapore. Thus,

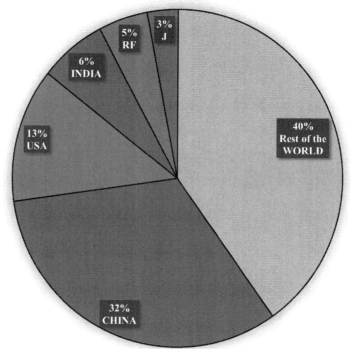

Figure 7.4 The Share of Most Polluting Countries in the Asia Compared with the Rest of the World
Source: Climate Watch Historical GHG Emissions (1990–2020) (2023). Washington, DC: World Resources Institute.

even if both Pakistan and Singapore became more globalized over time, gaining 15 and 14 more points on the globalization index respectively, they had very different globalization levels. In fact, even after 30 years of globalization and increased integration in the world, Pakistan's globalization level in 2020 was below that of Singapore in 1990. While cases like this are rare in the data analyzed herein, they should be accounted for to provide a more accurate analysis. Figures 7.6–7.8 presents the relationship between globalization and emissions in absolute terms to account for such potential differences in the globalization of countries with similar changes in globalization.

The findings in Figure 7.5 confirm an earlier conclusion on the relationship between globalization and the environment. A comparison of data in Figures 7.6 and 7.7 clearly shows that over time, countries in Asia became both considerably more globalized and more polluting, but the changes were not uniform, and some major differences exist between individual countries. Countries with similar emission levels, such as Indonesia and South Korea,

Environmental Threats to Security 113

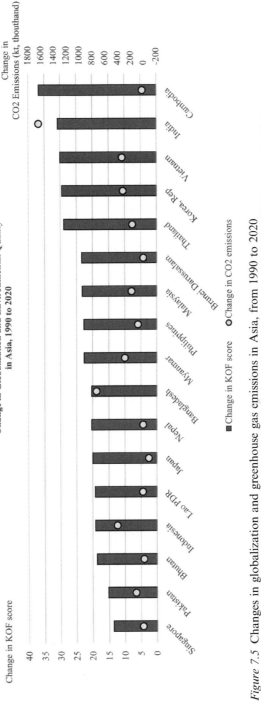

Figure 7.5 Changes in globalization and greenhouse gas emissions in Asia, from 1990 to 2020
Source: Climate Watch Historical GHG Emissions (1990–2020) (2023). Washington, DC: World Resources Institute.

114 *Luba Levin-Banchik*

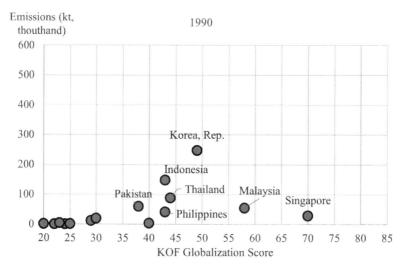

Figure 7.6 Relationship between globalization and greenhouse gas emissions in Asia 1990
Source: Climate Watch Historical GHG Emissions (1990–2020) (2023). Washington, DC: World Resources Institute.

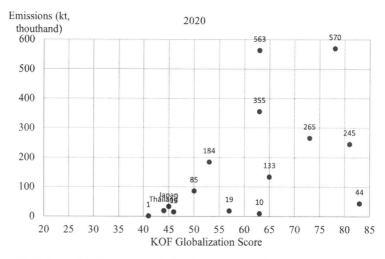

Figure 7.7 Relationship between globalization and greenhouse gas emissions in Asia 2020
Source: Climate Watch Historical GHG Emissions (1990–2020) (2023). Washington, DC: World Resources Institute.

may have very different levels of globalization. Countries with a similar level of globalization, such as the Philippines and Vietnam, may have very different levels of emissions. Increasing globalization in Asia does not necessarily translate into excessive emissions, as the cases of Cambodia, Brunei Darussalam, and Singapore indicate. The same conclusion on differences across countries in Asia holds even when the three most polluting countries in the region are analyzed in Figure 7.8. China and India, both making considerable progress towards becoming more globalized, demonstrate a noticeable difference in levels of greenhouse gas emissions, while Japan is both the most globalized and the least polluting among the three countries. Taken together, the literature survey and the analysis of evidence in Figures 7.1–7.8 show that globalization and the environment are related but have a complex and varied relationship. Globalization's role cannot be ignored, but it is unlikely to account, alone, for the environmental threats in the region. The remainder of the chapter discusses in-depth several examples of these environmental threats.

Environmental Threats to Food Security in Asia

According to The State of Food Security and Nutrition in the World 2022, the annual report published by the United Nations, more than half of the 768 million people in the world affected by hunger in 2021, or 425 million people, were in Asia (FAO, IFAD, UNICEF, WFP and WHO 2022). Analysis of the World Bank data shows that countries in South Asia are especially vulnerable to food insecurity. In 2019, more than a third of the population in South Asian countries,

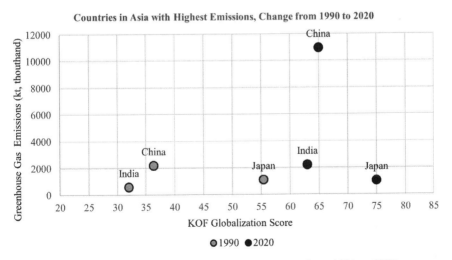

Figure 7.8 Countries with highest emmission CO2 change from 1990 to 2020
Source: Climate Watch Historical GHG Emissions (1990–2020) (2023). Washington, DC: World Resources Institute.

37.4%, were food insecure, nearly ten percentage points higher than the global level. In 2020, eight Asian countries, including Cambodia (50%), the Philippines (43.8%), Thailand (33.8%), Laos (31.8%), Bangladesh (31.7%), Nepal (37.8%), and Pakistan (32.6%) had a higher prevalence of food insecurity in their population than the world average. Asian countries with the lowest food insecurity included Japan (3.8%), Singapore (4.6%), the Republic of Korea (5.3%), Indonesia (6%), and Vietnam (7.6%).[4] While the environmental factors cannot alone explain such variability within the region, climate change is commonly regarded as one of the major drivers, alongside conflict, economic shocks, and inequalities, of food insecurity and malnutrition (FAO, IFAD, UNICEF, WFP, and WHO 2022).

A comprehensive analysis of food security in East and Southeast Asia by Lin et al. (2022:16–20) explains how climate change affects four pillars of food security—food availability, access to food, the stability of food supplies, and food utilization. The study suggests how climate effects, such as severe drought in Southeast countries, including Cambodia, Laos, Thailand, and Vietnam, and rising sea levels along the Mekong Delta in Vietnam, are among the factors that pose a threat to food security at the national, regional, and global levels. Yet, climate change can have potential benefits for food security in some regions, such as in parts of South Korea, as a result of geographical shifts in favorable conditions for food production.

Environmental factors impact food security in several ways. Most noticeably, there is an adverse impact on food production, such as on staple crops. Cambodia, for example, experiences one of the highest rice yield losses in Southeast Asia due to the increased temperatures during the growing season. Cambodia's rice agriculture is also dependent on rain-fed irrigation, which means that the lack or excess of rain can damage the crops. Moreover, the increased temperatures affect food production through the impact on the health and productivity of the labor force in agriculture (Climate Risk Profile: Cambodia, 2021:18–19).

In the Philippines, the low productivity of rice, which is the most significant crop in the country, can be attributed to climate shocks and their impacts, such as increasing temperatures, greater pest incidence, reduced labor productivity, and changing precipitation. According to the World Bank climate assessment, several of the top rice-producing provinces in the Philippines are highly exposed to typhoons, and the shift in the typhoon belt is likely to expand the exposure to additional rice-producing provinces. The impact of climate change extends beyond rice crops. Climate-change-related water shortage in the Philippines is projected to decrease the production of maze, sugarcane, bananas, corn, and other foods. The shortage of crops, fruits, and vegetables is expected to further increase food prices and, consequently, exacerbate the risk of malnutrition in the country (World Bank Group, 2022a:24–27). In his 2022 speech at the 77th UNGA, President Marcos of the Philippines emphasized that "food is not just a trade commodity nor a livelihood. It is an existential imperative and a moral one. It is the very basis of human security" (United Nations, 2022).

Climate change further threatens food security by damaging fisheries. Allison et al. (2009) compares the vulnerability of 132 national economies to the impacts of climate change on fisheries and find that Bangladesh, Cambodia, and Pakistan are among the ten most vulnerable economies in the world. The study suggests that Asian countries are especially vulnerable because of a combination of high fishery dependence, heavily exploited marine ecosystems, and high exposure of fisheries to climate change (Allison et al., 2009:184–188). In Bangladesh, for example, more than 12 million people rely on fisheries as their primary source of protein (World Bank Group, 2022b: 37). With the rapid increase in the population, the demand is likely to increase too. The population of Bangladesh has been increasing on average by more than 1.9 million people every year from 2011 to 2021.[5] Total fisheries production in Bangladesh has also been continuously increasing during that time, by roughly 148,000 metric tons, on average per year.[6] The increasing demand for seafood, puts a heavy strain on existing resources and affects biodiversity (Lin et al., 2022:2–3). The increasing demand is not limited to the national level but also extends to the regional and global levels because seafood is one of the top commodities exported by countries in East and Southeast Asia (Lin et al., 2022:2–4).

Work by Islam et al. (2014) examined the climate change effects on fishery-based livelihoods in Bangladesh. The study finds that exposure to cyclones and associated floods, which become more frequent and more violent over time, is the main determinant of the livelihood vulnerability in the analyzed coastal Bangladesh communities (Islam et al., 2014: 289). A Climate Risk Assessment by World Bank identifies six primary impacts of climate change on fishery production in Bangladesh: "cyclonic events (marine) as well as inland and coastal flooding, low flows of water and droughts, salinity intrusion, changes of the river bed level due to sedimentation and changes in morphological processes." All of these developments threaten existing aquatic ecosystems and fisheries. The study estimates that "Erratic and irregular rainfall patterns and temperature change will affect the readiness, maturity and gonad development of fishes in breeding season" (Climate Risk Country Profile: Bangladesh, 2021: 24). A meta-analysis of 98 studies by Siddique et al. (2022:1) reinforces this assessment, concluding that there are "indisputable negative impacts of climate change on hatchery production." The study's findings also suggests that temperature fluctuation was "The most significantly reported element that adversely impacted the broodstock development, breeding and spawning, hatching and larval development, and the incidence of fish diseases" in Bangladesh (Siddique et al., 2022:8).

Environmental Threats to Water Security in Asia

In 2020, nearly three of every four people in the world, 74% of the global population, had access to safely managed drinking water (UN-Water, 2021:37). In Asia, however, access to safe water varied greatly across the region. In some countries such as Nepal (18%), Laos (18%), Cambodia

(28%), Afghanistan (28%), Pakistan (36%), Bhutan (37%), and the Philippines (47%), less than half of the national population used safely managed drinking water. In other countries, such as Malaysia (94%), South Korea (99%), Japan (99%), and Singapore (100%), safe water was accessible to nearly all the population (UN-Water, 2021:37–52).

The water security of Nepal is one of the weakest in the Indo-Pacific (Nepal et al., 2021:68). Over 80 percent of annual precipitation in Nepal occurs during the monsoon period, causing excess during the wet season and scarcity during the dry season (World Bank Group, 2022c:42). As a result, one of the key issues with access to water is its underutilization due to high climate variability, inadequate infrastructure, and poor resource management. Nepal's mountainous topography, extreme weather events, such as floods and landslides, rapid urbanization, and population growth, are also among the main drivers of limited water availability in the country (Nepal et al., 2021; World Bank Group, 2022c:42).

Over the past four decades (1980 to 2020), Nepal experienced on average more than 40 flood events per year, making floods the most frequent natural hazard in the country. The number of flood events has doubled in recent years (World Bank Group, 2022c:11–12). Floods, alongside other natural hazards, endanger water security in Nepal by damaging already fragile and insufficient water infrastructure, such as drinking water supply facilities; determining the flow regimes of river systems; and serving for flooding irrigation method, which leads to a high loss of water (Nepal et al., 2021:72; Pandey, 2021). Water security is also affected by rising temperatures, which increase the frequency and severity of extreme weather events, increase variation in precipitation, reduce glacier volume that typically contributed to water flows during the dry season (World Bank Group, 2022c). As Nepal's Foreign Secretary Mr. Bharat Raj Paudyal summarized it, "The melting of glaciers and the drying-up of snow-fed rivers have been adversely affecting the lives and livelihoods of people downstream and rendering us one of the most vulnerable countries" (Government of Nepal, 2022).

Although access to safe water in Nepal is limited, with only less than twenty percent of the population having such access, the country has utilized only 8.2 percent of its available freshwater resources. This is far below the global average of about 18 percent. This suggests that with proper management and infrastructure, alongside other adaptation and mitigation strategies, Nepal can considerably improve its water security. Unlike Nepal, however, several Asian countries experience high or critical water stress, meaning that they have withdrawn more than 75% of their renewable freshwater resource (UN-Water, 2021). Among Asian countries, the water stress is highest in Pakistan (118%), Sri Lanka (91%), South Korea (85%), and Singapore (82%).[7]

In Pakistan, the level of water stress has increased dramatically over time. According to World Bank data, Pakistan was withdrawing 95.5 percent of its renewable freshwater resources in 1991 and by 1995 it passed the mark of 100 percent. In 2017, the level of water stress reached 122.7 percent, the highest for the country to date (Food and Agriculture Organization, AQUASTAT data, 2023). This means that Pakistan is experiencing acute water stress, which deteriorates over time as the country uses more freshwater than available, depleting resources. This trend of increasing water stress coincides with the trend of a rapidly increasing population. Pakistan was home to 119.2 million people in 1991, 133.1 million in 1995, and 216.4 million in 2017. In 2022 the population of Pakistan reached 235.8 million people, which nearly doubled, in just 30 years. Only 36 percent of Pakistani people, however, have access to safely managed drinking water (UN-Water, 2021). Numerous studies suggest that the growing gap between the water supply and demand, in combination with environmental changes, is expected to result in a major water crisis in the country (Climate Risk Country Profile: Pakistan, 2021:27; Mustafa, Akhter, and Nasrallah, 2013; Kirby and Ahmad, 2022). Kirby and Ahmad (2022:2051) study the combined effects and complex interrelationships between water security, food security, population growth, and economic growth in Pakistan. On the one hand, population growth and development increase the demand for groundwater, including for drinking and especially agriculture. On the other hand, climate change and rising temperatures also require more water to raise crops. Kirby and Ahmad conclude that such combined effects of development and climate change will further deteriorate water insecurity in Pakistan in the coming decades. Climate change poses additional threats to Pakistan's water security by increasing the frequency and severity of storms and rains (Pakistan Floods, 2022:12). In July and August 2022, for example, severe monsoon rains and resulting floods submerged a third of Pakistan's territory, affecting more than 33 million people, and leading to 1,700 deaths in the country (UN News, 2023b). The massive flood also destroyed critical infrastructure, including most of the water systems in the affected areas. Six months after the floods, the UN reported that more than 10 million people in the flood-affected areas did not have access to safe water (UNICEF, 2023). Thus, even when the monsoon season ends, the consequences of the floods and extreme weather events on water security persisted.

Rising Sea Level Threat to Security in Asia

On February 14, 2023, The United National Security Council held its first-ever debate on the phenomenon of the rising sea and its global implications (UN News, 2023a). In his remarks, UN Secretary-General Antonio Gutierrez emphasized that the sea-level rise poses "devastating security challenges" and has "unthinkable" consequences for the planet (United Nations Secretary-General, 2023). According to the United Nations, sea-level rise is a global phenomenon that has or is likely to have a direct impact on more a than third of the states in the world (Aurescu et al., n.d.:326). Many of these states are in Asia. A recent study finds that 70 percent of the total world population that lives in the territory vulnerable to sea-level rise is in Asia, with eight countries taking the lead: China, Bangladesh, India, Vietnam, Indonesia, Thailand, the Philippines, and Japan (Kulp and Strauss, 2019:3).

Countries with long coastlines and low-lying areas, such as Vietnam, and low-lying island states, such as Singapore, are especially vulnerable to rising sea levels. A World Bank study estimates that more than 12 million people in Vietnam face the risk of permanent inundation from the rising sea (Climate Risk Country Profile: Vietnam, 2021:17–18). The saltwater intrusion from the sea-level rise had already resulted in major crop damage and land loss, contaminating nearly 40,000 hectares of cultivated land and destroying 100,000 tons of food in Vietnam between 1976 and 2005 (Neumann et al., 2015:6558).

In Singapore, a small island city-state with little high ground for a retreat, the rise in sea-level is recognized as a major threat (Office of Legal Affairs of the United Nations, 2020). Speaking at the United Nations Climate Action Summit in September 2019, Prime Minister Lee Hsien Loong addressed Singapore's vulnerability to rising sea levels by stating that "For us, climate change is existential" (Prime Minister's Office Singapore, 2019). Shortly thereafter, Singapore's National Water Agency (PUB) officially extended its responsibility to include leading and coordinating the whole-of-the-government effort of protecting Singapore's coastline from sea-level rise. Currently, nearly a third of the country's territory is less than five meters above the global mean sea-level. The sea-level, however, is projected to rise by 1 meter by 2100, and it is possible that it will rise to up to 4 or 5 meters due to the combination of tides, storm surges, and land subsidence (Singapore's National Water Agency, 2023). The risk from the rising sea to Singapore is thus urgent and serious (Ministry of Foreign Affairs Singapore, 2022).

According to Shaw et al. (2022:1499), Asia is the most exposed region to sea-level rise. The globally average sea-level is rising at about 3.4 millimeters (0.13 inches) per year and is expected to accelerate over time due to three main factors: ice melting, expansion of water in the ocean as it absorbs heat, and excessive use of groundwater that leads to the sinking of the land (NASA EarthData, 2023; Nerem et al., 2018). The sea-level rise around Asia from 1900 to 2018 is similar to the global mean sea-level change, but in the recent decades, in the period from 1993 to 2018, it is higher than the global value (Shaw et al., 2022:1465). While climate change is the root cause of rising sea (United Nations Secretary-General, 2023), urbanization and development are additional factors that accelerate the threat from sea-level rise. Megacities, such as Jakarta, the capital of Indonesia, and Bangkok (officially called Krung Thep Maha Nakhon) the capital of Thailand are among the fastest-sinking cities in the world due to, in part, the excessive use of underground water by a rapidly increasing population. Some parts of Jakarta, the world's most populous island, are sinking 25cm (9.5 inches) a year. The risk of becoming submerged underwater is so grave that in 2019 the Indonesian government decided to create a new capital on the island of Borneo, where there is a much lower risk of natural disasters (BBC News, 2019).

Other megacities in Asia, such as Dhaka, Bangladesh, Mumbai, India, and Shanghai, China, all face serious impacts from the rising seas (United Nations Secretary-General, 2023). The 2021 China Sea Level Bulletin, published by the Ministry of Natural Resources of China, indicates that human activities, such as groundwater exploitation and high-rise building complex constructions increase the risk of the rising sea by intensifying land subsidence. The land subsidence is especially heavy in the coastal cities of Tianjin and Shanghai which experience higher-than-normal sea-level rise. The report estimates that in the next 30 years, the sea-level along the coast of Shanghai will rise by 70–175mm (The Ministry of Natural Resources, 2022: 12).

The sea-level rise poses a grave and multi-faceted threat to countries in Asia. Asuncion and Lee (2017) survey the research on how sea-level rise in the region impacts economic growth and development, focusing on projected losses of the gross domestic product (GDP), out-migration from vulnerable areas, and increased uncertainty in the tourism sector in the coastal areas. An extensive study of environmental threats in Asia by an international group of researchers, led by Shaw et al., (2022:1499–1500), suggests that one of the major threats from the sea-level rise is the threat of direct inundation, which will drive migration and displacement, and will have implications for regional development in terms of demands for job, housing, and food. The sea-level rise also threatens energy security in the region by exposing the industrial and energy systems to floods and sandstorms. The economic damages from the sea-level rise are estimated to reach hundreds of billions of dollars by 2050, with 13 of the 20 largest coastal cities with the highest flood losses located in Asia. There is also a risk to food security due to the intrusion of saline water into agricultural lands. Since the Asian coasts are projected to continue to have a higher than the global mean sea-level rise, the coastal population in Asia is especially vulnerable to disaster-related mortality (Shaw et al., 2022:1532).

In addition to the threats to human security, the sea-level rise in Asia has implications for regional and global military security. The increasing geopolitical tension between China and the United States and concerns over a potential military conflict in Taiwan highlight the significance of the region for strategic competition in shaping the emerging world order. As the United States increases its regional presence due to its national interests and requests from regional allies, the sea-level rise cannot be ignored. This is because the sea-level rise can expose and damage critical ports, infrastructure, and installations used by the U.S. military in cooperation with Asian countries (The White House, 2015). A country like the Philippines, for instance, has a geopolitical role due to its geographic proximity to Taiwan and provides the U.S. with expanded access to its military bases (Wingfield-Hayes, 2023). Yet, the Philippines is especially vulnerable to sea-level rise which in some areas of the archipelago is double the global average (Climate Risk Country Profile: Philippines, 2021; World Bank Group, 2022a). The risk of sea-level rise increases costs for military preparedness and can adversely affect military performance in case of a conflict, especially if it coincides with the time of extreme weather events, such as storms and floods, whose effects are amplified by the increased levels of the sea.

Another military security implication of the sea-level rise in the regional context relates to the territorial disputes in the South China Sea. China, Brunei, Indonesia, Malaysia, the Philippines, Taiwan, and Vietnam all claim and compete (at times with display or use of force) over the territory, natural resources, and fishing areas of the low-lying small islands in the South China Sea (Council on Foreign Relations, June 2023). Many of these islands are below sea level at high tide (Lally, 2010). Thus, there was cautious optimism that the rising sea-level would submerge the contested islands making the claims obsolete and putting an end to the conflict (VornDick, 2012). Others, however, suggested an opposite effect. It seems that today the rising sea-levels would accelerate the conflict by "increasing the urgency of territorial claims, requiring construction of new facilities, and increasing the likelihood of confusion and accidents between naval patrols of fishing vessels around newly submerged reefs" (Lally, 2010). As such, the rising sea-levels and their implications for human and military security for Asia, and consequently the world, cannot be ignored.

Conclusion and Future Prospects

This chapter analyzed environmental threats to security in Asia. It began with a discussion of how existing studies address the nexus between climate change and security, as well as the nexus between globalization and the environment. The chapter showed that there is a growing awareness that climate change can pose a major security risk to civilian and military infrastructure and population and hence can be considered a threat to both human and state security, both globally and in the region,

The chapter also showed that studies on globalization and the environment often conclude that the two phenomena have a complex relationship, as indicated by the common finding that globalization can have both positive and negative impacts on the environment and can itself be influenced by the processes related to the environment, such as environmental regulations. The analysis of the most recent data on globalization and greenhouse gas emissions presented in this chapter provided additional support for conclusions in the literature. The analysis showed that there is an increasing trend in both globalization and emissions in Asia, but the relationship between these trends is not uniform and major differences exist among Asian countries. The most globalized Asian countries are not necessarily the most polluting in the region, while the most polluting Asian countries are not necessarily the most globalized. Thus, in line with previous studies, the findings in this chapter suggest that globalization may be associated with negative trends in the environment in some countries (e.g. China), but with positive trends in the environment in others (e.g. Japan).

A detailed discussion of the examples of environmental threats to security, such as threats to water and food security, as well as threats posed by rising sea levels, showed how countries in Asia are vulnerable to the impacts of climate change. The threats of malnutrition and hunger, inundation, climate-forced displacement, lack of safe drinking water, overuse of renewable resources, damage to water and energy infrastructure, adverse effects on agriculture, public health, and geopolitical processes, extreme weather events and loss of human life and biodiversity are just some of the vulnerabilities in Asia as a consequence of climate change. The rising temperatures, population growth, increasing demand for ground freshwater, urbanization, and other processes related to development and globalization, all play a role in accentuating these vulnerabilities and shaping human and military security in Asia.

One question remains: Can the environmental threat to security in the region be managed or contained? There is no unequivocal answer to this question as there is evidence to support arguments by both those who have a pessimistic outlook and those who have an optimistic one.

According to a pessimistic outlook, it may be extremely challenging or nearly impossible to contain environmental threats for several reasons. First, just like globalization, environmental threats develop on multiple levels, including local, national, regional, and global levels. Thus, even if some countries make progress in areas such as the reduction of emissions, the lack of progress by other countries may offset these national gains. Imposing self-limitations by a nation on areas such as development and industrialization to better the environment may be perceived as an unreasonable task if such practice is not reciprocated by the neighboring countries and especially the competitors. For environmental threats to be contained there is a need for extensive and genuine cooperation by all nations on all levels, including national and global, an unlikely outcome in the current conflictual regional and international environment.

The second argument of those who have a pessimistic outlook is that it may already be too late to stop global warming and reverse its effects. An illustrative of this point is the appeals by the UN Secretary-General António Guterres to radically accelerate the pace of climate change containment. In 2018, he warned that climate change poses "a direct existential threat" to humankind and it is "moving faster than we are" (United Nations Secretary-General, 2018). In a more recent statement, the Secretary-General said that he remains "very worried about where the world stands on climate" and complained that "Countries are far off track in meeting climate promises and commitments. I see a lack of ambition. A lack of trust. A lack of support. A lack of cooperation. And an abundance of problems around clarity and credibility" (United Nations, 2023). A 2023 report by the United Nations' Intergovernmental Panel on Climate Change found that climate change "has caused substantial damages, and increasingly irreversible losses, in terrestrial, freshwater, cryosphere, and coastal and open ocean ecosystems," concluding that some environmental hazards can no longer be avoided or reversed (IPCC, 2023:18).

A third argument is that environmental processes, specifically the increasing deficit of resources such as water, clean air, arable lands, crops, and fish, have already resulted in popular unrest and disputes within and between countries. Numerous studies suggest that such conflicts will only intensify as the effects of climate change exacerbate. A manifestation of this perspective is a study of hydro-politics in South Asia that examines a water war thesis in the regional context (Mehsud and Khan, 2019). The study suggests that climate change and population growth have already resulted in water disputes between India and Pakistan, India and Nepal, China and India, and Pakistan and Afghanistan and that the contest over limited resources in combination with weak or non-existent water treaties, makes region especially vulnerable to war over water in the near future (Mehsud and Khan, 2019).

Lastly, even if globalization and development were to be dramatically backtracked to protect the environment, some of the major environmental hazards would persist (United Nations, 2023). Indeed, not all environmental threats result from man-made activity and thus humans may have limited control over some extreme weather events and threats, such as earthquakes or tsunamis. Consider the example of Japan, which is the only country in the region that reduced rather than increased its emissions, and yet became a place of a major 9.0-magnitude earthquake and a resulting 15-meter tsunami in March 2011. This Great East Japan Earthquake and tsunami killed more than 20,000 people and caused a nuclear accident in Fukushima Daiichi reactors leading to a high radioactive release (World Nuclear Association, January 2023).

A more positive outlook on future prospects suggests that the effects of climate change on global and regional security can be managed and, in some cases, diminished. First, there is increasing regional awareness and cooperation on tackling climate change. The pace of such diplomatic efforts may be slower than the pace of climate change, as indicated by the remarks of the UN's Secretary-General, but their presence is undeniable, and the increasing trend is promising. One example of such increased regional cooperation is the environmental diplomacy of the Association of Southeast Asian Nations (ASEAN), an intergovernmental organization of ten Asian countries. The organization consists of several bodies that aim to promote regional cooperation on the environment, including ASEAN Ministries Meeting on Environment, which meets once every two years, and ASEAN Senior Officials on Environment, which meets every year to coordinate environmental cooperation on seven priority areas. These include cooperation on nature conservation and biodiversity, coastal and marine environment, water resources management, environmentally sustainable cities, climate change, chemicals and waste, and environmental education. Thematically dedicated working groups are overseeing these priority areas and developing action plans to manage the environmental threats. Additional ASEAN bodies with a focus on the environment include the ASEAN Centre for Biodiversity, the ASEAN Institute for Green Economy, and numerous partnerships, such as ASEAN-Japan Dialogue on Environmental Cooperation. A detailed study of the state of climate change in the region, The ASEAN State of Climate Change Report, concludes that while "Southeast Asia is one of the most at-risk regions in the world to the impacts on climate change [...] the region has been making steady progress in several areas relevant to climate change adaptation and disaster risk reduction" (ASEAN State of Climate Change Report, 2021).

A related argument in favor of a more positive outlook suggests that globalization has increased awareness and greater global investment in the region. Non-governmental organizations, such as the Bill and Melinda Gates Foundation, provide funds to build resilience to climate effects in a variety of projects, such as climate-smart agriculture projects in rural Asia (Bill and Melinda Gates Foundation, 2022). Global intergovernmental organizations, such as the UN and World Bank, consider climate change in Asia as one of the most pressing issues. Nearly half, or 46 percent, of the new World Bank commitments in East Asia and the Pacific in fiscal year 2022 contributed to climate action, a total of more than $3.2 billion dollars. For South Asia, the World Bank's climate financing more than doubled in just a few years, rising from $1.4 billion in 2017 to $3.7 billion in 2021. This funding was nearly equally divided between supporting climate adaptation and climate mitigation actions in the region (The World Bank, 2023). In addition to funding, the World Bank provides guidance, climate action plan, and reports to help the region combat climate change.

All this indicates that managing and containing environmental threats in Asia is a common goal for the region and the global community. Much international, regional, and local effort is devoted to managing and mitigating the effect of climate change while preserving the development and benefits of globalization. Asia is one of the world's most affected and vulnerable regions to climate change, but ensuring regional security and protecting the region from environmental threats is of the foremost interest and practical relevance to the security of the world.

Notes

1 The 2023 edition of National Footprint and Biocapacity Accounts (data year 2022) combines Asia and the Pacific in a single region. For the purposes of data analysis on Asian environmental security, this chapter analyzes data for Asian countries only. See Figures 7.1 and 7.2 for the list of countries included in the analysis.
2 The analysis in this chapter does infer causation. Studies surveyed in the literature section of this chapter should be consulted for comprehensive statistical analyses. The goal of the analysis that follows is to visualize the connections between globalization and the environment and to set the stage for a more in-depth analysis of food security, water security, and rising sea levels as examples of environmental threats to security in Asia.
3 In addition to Carbon dioxide (CO_2), the World Bank's measure of total greenhouse gas emissions includes methane (CH4), nitrous oxide (N2O), hydrofluorocarbons (HFCs), perfluorocarbons (PFCs), and Sulphur hexafluoride (SF6). The total emissions of all these gasses for each nation per year are transformed into CO_2 equivalence for the purposes of comparison in the total greenhouse gas emissions.
4 Data was not available for Bhutan and India. The definition of regions and inclusion of countries in the region follows that of World Bank data at https://data.worldbank.org/country/8S.

5 Based on World Bank data on the total population in Bangladesh. Available at https://data.worldbank.org/indicator/SP.POP.TOTL?locations=BD. Accessed April 17, 2023.
6 Based on World Bank data on the "Total fisheries production (metric tons)" for 2011–2020. Available at https://data.worldbank.org/indicator/ER.FSH.PROD.MT?locations=BD. Accessed April 17, 2023.
7 Existing UN-Water (2021) data do not allow comparing Asia as a region, or a collection of sub-regions, to the global statistic, mainly due to the lack of reported data for countries such as China and India.

References

Allison, Edward H., *et al.*, 2009. "Vulnerability of National Economies to the Impacts of Climate Change on Fisheries." *Fish and Fisheries* 10 (2): 173–196.

ASEAN State of Climate Change Report. 2021. https://asean.org/wp-content/uploads/2021/10/ASCCR-e-publication-Correction_8-June.pdf.

Asuncion, Ruben Carlo, and Minsoo Lee. 2017. "Impacts of Sea Level Rise on Economic Growth in Developing Asia." Asian Development Bank Economics Working Paper Series 507. https://www.adb.org/publications/sea-level-rise-economic-growth-developing-asia.

Aurescu, Bogdan, *et al.* n.d. "Sea-level Rise in Relation to International Law." *International Law Commission*. A/73/10. https://legal.un.org/ilc/guide/8_9.shtml.

Baek, Jungho, Yongsung Cho, and Won W. Koo. 2009. "The Environmental Consequences of Globalization: A Country-specific Time-series Analysis." *Ecological Economics* 68 (8–9): 2255–2264.

BBC News. 2019. "Indonesia Picks Borneo Island as Site of New Capital." August 26, 2019. https://www.bbc.com/news/world-asia-49470258.

Bill and Melinda Gates Foundation. 2022. https://www.gatesfoundation.org/ideas/media-center/press-releases/2022/11/helping-african-and-asian-farmers-with-climate-change-adaptation.

Busby, Joshua. 2019. "A Clear and Present Danger: Climate Risks, the Energy System, and U.S. National Security," in *Impact of Climate Risk on the Energy System*. Council on Foreign Relations. https://www.cfr.org/report/impact-climate-risk-energy-system.

Busby, Joshua, and Nisha Krishnan. 2015. "Widening the Scope to Asia: Climate Change and Security." The Centre for Climate and Security: 23–30. https://www.strausscenter.org/wp-content/uploads/Climate_Change_Security_Busby_Krishnan.pdf

Climate Risk Country Profile: Bangladesh. 2021. *The World Bank Group*. https://climateknowledgeportal.worldbank.org/sites/default/files/country-profiles/15502-WB_Bangladesh%20Country%20Profile-WEB.pdf.

Climate Risk Country Profile: Pakistan. 2021. *The World Bank Group and the Asian Development Bank*. https://climateknowledgeportal.worldbank.org/sites/default/files/2021-05/15078-WB_Pakistan%20Country%20Profile-WEB.pdf.

Climate Risk Country Profile: Philippines. 2021. *The World Bank Group and the Asian Development Bank*. https://climateknowledgeportal.worldbank.org/sites/default/files/2021-08/15852-WB_Philippines%20Country%20Profile-WEB.pdf.

Climate Risk Country Profile: Vietnam. 2021. *The World Bank Group and the Asian Development Bank*. https://climateknowledgeportal.worldbank.org/sites/default/files/2021-04/15077-Vietnam%20Country%20Profile-WEB.pdf.

Climate Risk Profile: Cambodia. 2021. *The World Bank Group and Asian Development Bank*. https://climateknowledgeportal.worldbank.org/sites/default/files/2021-08/15849-WB_Cambodia%20Country%20Profile-WEB.pdf.

Climate Watch Historical GHG Emissions (1990–2020). *2023*. Washington, DC: World Resources Institute. www.climatewatchdata.org/ghg-emissions. World Bank. https://data.worldbank.org/indicator/EN.ATM.GHGT.KT.CE.

Council on Foreign Relations. June2023. "Territorial Disputes in the South China Sea." https://www.cfr.org/global-conflict-tracker/conflict/territorial-disputes-south-china-sea.

Dabla-Norris, Era, Masahiro Nozaki, and James Daniel. September2021. "Asia's Climate Emergency." *International Monetary Fund*. https://www.imf.org/en/Publications/fandd/issues/2021/09/asia-climate-emergency-role-of-fiscal-policy-IMF-dabla.

Dreher, Axel. 2006. "Does Globalization Affect Growth? Evidence from a New Index of Globalization." *Applied Economics* 38 (10): 1091–1110.

FAO, IFAD, UNICEF, WFP and WHO. 2022. *The State of Food Security and Nutrition in the World 2022. Repurposing food and agricultural policies to make healthy diets more affordable*. Rome, FAO. https://doi.org/10.4060/cc0639en.

Figge, Lukas, and Pim Martens. 2014. "Globalisation Continues: The Maastricht Globalisation Index Revisited and Updated." *Globalizations* 11(6): 875–893.

Food and Agriculture Organization, AQUASTAT data. 2023. "Level of Water Stress: Freshwater Withdrawal as A Proportion of Available Freshwater Resources – Pakistan." Accessed August 5, 2023.

Footprint Data Foundation. 2023. *York University Ecological Footprint Initiative, and Global Footprint Network: National Footprint and Biocapacity Accounts*. Accessed August 5, 2023. https://data.footprintnetwork.org.

Global Footprint Network's Data. Accessed August 7, 2023. https://data.footprintnetwork.org/?_ga=2.4440944.214332282.1690998573-2084092607.1690998573#/.

Government of Nepal. 2022. "Statement by Foreign Secretary and the Leader of Nepali Delegation Mr. Bharat Raj Paudyal at the General Debate of the 77th Session of United Nations General Assembly New York." September 27, 2022. https://mofa.gov.np/statement-by-foreign-secretary-and-the-leader-of-nepali-delegation-mr-bharat-raj-paudyal-at-the-general-debate-of-the-77th-session-of-united-nations-general-assembly-new-york/.

Gygli, Savina *et al*. 2019. "The KOF Globalisation Index–Revisited." *The Review of International Organizations* 14: 543–574.

Hyun, In-Taek, and Sung-Han Kim. 2007. "Introduction: The Environment-Security Nexus in Northeast Asia." In In-Taek Hyun and Miranda A. Schreurs (editors), *The Environmental Dimension of Asian Security*. Washington, DC: United States Institute of Peace Press, pp. 3–22.

International Monetary Fund. 2008. "Globalization: A Brief Overview." https://www.imf.org/external/np/exr/ib/2008/053008.htm.

IPCC. 2023. Summary for Policymakers. In: *Climate Change 2023: Synthesis Report. Contribution of Working Groups I, II and III to the Sixth Assessment Report of the Intergovernmental Panel on Climate Change* [Core Writing Team, H. Lee and J. Romero (eds.)]. IPCC, Geneva, Switzerland, pp. 1–34, doi:10.59327/IPCC/AR6-9789291691647.001.

Islam, Md Monirul *et al.*, 2014. "Vulnerability of Fishery-Based Livelihoods to the Impacts of Climate Variability and Change: Insights from Coastal Bangladesh." *Regional Environmental Change* 14: 281–294.

Kirby, Mac, and Mobin-ud-Din Ahmad. 2022. "Can Pakistan Achieve Sustainable Water Security? Climate Change, Population Growth and Development Impacts to 2100." *Sustainability Science* 17 (5): 2049–2062.

KOF Globalization Index. 2023. https://kof.ethz.ch/en/forecasts-and-indicators/indicators/kof-globalisation-index.html.

Kulp, Scott A., and Benjamin H. Strauss. 2019. "New Elevation Data Triple Estimates of Global Vulnerability to Sea-Level Rise and Coastal Flooding." *Nature Communications* 10 (1): 1–12.

Lally, Mike. 2010. "Spratly Islands Strategic Importance and Rising Sea Levels." *International Conflict and Environment Case Studies* 226. https://mandalaprojects.com/ice/ice-cases/spratly-submerge.htm#:~:text=%5B2%5D%20As%20sea%20levels%20rise,vessels%20around%20newly%20submerged%20reefs.

Lin, Hen-I., Ya-Yin Yu, Fang-I. Wen, and Po-Ting Liu. 2022. "Status of food security in East and Southeast Asia and challenges of climate change." *Climate* 10, 40.

Maddock, Rowland Thomas. 1995. "Environmental Security in East Asia." *Contemporary Southeast Asia* 17 (1): 20–37.

Mehsud, Muhammad Imran, and Tariq Anwar Khan. 2019. "Water War Thesis: Perspective from South Asia." *Journal of Political Studies* (2019). http://pu.edu.pk/images/journal/pols/pdf-files/9_spec_19.pdf.

Ministry of Foreign Affairs Singapore. 2022. "Minister for Foreign Affairs Dr Vivian Balakrishnan's National Statement at the General Debate of the 77th Session of the United Nations General Assembly in New York, 24 September 2022." September 25, 2022. https://www.mfa.gov.sg/Newsroom/Press-Statements-Transcripts-and-Photos/2022/09/20220925-UNGA-National-Statement.

Ministry of Foreign Affairs Singapore. 2022. "Minister for Foreign Affairs Dr Vivian Balakrishnan's National Statement at the General Debate of the 77th Session of the United Nations General Assembly in New York, 24 September 2022." September 25, 2022. https://www.mfa.gov.sg/Newsroom/Press-Statements-Transcripts-and-Photos/2022/09/20220925-UNGA-National-Statement.

Morton, Katherine. 2008. "China and Environmental Security in the Age of Consequences." *Asia-Pacific Review* 15 (2): 52–67.

Mustafa, Daanish, Majed Akhter, and Natalie Nasrallah. 2013. Understanding Pakistan's Water-Security Nexus. *United States Institute of Peace*. https://www.usip.org/sites/default/files/PW88_Understanding-Pakistan's-Water-Security-Nexus.pdf.

NASA EarthData. 2023. "Sea Level Change Data Pathfinder - Find Data." https://www.earthdata.nasa.gov/learn/pathfinders/sea-level-change/find-data#gmslhttps://www.earthdata.nasa.gov/learn/pathfinders/sea-level-change.

Nepal, Santosh *et al.* 2021. "Achieving Water Security in Nepal Through Unraveling the Water-Energy-Agriculture Nexus." *International Journal of Water Resources Development* 37 (1): 67–93.

Nerem, Robert S. *et al.* 2018. "Climate-Change–Driven Accelerated Sea-Level Rise Detected in the Altimeter Era." *Proceedings of the National Academy of Sciences* 115 (9): 2022–2025.

Neumann, James E. *et al.* 2015. "Risks of Coastal Storm Surge and the Effect of Sea Level Rise in the Red River Delta, Vietnam." *Sustainability* 7 (6): 6553–6572.

Office of Legal Affairs of the United Nations. 2020. *Note No. SMUN054/2020*https://legal.un.org/ilc/sessions/72/pdfs/english/slr_singapore.pdf.

Pakistan Floods. 2022. Post-Disaster Needs Assessment. October 2022. The Government of Pakistan, Asian Development Bank, European Union, United Nations

Development Programme, World Bank. https://www.undp.org/pakistan/publications/pakistan-floods-2022-post-disaster-needs-assessment-pdna.

Panayotou, Theodore. 2000. "Globalization and Environment." *CID Working Paper* No. 53. Harvard University, Cambridge, MA, July 2000. https://dash.harvard.edu/bitstream/handle/1/39569837/053.pdf?sequence=1&isAllowed=y.

Pandey, Chandra Lal. 2021. "Managing Urban Water Security: Challenges and Prospects in Nepal." *Environment, Development and Sustainability* 23 (1): 241–257.

Prime Minister's Office Singapore. 2019. "PM Lee Hsien Loong at the Climate Action Summit 2019." https://www.pmo.gov.sg/Newsroom/PM-Lee-Hsien-Loong-at-the-Climate-Action-Summit.

Shaw, Rajib et al. 2022. "Asia." In: *Climate Change 2022: Impacts, Adaptation and Vulnerability. Contribution of Working Group II to the Sixth Assessment Report of the Intergovernmental Panel on Climate Change.* Cambridge University Press, Cambridge, pp. 1457–1579, doi:10.1017/9781009325844.012.

Siddique, Mohammad Abu Baker et al. 2022. "Impacts of Climate Change on Fish Hatchery Productivity in Bangladesh: A Critical Review." *Heliyon*: e11951.

Singapore's National Water Agency. 2023. "Sea Level Rise." https://www.pub.gov.sg/Pages/sealevelrise.aspx.

Stobierski, Tim. April2021. "4 Effects of Globalization on The Environment." *Business Insights Blog*, Harvard Business School Online. https://online.hbs.edu/blog/post/globalization-effects-on-environment#:~:text=Decreased%20Biodiversity,reduce%20biodiversity%20around%20the%20globe.

The Ministry of Natural Resources. 2022. "2021 China Sea Level Bulletin." https://www.chinawaterrisk.org/research-reports/2021-china-sea-level-bulletin.

The White House. 2015. "Findings From Select Federal Reports: The National Security Implications Of A Changing Climate." The White House. https://obamawhitehouse.archives.gov/sites/default/files/docs/National_Security_Implications_of_Changing_Climate_Final_051915.pdf.

The World Bank. 2023. "Climate and Development in East Asia and Pacific Region." https://www.worldbank.org/en/region/eap/brief/climate-and-development-in-east-asia-and-pacific-region.

UN News. February2023a. "Sea Level Rise Poses 'Unthinkable' Risks for the Planet, Security Council Hears." February 14, 2023. https://news.un.org/en/story/2023/02/1133492.

UN News. March2023b. "UN Continues to Support Pakistan Flood Response" March 7, 2023. https://news.un.org/en/story/2023/03/1134302.

UN Web TV. 2022. "Viet Nam - Deputy Prime Minister Addresses General Debate, 77th Session." 2022. September 24, 2022. https://media.un.org/en/asset/k1j/k1jg0awnmq.

UNICEF. 2023. "More than 10 Million People, Including Children, Living in Pakistan's Flood-affected Areas Still Lack Access to Safe Drinking Water." March 21, 2023. https://www.unicef.org/press-releases/more-10-million-people-including-children-living-pakistans-flood-affected-areas#:~:text=The%20floods%20damaged%20most%20of,Representative%20in%20Pakistan%2C%20Abdullah%20Fadil.

United Nations Secretary-General. 2018. "Secretary-General's Remarks on Climate Change [as delivered]." September 10, 2018. https://www.un.org/sg/en/content/sg/statement/2018-09-10/secretary-generals-remarks-climate-change-delivered.

United Nations Secretary-General. 2023. "Secretary-General's Remarks to the Security Council Debate on "Sea-level Rise: Implications for International Peace and Security." February 14, 2023. https://www.un.org/sg/en/content/sg/statement/2023-02-14/secreta

ry-generals-remarks-the-security-council-debate-sea-level-rise-implications-for-international-peace-and-security?_gl=1*6l2oc3*_ga*NTU1Mzk2NDI5LjE2NjExMjc1MjA.*_ga_TK9BQL5X7Z*MTY3Nzg2ODE4Ni42LjAuMTY3Nzg2ODE4Ni4wLjAuMA.

United Nations. 2022. "Philippines - President Addresses United Nations General Debate, 77th Session (English) | #UNGA." September 20, 2022. https://www.youtube.com/watch?v=2Cr7eMt7aGI.

United Nations. 2023. "Press Conference by Secretary-General António Guterres at United Nations Headquarters." SG/SM/21840. June 15, 2023. https://press.un.org/en/2023/sgsm21840.doc.htm.

UN-Water. 2021. *Summary Progress Update 2021 – SDG 6 – Water and Sanitation For All.* Version: July 2021. Geneva, Switzerland. https://www.unwater.org/sites/default/files/app/uploads/2021/07/SDG-6-Summary-Progress-Update-2021_Version-July-2021.pdf.

VornDick, Wilson. 2012. "Thanks Climate Change: Sea-Level Rise Could End South China Sea Spat." *The Diplomat.* November 8, 2012. https://thediplomat.com/2012/11/can-climate-change-wash-away-south-china-sea-dispute/.

Wingfield-Hayes, Rupert. 2023. "US Secures Deal on Philippines Bases to Complete Arc Around China." February 2, 2023. *BBC News.* https://www.bbc.com/news/world-asia-64479712.

World Bank Group. 2022a. *Philippines Country Climate and Development Report.* CCDR Series; World Bank, Washington, DC. http://hdl.handle.net/10986/38280. License: CC BY-NC-ND. https://openknowledge.worldbank.org/entities/publication/3f76eedd-4ab6-5250-ab4e-75f39593f1b3.

World Bank Group. 2022b. *Bangladesh Country Climate and Development Report.* CCDR Series; World Bank Group, Washington, DC. http://hdl.handle.net/10986/38181. License: CC BY-NC-ND. http://hdl.handle.net/10986/38181.

World Bank Group. 2022c. *Nepal Country Climate and Development Report.* CCDR Series. World Bank, Washington, DC. http://hdl.handle.net/10986/38012. License: CC BY-NC-ND. http://hdl.handle.net/10986/38012.

World Nuclear Association. January2023. "Fukushima Daiichi Accident." https://world-nuclear.org/information-library/safety-and-security/safety-of-plants/fukushima-daiichi-accident.aspx.

Wu, Cheng-Feng et al. 2022. "Impact of Globalization on the Environment in Major CO_2-Emitting Countries: Evidence Using Bootstrap ARDL With a Fourier Function." *Frontiers in Public Health* 10. doi:10.3389/fpubh.2022.907403/.

8 Health Threats to Security

Jeremy Youde

Introduction and Overview

Global health and disease, security, and globalization are inextricably interconnected in both positive and negative ways, and this is particularly true in Asia. The ease and speed with which people and goods can cross borders mean that a disease outbreak anywhere in the world can rapidly spread around the globe. Understanding the importance of health security to Asia requires us to consider the interplay between globalization and health. The highly regionalized and globalized relationships Asian states have with each other and the rest of the world both heighten vulnerability to ill health outcomes and increase opportunities for cross-border collaboration and cooperation to stop ill health before it spreads too far.

This chapter begins by looking at the concept of health security, the securitization of health, and the interplay between globalization and health security in Asia. It then turns to a series of short case studies of SARS (Severe Acute Respiratory Syndrome), non-communicable diseases, and COVID-19 (Corona Virus Disease) to examine the successes and failures the region has had in putting health security into practice. Each of these vignettes highlight the ongoing collaborations and challenges faced throughout Asia as its governments try to put health security into practice. The chapter concludes by discussing the future of health security in Asia and how states within the region might address these ongoing challenges.

Theoretical Orientation and Evolving Milieu

The end of the Cold War, the emergence of new diseases like HIV/AIDS, and a shift in the thinking of policymakers at all different levels have contributed to the securitization of health. As time has gone on, though, there has also been resistance to securitizing health with various scholars arguing that claims of securitizing health have been overblown, that securitizing health harmfully narrows the global health agenda, and that securitization is an inappropriate frame for understanding the importance of global health. This is at the heart of what Enemark calls the "biosecurity dilemma"—the fact

DOI: 10.4324/9781003473206-8

that "security-oriented efforts to prevent or respond to disease outbreaks... have the potential to generate harms as well as benefits" (2017:180).

Global health has garnered unprecedented attention over the past generation. It has moved from the backwaters of international diplomacy to assuming a prominent place on the international policy agenda. International summits have focused on the effects of ill health on development, security, gender equity, and democracy. The Group of Eight (G8) has devoted two of its meetings to global health. Official development assistance (ODA) for health has increased by nearly 600 percent over 25 years, far outstripping growth in other areas and counteracting other trends in foreign aid (Institute for Health Metrics and Evaluation, 2015:9–11). The United Nations Security Council has even devoted special sessions to discussing health's ramifications on the international community.

In addition, there have been concerted academic and policy efforts to connect health with the notion of human security. This idea flips security on its head by prioritizing the security of people over the security of the state. Human security focuses its analytical attention on the challenges that most directly threaten people in their lived experiences. While it is undoubtedly true that a nuclear weapon threatens a person's or a community's security, it is an incredibly distant threat—particularly in comparison to ill health, a lack of food, or the absence of educational opportunities. As Curley and Thomas assert, "The security of the state is dependent on the security of individuals. If they are not secure, the state is not secure" (2004:17). Caballero-Anthony goes further to argue that shoehorning health into traditional notions of security is insufficient and misses the point in a regionalized and globalized world. She argues that infectious disease outbreaks "cut across related issues of poverty, natural disaster, migration, drug trafficking, and others, and in turn they require the involvement of a wide range of actors" (2006:106–107).

Health security is inextricably linked to and with globalization. Globalization leads to all sorts of changes—both positive and negative—for people, animals, and the planet. The same forces that bring people together and make it easier to share information can also create greater divisions and make it harder to stop the spread of an infectious disease. Diseases can hitch a ride around the world as people and goods cross borders, and there is a strong correlation between trade and travel routes and the spread of pathogens (McNeill, 1998). "Many of the social, economic, and environmental problems that benefit the opportunistic microbial world are caused or exacerbated by globalization in other contexts," writes Fidler (1997:33). With the high degree of economic growth, the high population densities, and its growing political importance, Asia is incredibly globalized in many respects, and its futures are bound up with the positive and negative effects of globalization.

Why is health security particularly pertinent and relevant to Asia? It should be nearly self-evident as the world emerges from a global pandemic that has cost literally millions of lives and trillions of dollars that health security matters, but there are two unique factors that make the issue particularly pressing for Asian states. First, there is a history of disease epidemics beginning within Asia. This includes recent outbreaks like H5N1 influenza, SARS, and COVID-19, among others. In a more historical vein, recent work by biologists and geneticists suggests that all three major waves of the bubonic plague—in the 6th, 14th, and 19th centuries—originated in China and spread to other parts of the world via trade routes (Achtman, 2012). This does not mean that there is anything inherently diseased about Asian states; rather, acknowledging this history highlights the first-hand experience the region has with significant disease outbreaks.

Second, Asian states have experienced the health, economic, political, and social consequences of disease outbreaks directly, giving them a unique vantage point for understanding why shortcomings in health security are so consequential. The SARS epidemic in 2002 and 2003 is one of the clearest examples of this. Though SARS itself caused only approximately 8000 confirmed cases and roughly 800 deaths, the ripple effects of the outbreak were massive. Early estimates put the economic effects of SARS at $30–100 billion—or roughly $3–10 million per case (Keogh-Brown and Smith, 2008). The outbreak depressed gross domestic product growth rates, devastated the tourism and hospitality industries, and reduced foreign direct investment. The outbreak also had political effects, creating a legitimacy crisis for the Chinese government (Price-Smith, 2009; Huang, 2004). "The possibility of an economic recession caused by SARS, therefore, posed a direct threat to the regime's material interests, and to perceptions of its legitimacy," Price-Smith (2009) writes.

One good way to examine the vicissitudes of health security in Asia is through a series of brief case studies of three key health issues that have challenged the region in recent years—SARS, noncommunicable diseases, and COVID-19. None of these case studies can provide a comprehensive overview of these outbreaks, but each shows the interplay in positive and negative ways between globalization and health security in the region.

Case Studies

SARS

New and novel pathogens present unique problems for health security, and severe acute respiratory syndrome (SARS) illustrates the dilemma in stark relief. SARS shows how health issues quickly become political, economic, and social issues, too, and the ways in which existing systems can (and cannot) be adapted to respond to an unanticipated outbreak. It also illustrates the close connections between globalization and health. In their review of the political responses to SARS in Asia, So and Pun bluntly state, "It is well known that SARS is a product of globalization. Otherwise, it could not possibly spread so fast to so many countries in such a short time" (2004:5).

SARS is a highly contagious viral respiratory illness that spreads person-to-person through coughs and sneezes. The initial symptoms of SARS are indistinguishable from many other respiratory illnesses, which can make it hard to diagnose quickly. There is still no vaccine or treatment for SARS. SARS' origins remain undetermined, but most scientists believe that the disease entered the human population from animals.

This new disease first appeared in November 2002 in Guangdong, a province along China's southeastern coast that borders Hong Kong. Disease surveillance systems picked up media reports of unusual respiratory illnesses, and the WHO requested additional information from the Chinese government in early December, and the government reported it was merely an influenza outbreak (Heymann 2006:351). In January 2003, more reports about an atypical respiratory illness appeared, this time noting "unusual increases in antiviral drug sales by a pharmaceutical company based in Guangdong" (Weir and Mykhalovskiy, 2010:88). When the WHO received reports about more than 100 deaths from an unknown infectious disease on 10 February, it again contacted the Chinese government for more information. Officials told the WHO that the outbreak was under control and claimed there was no need for WHO's involvement (Heymann, 2006:351). On 10 March, they officially gave the disease the name SARS and established a common diagnostic checklist for identifying potential new cases. Over the course of the outbreak from November 2002 to July 2003, the WHO identified 8098 cases of the disease in 37 different countries. Of these, 774 people died.

SARS' dramatic spread can be traced back to a specific time and place. On February 21, 2003, a doctor who was in town for a family wedding checked in to Room 911 of the Hotel Metropole in the Kowloon section of Hong Kong. The doctor was from Guangdong, and he had been treating cases of atypical pneumonia (Wong, 2004). Shortly after checking in, he began to feel ill, and his condition rapidly worsened. He soon went to the hospital, where he died on 4 March. Unfortunately, other hotel guests staying on the same floor fell ill themselves over the next few days. These other guests were Singaporean, Canadian, Chinese, and an American bound for Vietnam. Over the next few days, they all boarded planes for their intended destinations—and, in that simple act of international air travel, managed to spread SARS far beyond China. The first cases of SARS outside of China appeared in Vietnam on February 26, 2003, and the disease soon appeared in more countries. Within four months of the doctor's hotel stay, more than 4000 cases and 550 deaths of SARS outside China and Taiwan could be directly or indirectly traced back to the Hotel Metropole (Fleck, 2003:625). This rapid spread was not the result of conscious action or a desire to spread the disease. Instead, the virus unwittingly took advantage of his movements and those of the other people on his floor to extend its geographical spread and flout international borders.

The response by various governmental institutions to the SARS outbreak speaks to how actors tried to manage globalization. The Chinese government, for example, actively sought to suppress information about SARS and initially denied that there was a problem (Price-Smith, 2009:141). During a WHO fact-finding mission during the outbreak, one hospital in Beijing loaded 31 SARS patients into ambulances and drove them around the city to hide them from officials. Another hospital moved approximately 40 SARS patients to a different facility while WHO personnel were conducting their investigation. In both instances, hospital personnel claimed that they were ordered to take these actions by government officials. Lower-level government bureaucrats also had strong incentives to distort information about SARS as it went to higher officials because they feared that any problems found within their jurisdictions could cause them to lose their jobs or be passed over for future promotions (Huang, 2003:11). The government prohibited public discussion of the disease, and it maintained that it did not need assistance from international organizations or other groups.

Despite these strenuous efforts at the domestic level, the Chinese government could not prevent information and rumors about SARS from getting out. A survey found that nearly 41 percent of urban residents in China had heard about the disease even though the government officially denied its existence. Much of this information came via text messages, which became so ubiquitous that government officials in Guangzhou felt compelled to hold a press conference to refute them (Huang, 2003:12). The ability of information—both reliable and unreliable—to circumvent official government channels is one of the hallmarks of globalization, as communication flows make it easier to challenge official narratives. On the flip side, though, that also means that it can be harder to correct misinformation.

While the Chinese government denied SARS's existence, the WHO instead implemented an incredibly aggressive response. This was all the more remarkable because the organization technically lacked the international legal authority to override national sovereignty. At the time, the International Health Regulations (IHR)—an international treaty that governs how states should respond to infectious disease outbreaks—only required states to report human cases of cholera, yellow fever, and plague. SARS fell outside the IHR's mandate and thus severely limited the WHO's ability to mount a response. If the Chinese government did not want to report cases of SARS or cooperate with the WHO, that was entirely within its legal rights. Its actions reflected its Westphalian sovereignty, even at a time when international borders were proving irrelevant to containing the spread of a new pathogen (Fidler, 2003:490).

When disease surveillance systems first picked up reports of deaths due to an unknown infectious disease in China, the WHO approached the Chinese government for more information. This happened on multiple occasions, and in each instance, government officials told the WHO that they did not require any assistance. The WHO escalated its involvement against SARS when it issued a global health alert about a severe atypical pneumonia that placed health workers at particular risk on March 12, 2003. Three days later, it issued a rare emergency advisory, recommending postponing any nonessential travel to Hong Kong and Guangdong—the epicenters of the outbreak (Curley and Thomas, 2004:21–22). The combination of domestic and international pressures did eventually force the Chinese government to change its tactics. On April 4, the head of China's Center for Disease Control publicly apologized for failing to keep the Chinese public and international community informed about the outbreak. Less than a week later, Jiang Yanyong, a prominent member of the Communist Party, publicly accused the government of covering up the outbreak in Beijing. Minister of Health Zhang Wenkang and Beijing Mayor Meng Xuenong were both subsequently fired for not stopping the outbreak—the first of more than 120 who lost their jobs or were disciplined for their lax responses. After the WHO publicly chastised the Chinese government for its failures on April 16, it responded by declaring a national war on SARS (Price-Smith, 2009:141–142). On April 17, the government mobilized a large public campaign against SARS, publicly releasing the number of cases in each province and making government officials responsible for aggressively addressing the SARS outbreak within their jurisdictions. Tens of thousands of people were quarantined, and 80 million people in Guangdong were mobilized to clean the streets in an effort to kill the virus. The party even created a two billion yuan (approximately US $242 million) fund for SARS prevention and control to upgrade facilities and make free treatment available to SARS patients (Huang, 2004:11–13).

Asian governments' experiences with SARS demonstrated the high direct and indirect costs that come with large disease outbreaks, the negative effects of failing to share information, and the ease with which outbreaks can travel across borders. These lessons have continued to reverberate throughout the region to this day.

Non-Communicable Diseases

Non-communicable diseases present a unique challenge to health security in Asia and elsewhere throughout the world. Outbreaks like SARS or H5N1 influenza tend to emerge seemingly out of nowhere, spread quickly, and then fade into the background. They seem to strike at random. Non-communicable diseases, including conditions like stroke, heart disease, and cancer, are slower to emerge, require ongoing attention to treat, and are often considered "lifestyle diseases." Their growth throughout Asia challenges a number of the existing strategies for addressing health concerns, and adequately addressing them will require a degree of international coordination and resource sharing that goes beyond current levels.

The discourse around health security tends to prioritize a focus on infectious disease outbreaks, but the reality is that non-communicable diseases account for 71 percent of all deaths around the world in 2016. This is a dramatic shift, and it has significant implications for the meaning of health security in Asia in the future. That same year, the World Health Organization reported that South Asia had the second-highest rate of deaths due to infectious diseases—approximately 20 percent. Just five years earlier, though, more than half of all deaths in the region were caused by infectious diseases (Sciubba, 2022:98). There is a great deal to celebrate about this shift in causes of death, but it raises profound questions for health care systems in the region. Bollyky (2018) argues that much of the reason that these dramatic shifts occurred was due to external support and assistance. These interventions addressed the infectious diseases themselves, but largely failed to build the ongoing infrastructure necessary to treat non-communicable diseases over the long term. Donor support has typically focused on discrete, disease-specific, horizontal interventions that are not well-suited for providing the sort of long-term care necessary for treating non-communicable diseases. As a result, without serious efforts from internal and external sources, the gains in life expectancy resulting from the decrease in infectious diseases could be wiped out by rising rates of untreated non-communicable diseases.

Making this problem all the more pressing is the fact that non-communicable diseases have been "spectacularly unsuccessful in attracting development funding for management and prevention in low- and middle-income countries" (Magnusson, 2020:627). Data collection by the Institute for Health Metrics and Evaluation finds that development assistance for health has grown dramatically—nearly 1900 percent between 1990 and 2021—but it remains a very low percentage of overall development assistance for health levels. In 2021, development assistance for health spending that focused on non-communicable diseases totaled a bit more than $1 billion—and this was a decrease of 2.6 percent from 2020. That same year, total development assistance for health (not including funds earmarked for COVID-19) totaled $45.6 billion (Institute for Health Metrics and Evaluation, 2023). That means that non-communicable diseases are responsible for nearly three-quarters of all deaths around the world, but receive just over 2 percent of international health assistance funding. This disjuncture does not bode well for any country's ability to adequately address the pressing healthcare needs posed by non-communicable diseases.

The increases in mortality and morbidity caused by non-communicable diseases in Asia reflect the demographic transition, in which a smaller number of people die from infectious diseases and so-called "lifestyle diseases" are responsible for more illness and death. The World Health Organization identifies four key drivers associated with the increasing rate of non-communicable diseases: tobacco use, physical inactivity, increased alcohol usage, and unhealthy diets (World Health Organization, 2023). Environmental factors, like increasing air, water, and soil pollution, can also play a significant role, particularly in rapidly urbanizing areas (Dhimal et al., 2021). Urbanization is also closely linked to increasing rates of non-communicable diseases, as people moving into new areas may be exposed to more pollution or undergo changes in their diet and physical activity that can lead to illness (Goryakin et al., 2017). Demographic projections anticipate that Asia will experience the highest rates of urbanization through 2050 and will, by the middle of the century, be home to more than half of the world's urban population (Birch and Wachter, 2011:4). This reality makes the challenges of non-communicable diseases for Asian states all the more pressing and will require these governments to implement and support ongoing monitoring, surveillance, and intervention programs and universal health care programs—all of which will require human and financial resources that go beyond current health spending in these states. As a result, it will take sustained efforts to maintain the region's ongoing commitment to health security.

Asian states have implemented a number of strategies—on both national and regional levels—to try and address rising rates of non-communicable diseases. On a regional level, the member-states of the South-East Asia Regional Office of the World Health Organization in 2022 endorsed an Implementation Roadmap that prioritizes primary health care and universal health coverage as comprehensive pillars of establishing ongoing surveillance and regular access to health professionals to reduce mortality and morbidity from non-communicable diseases. The Roadmap also provides technical expertise to national governments to help them implement the necessary policies and identify viable funding sources. Strategies include engaging civil society and the private sector, integrating NCD control into poverty alleviation programs, introducing and enforcing policies to reduce the harmful use of tobacco and alcohol, and relying on cost-effective health interventions that can be sustained in a variety of environments (World Health Organization, 2022). Similarly, the member-states in the Western Pacific Regional Office of the World Health Organization report increasing levels of capacity building to allow for the implementation of a comprehensive strategy. This includes increased staffing in public health offices; imposing taxes on alcohol, tobacco products, and food products high in sugar and fat; creating and implementing nationally coordinated strategies; and building surveillance systems that can track mortality by cause of death. Despite this progress, the WHO has called on the region to go further to limit the availability and desirability of alcohol, tobacco, and unhealthy foods through higher taxation and advertising bans (World Health Organization, 2021). Additional work suggests that blending allopathic medical strategies with traditional and complementary medical techniques leads to higher rates of acceptance and uptake, particularly among older community members (Chung et al., 2021).

Much of the work at the national level mirrors and contributes to these broader regional strategies. In China, for example, the government has focused on and received good marks for its increased surveillance capabilities and its efforts to introduce more systematic approaches to NCD governance. At the same time, its efforts to reduce the use and accessibility of tobacco lags, as do its systems for building and maintaining systems that will support older adults (Zhu et al., 2017). Meanwhile, in Vietnam, government efforts have shown some success in reducing tobacco consumption, but much less so in reducing the use of alcohol (particularly among males), unhealthy diets, and lack of physical exercise (Duyen et al., 2020).

One element that stands out in many of the regional and national strategies addressing non-communicable diseases in Asia is that they tend to prioritize, or at least have greater initial success with, a focus on individual-level behaviors. Most of the work seems to assume that people can make choices to eat healthier, reduce their tobacco and alcohol consumption, and increase their physical activity on their own. It is undoubtedly true that no one forces another person to reduce their physical activity or to eat unhealthy meals, but the heavy focus on individual-level behaviors obscures the larger structural issues at play that contribute to these choices—or restricts people from being able to make a meaningful choice. Advertising bans, taxation, and increased availability of processed foods are all inevitably tied to issues of globalization, trade policy, and commercial interests. Without addressing the *commercial* determinants of health (Lee and Freudenberg, 2022), it will be next to impossible to address the underlying causes of increased rates of non-communicable diseases in Asia—or any other region. At the same time, it is impossible to disentangle a whole host of complex issues from rising NCD rates—difficult policy areas like urban planning and infrastructure, climate change, and agricultural policy.

Asia's relative lack of addressing the broader structural issues that give rise to increased rates of non-communicable diseases mirrors experiences in the rest of the world. It is possible that some existing structures designed to address infectious diseases could potentially be adapted for use in NCD settings; for example, surveillance systems for tracking infectious diseases could be augmented or adapted to monitor rates of, say, heart disease. The challenges in such work are twofold. First, there needs to be a mechanism for establishing and maintaining an ongoing relationship. Rather than a situation where someone goes to a health clinic (assuming one is available) only when they feel ill, NCD surveillance requires ongoing monitoring and regular evaluations to track changes. Second, there remains the issue of funding. International donors have made global health a significant priority—but they have largely conceptualized global health as infectious diseases. To support and fund these sorts of ongoing interventions will require either a shift in the mindset of donor states and organizations and/or increased financial and human capital capacity within Asian states themselves.

COVID-19

The COVID-19 pandemic has been the largest infectious disease outbreak in the world since the 1918 influenza pandemic, and its lingering effects will continue to reverberate for years. COVID-19, and health security in Asia in general, are inextricably intertwined with larger geopolitical contests and questions. It is a clear manifestation of the reality that public health is inherently political and that we cannot fully understand the decisions that states and regional organizations make outside of the geopolitical context. For example, Economy (2020) distinguishes between the international responses to COVID-19 by the United States and China in terms of political competition. The initial response by the Trump Administration, she argues, reflected an abdication of global leadership, while the Chinese government "sought to grasp the mantle of global leadership"—though with its own shortcomings and reasons for criticism (Economy, 2020:369).

The interplay between public health and geopolitical competition does not simply originate with COVID-19; it has been a relatively underappreciated element of geopolitics throughout the 21st century. Leon (2015) notes that both India and China have become increasingly important players in development assistance for health, though without necessarily adhering to the traditional tenets of the existing global health governance system.

The responses to COVID-19 throughout Asia also demonstrate how past experience dealing with (or failing to deal with) pandemics can have a significant effect on how prepared states were for dealing with the effects of the pandemic. The experiences with SARS and MERS (Middle Eastern Respiratory Syndrome)—both from the same virus family as COVID-19 and outbreaks that had disproportionate effects on Asian states—in particular bolstered the strategies that countries already had in place to address an infectious disease outbreak.

As might be expected in the midst of a fast-moving and unprecedented event, evaluations of the responses to the outbreak vary considerably. It is also important to stress that there was no single response to COVID-19 among Asian states.

Asian states—both on an individual level and as a region—received significant praise for their non-pharmaceutical interventions for helping to limit the pandemic's spread before vaccines were widely available. Patel and Sridhar (2020) commented favorably on the "zero COVID" responses for navigating the "challenge of devising new strategies that give precedence to the health of citizens, while minimizing further economic damage, often in climates of reduced public compliance and government mistrust." They singled out the responses from the New Zealand and Taiwan governments for being proactive and adapting existing surveillance systems to monitor the spread. Others have taken more critical stances. Amul et al. (2021:91) see more of a spectrum of policy responses, from "rigorously enforced full lockdowns" in Singapore to "relative 'laissez-faire'" policies in Myanmar. They further note that countries that more explicitly framed their COVID response in terms of national security and put the police and the military at the lead, like the Philippines, saw lower rates of public compliance and higher numbers of allegations regarding human rights violations. Trust in the government and coherent national communication strategies also varied significantly, but played large roles in the efficacy of the response.

The role of regional organizations also came in for an ambiguous assessment. ASEAN's initial response received high marks for being quick, efficacious, and collaborative with international partners. As time went on, though, the limits to ASEAN's power and authority came to the forefront. Unlike the

European Union, ASEAN is not a supranational union—and one that strenuously advocates for national sovereignty and non-interference (Ramcharan, 2000). As a result, its ability to coordinate region-wide policies around trade and travel restrictions was limited (Amul et al., 2021:105–106).

One key variable that seems to distinguish evaluations of the efficacy of a government's response to COVID throughout Asia is state capacity. This idea draws on Price-Smith's (2001) recognition of state capacity as a leading independent variable for understanding responses to infectious disease outbreaks, with political will and social cohesion acting as intervening variables. State capacity refers to a country's ability to maximize prosperity and stability, maintain control over its territory, protect its populace, and adapt to crises (Price-Smith, 2001:25). Yen et al. (2021) apply a state capacity framework to examine national-level responses to COVID in five Asian states and find that states with higher levels of state capacity like Taiwan, South Korea, and Singapore responded more quickly with a broader array of tools and greater level of resources than lower capacity states like Thailand and Indonesia. An and Tang (2020) pick up on a similar analytical vein, arguing that the existence of sufficient institutional infrastructure that resonates with a polity's underlying culture is what allows state capacity to operate in a meaningful way. These issues of state capacity, they argue, matter more than crude measures of national wealth alone.

Perhaps no Asian state has received as much scrutiny for its COVID response—both positively and negatively—than the People's Republic of China. The first cases of what came to be known as COVID appeared in Wuhan, the Chinese government made the first report of a potential new infectious disease outbreak to the World Health Organization on December 31, 2019, and the powers its government holds are vastly more significant than many of its Asian counterparts. The Chinese government was initially praised by the World Health Organization for its proclivity to share information, but the organization came to criticize it for stonewalling independent investigations into the outbreak's origins. The World Health Organization's early praise of China's response, even in the midst of questions about whether it was being fully transparent about its reporting, may reflect a strategic calculation on the part of the WHO's senior leadership to maintain good relations with China. There may have been a fear that criticizing China too harshly would have prevented the WHO from having any access to the country while building a positive relationship could open opportunities for future collaborations (Brown and Ladwig, 2020).

It also became the enemy of the Trump Administration in the United States. Trump blamed China for unleashing the virus on the world, employed racist language in describing the virus, and went so far as to withdraw the United States from the World Health Organization because "China has total control over" it (BBC, 2020). Ironically, Trump initially and repeatedly praised the Chinese government for "working really hard" and "making tremendous progress" (Ward, 2020). These varying responses reflect the interplay between the responses to COVID-19 and larger geopolitical competition that have been at play throughout the entire pandemic.

China eventually pursued a "zero-COVID" policy, which relied on mass testing, strict lockdowns, and quarantines in government facilities. Indeed, when the outbreak initially appeared, the government locked down the city of Wuhan and its 11 million residents. It argued that this strict and aggressive approach allowed the country to keep the number of cases and deaths relatively low—though questions exist about the accuracy of official case counts and death statistics (Baptista and Goh, 2023). After three years, though, the Chinese government abruptly abandoned the "zero-COVID" policy in late 2022. The sudden policy reversal led to widespread confusion, a surge in hospital admissions, and a lack of clear guidance. This period of uncertainty even witnessed public demonstrations critical of the central government—a rare event, particularly coming right after President Xi Jinping received another term and further consolidated his power.

The policy responses to COVID illustrate some key ongoing opportunities and challenges for health security in Asia. First, previous experience can positively inform future-oriented strategies. Many Asian states have learned from their experiences with previous outbreaks, such as SARS and MERS, and created public health and disease surveillance systems that can respond when new outbreaks occur. Second, separating geopolitics from global public health is impossible. Health is inherently political, and actions taken (or not taken) in response to outbreaks are inevitably filtered through geopolitical lenses. The praising and shaming of the Chinese government's COVID policies reflect tensions with the United States government, questions from international partners about its transparency, and efforts to keep China within the larger realm of international health diplomacy. Third, the contemporary global health governance architecture can help governments navigate the health-related challenges associated with globalization, but its systems are also in need of updating. In particular, the system can offer states few direct and ongoing resources, and it can be difficult to mobilize as quickly as is necessary in a globalized world.

Conclusion and Future Prospects

Health's importance is unlikely to diminish in the coming years. The interconnections among Asian states and between Asia and the rest of the world are such that disease outbreaks and ill health will necessarily have effects throughout the region. Furthermore, recent evidence shows that health problems go beyond population health; they have direct and significant political, economic, and social effects, too.

The future of health security—both in Asia and globally—is currently hazy. On the one hand, there is clear evidence of the importance of and need for robust cooperation. A disease outbreak in one part of the world necessarily challenges the rest of the world, and no country can effectively address an outbreak on its own. On the other hand, there is increased skepticism about the value of multilateralism—or at least multilateralism as has been practiced during the post-World War II era. Some of this is because these structures are out of date and reflect political realities that simply no longer exist. Some of this, though, is because of the increased wariness of multilateral institutions and a lack of willingness to undertake any actions that might be seen as eroding a state's sovereignty. Within Asia, China has expressed an ambivalent attitude toward multilateralism—wanting to assume a more prominent role in world affairs, but often doing so by going around existing institutions or creating new ones. ASEAN, too, has brought its member-states together in important ways—but the organization remains firmly committed to its principles of non-interference and state sovereignty.

One of the other challenges in addressing health security in Asia going forward is the changing nature of health concerns facing governments. Most of the global health governance infrastructure is oriented toward addressing infectious diseases, but the overwhelming health challenge facing Asian—and all—states is the rapid increase in non-communicable diseases. In addition, much of the current thinking around controlling non-communicable diseases focuses primarily on individual behavior changes without addressing larger systemic factors, like trade regimes, the ability to regulate alcohol and tobacco, and environmental degradation.

References

Achtman, Mark. 2012. "Insights from genomic comparisons of genetically monomorphic bacterial pathogens." *Philosophical Transactions of the Royal Society B: Biological Sciences* 367(1590): 860–867.

Amul, Gianna Gayle, Michael Ang, Dia Kraybill, Suan Ee Ong, and Joanne Yoong. 2021. "Responses to COVID-19 in Southeast Asia: Diverse paths and ongoing challenges." *Asian Economic Policy Review* 17 (1): 90–110.

An, Brian Y. and Shui-Yan Tang. 2020. "Lessons from COVID-19 responses in East Asia: Institutional infrastructure and enduring policy instruments." *American Review of Public Administration* 50(6–7): 790–800.

Baptista, Eduardo and Brenda Goh. 2023. "China defends its COVID response after WHO, Biden concerns." *Reuters*, 5 January. https://www.reuters.com/world/china/biden-raises-concern-over-chinas-covid-response-after-who-questions-data-2023-01-05/ (accessed 18 May 2023).

BBC. 2020. "Coronavirus: Trump moves to pull US out of World Health Organization." 7 July. https://www.bbc.com/news/world-us-canada-53327906 (accessed 18 May 2023).

Birch, Eugenie L. and Susan M. Wachter. 2011. "World urbanization: The critical issue of the twenty-first century." In *Global Urbanization*, Susan M. Wachter and Eugenie L. Birch, eds. Philadelphia: University of Pennsylvania Press.

Bollyky, Thomas J. 2018. *Plagues and the Paradox of Progress: Why the World is Getting Healthier in Worrisome Ways*. Cambridge: MIT Press.

Brown, Theodore M. and Susan Ladwig. 2020. "COVID-19, China, the World Health Organization, and the limits of international health diplomacy." *American Journal of Public Health* 110 (8): 1149–1151.

Caballero-Anthony, Mely. 2006. "Combating infectious diseases in East Asia: Securitization and global public goods for health and human security." *Journal of International Affairs* 59 (2): 105–127.

Chung, Vincent C.H., Charlene H.L.Wong, Claire C.W.Zhong, YanYin Tejoe, Ting HungLeung, and Sian M.Griffiths. 2021. "Traditional and complementary medicine for promoting healthy ageing in WHO Western Pacific Region: Policy implications from utilization patterns and current evidence." *Integrative Medicine Research* 10 (1): 100469.

Curley, Melissa and Nicholas Thomas. 2004. "Human security and public health in southeast Asia: The SARS outbreak." *Australian Journal of International Affairs* 58 (1): 17–32.

Dhimal, Meghnath, Tammana Neupane, and Mandira Lamichhane Dhimal. 2021. "Understanding linkages between environmental risk factors and noncommunicable diseases–a review." *FASEB BioAdvances* 3 (5): 287–294.

Duyen, Nguyen Thuy, Hoang Van Minh, Nguyen Van Huy, Kim Bao Giang, Tran Thu Ngan, Nguyen Xuan Long, Dang Kim Khanh Ly, Vu Thu Trang, and Vu Dung. 2020. "Patterns of behavioral risk factors for noncommunicable diseases in Vietnam: A comparative scoping study." *Health Psychology Open* July–December: 1–15.

Economy, Elizabeth. 2020. "The United States, China, and the great value game." In *COVID-19 and World Order*, Hal Brands and Francis J. Gavin, eds. Baltimore: The Johns Hopkins University Press.

Enemark, Christian. 2017. *Biosecurity Dilemmas: Dreaded Diseases, Ethical Responses, and the Health of Nations*. Baltimore: The Johns Hopkins University Press.

Fidler, David P. 1997. "The globalization of public health: Emerging infectious disease and international relations." *Indiana Journal of Global Legal Studies* 5 (1): 11–51.

Fidler, David P. 2003. "SARS: Political pathology of the first post-Westphalian pathogen." *Journal of Law, Medicine, and Ethics* 31 (4): 485–505.

Fleck, Fiona. 2003. "How SARS changed the world in less than six months." *Bulletin of the World Health Organization* 81 (8): 625–626.

Goryakin, Yevgeniy, Lorenza Rocco, and Marc Suhrcke. 2017. "The contribution of urbanization to non-communicable diseases: Evidence from 173 countries from 1980 to 2008." *Economics and Human Biology* 26: 151–163.

Heymann, David L. 2006. "SARS and emerging infectious diseases: A challenge to place global solidarity above national sovereignty." *Annals of the Academy of Medicine of Singapore* 35 (5): 350–353.

Heymann, David L. and Alison West. 2015. "Emerging infections: threats to health and economic security." In *The Routledge Handbook of Global Health Security*, Simon Rushton and Jeremy Youde (eds.), 92–104. New York: Routledge.

Huang, Yanzhong. 2003. "The politics of China's SARS crisis." *Harvard Asia Quarterly* 7 (4): 9–16.

Huang, Yanzhong. 2004. "The SARS epidemic and its aftermath in China: a political perspective." In *Learning from SARS: Preparing for the Next Disease Outbreak: Workshop Summary*, Stacey Knobler, Adel Mahmoud, Stanley Lemon, Alison Mack, Laura Sivitz, and Katherine Oberholtzer (eds.), 116–136. Washington: National Academies Press.

Institute for Health Metrics and Evaluation. 2015. *Financing Global Health: Development Assistance Steady on the Path to Global Goals*. Seattle: Institute for Health Metrics and Evaluation.

Institute for Health Metrics and Evaluation. 2023. *Financing Global Health 2021: Global Health Priorities in a Time of Change*. Seattle: Institute for Health Metrics and Evaluation.

Keogh-Brown, MarcusRichard and Richard David Smith. 2008. "The economic impact of SARS: How does the reality match the predictions?" *Health Policy* 88 (1): 110–120.

Lee, Kelley and Nicholas Freudenberg. 2022. "Public health roles in addressing commercial determinants of health." *Annual Review of Public Health* 43: 375–395.

Leon, Joshua K. 2015. *The Rise of Global Health: The Evolution of Effective Collective Action*. Albany: SUNY Press.

Magnusson, Roger. 2020. "Non-communicable diseases and global health politics." In *Oxford Handbook of Global Health Politics*, Kelley Lee, Colin McInnes, and Jeremy Youde, eds. New York: Oxford University Press.

McNeill, William H. 1998. *Plagues and Peoples*. New York: Anchor Books.

Patel, Jay and Devi Sridhar. 2020. "We should learn from the Asia-Pacific responses to COVID-19." *Lancet Regional Health Western Pacific* 5: 100062.

Price-Smith, Andrew T. 2001. *The Health of Nations: Infectious Disease, Environmental Change, and Their Effects on National and International Security*. Cambridge: MIT Press.

Price-Smith, Andrew T. 2009. *Contagion and Chaos: Disease, Ecology, and National Security in the Era of Globalization*. Cambridge: MIT Press.

Ramcharan, Robin. 2000. "ASEAN and non-interference: A principle maintained." *Contemporary Southeast Asia* 22 (1): 60–88.

Sciubba, Jennifer D. 2022. *8 Billion and Counting: How Sex, Death, and Migration Shape Our World*. New York: W.W. Norton.

So, Alvin Y. and Ngai Pun. 2004. "Introduction: globalization and anti-globalization of SARS in Chinese societies." *Asian Perspectives* 28 (1): 5–17.

Ward, Myah. 2020. "15 times Trump praised China as coronavirus was spreading across the globe." *Politico*, 15 April. https://www.politico.com/news/2020/04/15/trump-china-coronavirus-188736 (accessed 18 May 2023).

Weir, Lorna and Eric Mykhalovskiy. 2010. *Global Public Health Vigilance: Creating a World on Alert*. New York: Routledge.

Wong, Oscar. 2004. "Severe acute respiratory syndrome (SARS): wild game chefs and healthcare workers." *Occupational and Environmental Medicine* 61 (1). http://www.occenvmed.com/cgi/content/full/61/1/e1.

World Health Organization. 2021. *Progress on the Prevention and Control of Non-communicable Diseases in the Western Pacific Region: Country Capacity 2019*. Manila: Western Pacific Regional Office of the World Health Organization.

World Health Organization. 2022. *Implementation Roadmap for Accelerating the Prevention and Control of Non-Communicable Diseases in South-East Asia, 2022–2030*. New Delhi: South-East Asia Regional Office of the World Health Organization.

World Health Organization. 2023. "Noncommunicable diseases." https://www.who.int/health-topics/noncommunicable-diseases#tab=tab_1 (accessed 3 May 2023)

Yen, Wei-Ting, Li-Yin Lui, Eunji Won, and Testriono. 2021. "The imperative of state capacity in public health crisis: Asia's early COVID-19 policy responses." *Governance* 35 (3): 777–798.

Zhu, Xiao-Lei, Jie-Si Luo, Xiao-Chang Zhang, Yi Zhai, and Jing Wu. 2017. "China's efforts on management, surveillance, and research of noncommunicable diseases: NCD Scorecard Project." *Annals of Global Health* 83 (3/4): 489–500.

9 Towards Regional Security Cooperation

Janicke Stramer-Smith

Introduction and Overview

The "ASEAN Way" is used to describe a corporate culture among the members of the Association of Southeast Asian Nations (ASEAN).[1] Its trademark is informality and decision-making procedures based on consultation and consensus with an emphasis on dialog and negotiation rather than an outcome. The "Asian Way" embodies the way in which Asian countries have been cooperating beyond just the ASEAN club. The extensive web of ASEAN-related governmental organizations in the region subscribes to the same core values. The "Asian Way" also embraces the idea of non-intervention in the affairs of other states. While this strict adherence to the sovereignty principle differs from the "EU Way" by which states can be criticized and even punished for internal behavior that goes against the rules of the union.

This chapter is organized as follows: The first section will sketch and assess the evolution of security cooperation in the Asia Pacific region, with a focus on the post-Cold War security challenges both traditional and non-traditional security (NTS). Specifically, it evaluates the Asian states' ability to meet current and future security challenges in an increasingly globalized and interconnected world. Section two examines the role and effect of globalization on regional security. Globalization continues to be a hotly contested concept. In the vein of Lui Hebron and John F. Stack Jr., the concept of globalization as used in this chapter is seen as ever-evolving (Hebron and Stack Jr., 2016). The third section discusses the various evolving traditional and non-traditional security challenges facing the Asia-Pacific region. None of the issues the region faces are really new. Most of the multilateral organizations trying to deal with these are also not new. Rather both the security threats and the efforts to counter them are ever-evolving. It will use the case study of the ASEAN Regional Forum (ARF) and the Asian Pacific Economic Cooperation (APEC) to take a closer look at two primary areas of security cooperation in the political and economic areas. They have been key organizations in paving the way for multilateral security cooperation in the political and economic spheres. While ARF and APEC are not designed to facilitate ambitious security cooperation, the question remains whether they will hinder or help security cooperation with the inevitable rise of China in this age of globalization. The concluding section discusses the myriad of security challenges, both traditional and non-traditional, facing the region, and whether the existing network of multilateral security cooperation is robust enough to create pathways for peace and cooperation.

Theorizing Asian Security

Theoretically, there are four primary strains that inform studies on Asian security. Realism purports that the "Asian Way" of informality and consensus-driven processes will not be effective enough to counter traditional security threats. Realists are mostly concerned with U.S.-dominated bilateralism and the balance between the U.S. and China. Offensive realists argue the U.S. should try to constrain the rise of China and reassert its leadership in the region through U.S.-dominated bilateralism (Fleitz et al., 2016; Mearsheimer, 2010, 2014b, 2014a). The defensive realists argue the United States should opt for a partnership with China on managing regional security issues (Kirshner, 2012; Raditio, 2019). Both strains disregard the importance of NTS threats, such as environmental, public health, and human security issues. Thus, realism is not able to engage in the discussion about the ramifications of an expanded set of security issues facing the region and how the complex network of multilateral institutions can enhance regional security through economic and social integration. The failure of realists to include these types of threats in their examination of major power competition and rivalry, means they are missing the interplay between non-military and military security threats.

Similarly, Institutionalists lament the lack of a formal structure and rules from which to counter security threats and from which to hold members accountable (Jones and Smith, 2001; Kipgen, 2020). While the "Asian way" is viewed as mostly successful in creating peaceful relations among its members, it also has some inherent weaknesses in dealing with more comprehensive security issues, such as human rights violations, financial crises, and ecological disasters. It has been argued that the core principle of non-interference in the internal politics of member states and the subordination of issues to the national security agenda has hindered important responses from the organization (Loke, 2005). For institutionalists, this puts a question mark on the ability to counter both traditional and NTS threats.

The Liberal strain is more optimistic about the ability of the "Asian Way" to allow for a multilateral approach to traditional and NTS through complex cooperation and networks with ASEAN as the central facilitator. The repetition and deepening of norms and cooperation create a culture of cooperation and compliance to peaceful relations among members (Caballero-Anthony, 2018, 2022). The fact that great powers like the U.S. and China operate through the extensive ASEAN network of organizations is a testament to its centrality in security cooperation. From this perspective, the "Asian" way should be able to constrain the ambitions of powerful global and regional players like the United States and China and facilitate mutual cooperation towards regional security through repeated interactions within the ASEAN network.

Finally, the Constructivist approach highlights the importance of a broadened conceptualization of security threats as more relevant to the East and Southeast Asian states. They argue that the use of the securitization framework can be relevant to redefining the referent object as human security rather than the survival of the state (Buzan and Wæver, 2009; Buzan, Wæver, and Wilde, 1998). While states are still relevant actors in managing security issues, there has been a proliferation of security actors, such as the secretary generals of various regional and international organizations, who play an important role in addressing NTS challenges through the complex network of multilateral institutions in the region (Caballero-Anthony, 2018). While there has been a focus on NTS challenges and the ability of the Asian countries and their network of multilateral institutions in managing these threats, the traditional security threats persist. Globalization presents an additional challenge of addressing both the old security dilemmas and the new security threats.

There is a spillover effect from NTS threats to traditional security issues. When weak states suffer natural disasters it often leads to economic and human insecurity. Migration and displacement can put pressure on the entire region, destabilizing the regional economy and increasing tension between states. Thus, one state's problem becomes a collective problem. Effective security governance at the regional and international levels becomes paramount to overcoming such challenges and preserving political and economic stability. Looking at Asian security in a multilateral framework it could be relevant to frame security actors as security governors as defined by Deborah Avant, Martha Finnemore, and Susan Sell. According to their definition, security governors are security actors with legitimacy and authority to exercise power over a certain policy area across borders. Security governors are then a complex set of actors at different levels and in different areas who can set security agendas and implement rules in their area (Avant, Finnemore, and Sell, 2010). In the Asian context, the ASEAN-centric network of interwoven institutions will be more effective than individual states in working towards cooperation on solving the expansive range of NTS threats from pandemics to climate change. There are several vulnerable states in Southeast Asia, such as Indonesia and the Philippines, who lack the capacity to mitigate NTS threats, particularly environmental disasters and climate change.

The Evolution of Security Cooperation

The primary contribution of the ASEAN network has been to foster peaceful relations amongst its member states. Prior to ASEAN, conflicts between Southeast Asian countries were prevalent, which made the region fragile and less prosperous. The ASEAN way worked well to create a partnership among states with different regime types, ideologies, ethnic and religious differences due to its focus on sovereignty and non-interference in internal affairs. In one sense, this is a very realist organization, which is probably one of the reasons it has been successful in binding this region together despite internal differences. However, in more recent years it has faced more NTS threats, many of which are normative in nature, such as human rights abuses in Myanmar, natural disasters, and economic crises. The expansive web of interwoven security organizations has struggled to address these issues because it requires a more liberal normative approach to the partnership between the various states involved. The diversity of the Asia-Pacific region and the complex history and relationship between some of the major and medium powers, such as China, South Korea, and Japan, is one reason for the relatively slow progress on regional security cooperation and the preference for consultation and dialogue over a rule-based partnership (Caballero-Anthony, 2022). Furthermore, the bilateral dominance of the U.S. as an external security governor in the region since the end of World War II and the Cold War makes security cooperation tenuous. In response, the preference has been to rely on multilateralism to promote engagement, trust, and confidence-building in working toward regional security cooperation (Song, 2016).

Globalization and Asian Security

Globalization has had varying effects on Asian security. There has been increased regional cooperation as countries seek partners in confronting the negative side effects of globalization, such as global and regional financial crises, mitigation of climate change and pollution, and external pressures stemming from increased global trade. Some argue that increased regionalization in Asia has facilitated voluntary actions and dialog between Asian states to mitigate a variety of security threats through cooperation in the complex web of regional organizations (Hettne, 2002). This may be seen as a positive effect of globalization. However, when globalization causes financial crises, like the 1997 crisis, the effect of political and economic turmoil has had a negative social impact in terms of poverty and lack of resources (Jayasuriya, 2004).

Most scholarship on the effect of globalization in Asia has focused on its impact on economic security, arguing that it has caused a significant shift in economic development and growth from the Southeast Asian states to China. This has affected the power balance with China stepping into a more prominent regional role and challenging U.S. primacy in the region. The rise of China has once again placed traditional security threats at the front and center of security issues facing the region. China's territorial claims have heightened tensions with regional and global powers, thus, increasing the risk of conflict in the region. Some argue that to mitigate these negative effects, security governance is best placed beyond the state within the web of intergovernmental organizations under the ASEAN umbrella (Nesadurai, 2012). It is still unclear if the effect of increased globalization on Asian security will be mostly negative or positive. This will likely depend on how the balance of power is resolved between the two world powers, China and the United States, and the ability of regional organizations to respond to internal disputes and external pressures, as a result of continued globalization in all aspects of economic, political, and environmental areas.

Moving Towards Regional Security Cooperation

Security cooperation in the Asian context did not see a significant shift between the pre- and post-Covid time period. Instead, the turning point in terms of increased conflict or cooperation has been the end of the Cold War, globalization, post-2009 era with the rise of China and its ambitious foreign policy, and perhaps the war in Ukraine will also prove to be a turning point.

Non-traditional Security Threats

Regional security cooperation and ASEAN and related organizations are products of the Cold War. The question became whether these institutions were relevant to solving new security dilemmas in the post-Cold War/Globalization world order, such as the Asian financial crisis, violent internal challenges, and environmental disasters (Jones and Smith, 2001). While the war in Ukraine is taking place far away from the Asian region, the rise of China as a contender to American primacy, economically and militarily, at the global level will have an impact on security cooperation within the Asia-Pacific region and the ability of institutions, such as ASEAN and its related organizations, in addressing regional security threats, whether traditional or non-traditional. The expansion of the list of NTS challenges facing the world in the age of globalization was highlighted by UN Secretary-general Kofi Annan in his address to the UN General Assembly at the 2005 World Summit Meeting. He stated that security challenges in the twenty-first century range from infectious diseases, climate change, migration, terrorism, nuclear proliferation, and mass atrocities (Annan, 2005). East and Southeast Asia have confronted most of the security issues, including a few more, in the last three decades.

Economic Security

Economic security has figured as an important issue for a long time. Yet, the 1990s and early 2000s saw a significant shift in focus on an expanded version of economic security following the 1997–1998 Asian financial crisis to include sustainable economic growth and human security as a vital part of understanding the Asian experience. Governments in Thailand, China, Vietnam, and Singapore have paid attention to the economic security of the poor, as well as the rich, as a result of the negative impact of the Asian financial crisis. Thus, there seems to be an understanding that political stability and economic security are tied to human security. Political and economic elites realize they depend on the rural poor, who account for a majority of the population, for their own economic advancement (Nesadurai, 2012). Globalization has posed new challenges to the balance between economic development and human security by undermining the state's capacity to ensure economic security for its own population. Studies have shown that institutional capacity is key to meeting the challenges of globalization, not just at the national level, but also at the regional and international levels within the network of security organizations to which these states belong (Nesadurai, 2012). There has been a reckoning that no state can on its own mitigate the economic and human security problems engendered by globalization. At the regional level, tracking two mechanisms (intergovernmental cooperation) and tracking three mechanisms (cooperation between civil society organizations) can help negotiate new ways of dealing with security problems. However, the usefulness of multilateral security cooperation depends on each state's relationship with powerful nations, such as China or the United States. In the case of Taiwan, economic security is indistinguishable from national security due to its conflict with China. Another example is the decision by the Japanese government not to pursue the formation of the Asian Monetary Fund in the wake of the Asian financial crisis because the United States opposed the idea.

Environmental Security

The Asian region also faces a significant security threat from environmental disasters, both natural and human-caused. Security organizations in the region have been faced with several challenges in addressing the human security aspect of natural disasters. The principle of non-interference and the need to respond quickly to the negative impacts of earthquakes, tsunamis, and volcanoes makes it challenging to coordinate an organized multilateral response. Especially in areas with vulnerable populations and a low governmental capacity to respond, such as Indonesia, Myanmar, and the Philippines (Hauger, 2012). The difficulty in addressing environmental security threats and the consequences of climate change and natural disasters is partly due to the adherence to the non-intervention principle. While states and organizations can provide humanitarian aid, they cannot collectively address or criticize governments if they commit human rights abuses or discrimination against populations facing displacement and economic and human insecurity.

Global warming, as a result of unsustainable economic growth models due to the increased pressure of globalization, is particularly evident in the Asian region (Lane and Dieterlen 2017). Southeast Asian states have struggled to lift its vast populations out of poverty and have used unsustainable industrialization to address problems of poverty and economic growth (Bosello et al., 2016). The climate effects of fossil fuels and greenhouse gas emissions have led to environmental degradation that is particularly dangerous for Southeast Asian states, such as the Philippines and Indonesia, as sea levels rise as a result of rising temperatures. This could lead to serious national security issues, such as poor public health, displacement, and mass migration, which can affect the entire region (Harris, 2003). To mitigate these negative effects of globalization on global warming, some point to the importance of the ASEAN network in creating policies and mechanisms to increase the flow of aid to convert economies to the use of renewable energy and sustainable industrialization (Lee et al., 2013).

Covid-19

Covid-19 presented the Asian region with a number of security challenges spanning a wide spectrum from human security to public health security to economic security as the pandemic disproportionately hurt poor and disadvantaged population groups. Countries, such as the Philippines, already struggling with the capacity to address poverty and human and economic insecurity, were ill-prepared to respond to the negative impact of the pandemic. In fact, even countries, such as South Korea, China, and Japan, which have enjoyed a relatively high capacity in addressing public health and economic challenges, struggled as they resorted to shutting down their borders and stifling their economies to reduce the spread of the virus. The globalization component is very pertinent to the economic outcomes of the pandemic. Global production slowed, affecting supply chains. The lack of goods reaching consumers led to rising costs and financial strain, and eventually inflation and a rising cost of living. However, it did not lead to an increase in conflict between states in the region, rather the increase in conflict was seen between the United States and Europe on the one side and China on the other side, as China was viewed with suspicion regarding the origin of the virus.

In sum, the regional security cooperation in Asia faces a number of NTS threats and will continue to do so. However, traditional security threats may hinder further integration and cooperation in response to NTS issues.

Traditional Security Threats

The rise and pre-eminence of NTS as the primary concern for East and Southeast Asian countries may now take a back seat to traditional security threats, as China has taken an active role as a peace negotiator to the war in Ukraine, even as it has yet to condemn the actions by Russia. Many see this as a bid to rival the United States as a power player on the global stage, inserting itself in a conflict outside its own region. This move elevates the competition and enmity between the United States and China. The question is: what will this mean for a continued move towards regional cooperation on security in the Asia-Pacific region? And, how will small and medium states in the region try to balance against a rising China either collectively or through bilateral arrangements?

Most of the big crises facing the network of regional security operations in the next few years are related to a rising China with an assertive foreign policy agenda. The East and Southeast Asian region is facing numerous security challenges ahead. The first is related to territorial claims in the South China Sea and rising tensions between Taiwan and China. The second is related to China's posturing as a global superpower and alternative to Western, i.e., U.S. leadership. Scholars and political leaders are pointing to the real possibility of a Cold War 1.5. China's recent agreement with Russia to deepen its strategic partnership points is a sign that Beijing wants to project its own agenda and will not be as open to Western overtures (Al Jazeera, 2023). The third is related to China's agenda in the Pacific engendered in the Belt and Road Initiative. One such example is the Thai government's pivot towards China away from the United States. This move is directly attributable to the economic benefits Thailand expects to gain from this partnership (Ruengkitkrisin, 2019; Sawasdipakdi, 2021).

The South China Sea Dispute

The frontline of hegemonic tension between the U.S. and China is the dispute over the South China Sea. Before 2009, it was not a major policy issue, but escalating tensions over maritime boundaries and sovereignty have had an impact on the U.S.' bilateral relationship with several of the ASEAN countries. For some ASEAN states, China's claim to the South China Sea is perceived as a threat prompting them to strengthen their bilateral relationship with the United States as a deterrent against China's assertiveness and growing power in the region. The issue also had an effect on their collective relationship with the U.S. as seen in the invitation for the U.S. to join both the East Asia Summit (EAS) in 2012 and the ASEAN Defense Ministers Meeting-Plus (ADMM-Plus) in 2010. The constellation of relationships between the ASEAN members and the U.S. and China are dependent on differing national interests and existing economic, political, and security relationships. When the South China Sea was raised as an issue at the 6th EAS meeting in 2011, only Laos and Cambodia, both closely aligned with China, did not speak on the issue (Song, 2016). There had been attempts to raise the issue of the South China Sea since the 1990s. There were even serious efforts to create a regional Code of Conduct for the South China Sea, but the principles of consensus and dialogue paired with China's refusal to negotiate made the attempt unsuccessful. Instead, a weaker political agreement lacking enforcement mechanisms was reached in 2002; it was called the Declaration on the Conduct of Parties in the South China Sea. It took until 2012 for this declaration to be finally adopted due to differences among the members on various issues. In the end, the document only calls for "self-restraint in the conduct of activities that would complicate or escalate disputes and affect peace and stability" (ASEAN, 2012).

China is not the only country staking a claim to the South China Sea, the Philippines, Vietnam, Malaysia, and Brunei have all staked their own claims. ASEAN has remained neutral neither supporting nor opposing these claims. Thus, the multilateral network has yet to be effective in resolving any of these disputes. Under the Obama administration, U.S. policy on the South China Sea was articulated as one of growing concerns by then-Defense Secretary Robert Gates at the Shangri-La Dialog meeting in Singapore (Song, 2016). U.S. interests in the South China Sea are formulated as a commitment to free and open commerce. As the South China Sea is one of the most important shipping lanes in the world it is seen as vital that there is open access by all to the global commons of the sea. Thus, the U.S. takes any discrimination again U.S. corporations in pursuing legitimate economic activity seriously. These types of statements by U.S. officials were repeated in the various forums from EAS to ARF throughout the Obama administration to make it clear that the U.S. sees it in its national interests that there is open access to Asia's maritime commons and respect for international law in the South China Sea.

The issue is complex partly due to the geography of the South China Sea with multiple groupings of islands that are in some form subject to territorial claims or sovereignty disputes. The only undisputed islands are the Natuna islands which are firmly recognized as under Indonesian sovereignty. While the South China Sea is governed under the Law of the Sea, the claims to sovereignty of the land territory complicate the matter, because the maritime boundaries are calculated from land into the sea. Depending on which baseline is used, some of the disputed islands would be within that boundary (IMO, 1982). The issue goes back to the fact that Article 7 in the Law of Sea does not directly indicate how to apply straight baselines in areas with low water, and how close to one another or how far offshore islands need to be. Thus, Vietnam, China, and Taiwan have all defined extensive baselines from their coastlines that would give them sovereignty over the fringes of the islands. The two Archipelagic states, the Philippines and Indonesia, have also laid claim to baselines that would give them sovereignty over outlying islands. In fact, most of the coastal states bordering the South China Sea have laid broad claims to maritime jurisdictional zones (Schofield, 2016).

This leaves the question: Can the "Asian Way" of dialogue and consultation resolve these issues or are rule-bound agreements necessary? Looking at just the South China Sea issue from its first mention at an ASEAN meeting in 1992, the multilateral institutions that encompass the Asia-Pacific region have not been successful in resolving territorial claims through repeated actions of corporation and dialog in various areas, nor at curbing Chinese ambitions. Most of the progress has been through bilateral agreements, such as that between China and Vietnam in 2000 on the maritime boundary in the Gulf of Tonkin/Beibu Gulf, an agreement between Indonesia and Vietnam continental shelf boundary of 2003, the Indonesia and Singapore agreements in 1973 and 2009, and talks between Malaysia and Brunei about territorial sea boundaries in 2009 (Schofield, 2016). These agreements offer some hope that the "Asian Way" can be effective in resolving this issue going forward when states work bilaterally. The collection of medium and small Asian states faces a big dilemma in the South China Seas, with the maritime ASEAN countries at odds with China (Darmawan, 2021).

Multilateral agreements seem to be harder to reach, especially in the face of rising hegemonic tension between the U.S. and China. Part of China's regional posturing is to deter the United States from interfering in regional affairs. The biggest challenge to multilateral security cooperation is therefore the rise of China and its increasingly assertive foreign policy in the region, as it shifts the balance of power. Smaller states, even if operating collectively through the centrality network of ASEAN organizations, will need an outside power, like the U.S. to counter-balance China. If not, they will have to align themselves with China to survive. A third option is to find a way for the United States and China to share power in the region. The case study on the ARF and APEC will consider the ability of these organizations in facilitating a move towards closer security cooperation in the economic and political spheres.

The ARF and APEC Case Studies

The case study focuses on the efforts underway towards regional security cooperation via the ASEAN Regional Forum (ARF) and APEC's common collective culture of cooperation and security. While economic security may impinge on the cultural side of security, these case studies consider the challenges and questions being raised in this evolving new world, and how they will survive. Some argue that the existing cooperative framework within the organization of ASEAN, ARF, APEC, and beyond will not be successful in dealing with the security challenges brought on by globalization. In part, due to the lack of coherence and the principles of the dialogue, consensus, and non-interference approach, which make the institutions ill-equipped to deal handle the pressures of the age of globalization (Jones and Smith, 2001). Others argue that it is exactly due to these principles that security cooperation between a set of unequal and institutionally diverse states has managed to stave off intense conflict (Loke, 2005).

The role/impact of traditional and non-traditional security threats on the regional (ARF[2] and APEC[3]), international, and human security level of analysis is examined. The ARF, the political forum, and APEC, the economic forum, are based on the same principles of dialogue and consultation as ASEAN. Together, they are the core of a strategic framework for defining national security in East and Southeast Asia. The lack of deep institutionalization makes them less effective mechanisms, however, for conflict management and resolution (Tan, 2017). While the region is politically fragile due to the diverse nature of security threats and regimes, basic stability relies on U.S. military presence (Almonte, 1997). Yet, much will depend on the evolution of the U.S.–China relationship on regional economic and political issues going forward. The region will certainly face significant challenges in an increasingly globalized world.

The fact that Russia and China are both members of these organizations and have recently aligned themselves against Western dominance and U.S. bilateralism presents a challenge to the coherence and cooperation amongst the diverse member states of ARF and APEC. Russian President Vladimir Putin and Chinese President Xi Xipeng's joint statement in February 2022, ahead of the invasion in Ukraine, criticizing the efforts by the United States and its European allies "to impose their own democratic standards" and asserting that "such attempts at hegemony pose serious threats to global and regional peace and stability" (Kremlin, 2022) sends a strong message to China's Asian neighbors that China wants to set the agenda for regional cooperation.

ARF

The ARF was formed in 1994 with the idea that it would enhance security cooperation among its members evolving from a mechanism of confidence-building to preventive diplomacy until it would reach the stage of conflict resolution. It relies on track-two institutions, national-security think tanks and intellectual institutions, for informal dialogue and consultation (Almonte, 1997). However, China asked that conflict resolution be amended to "approaches to conflicts" because it saw the concept of conflict resolution as a Western invention, based on democratic principles to which it does not adhere (Tan, 2017). The ARF was not able to move beyond the confidence-building stage until 2011 due to differences in preferences between its democratic activist members advocating for concrete preventive diplomacy measures, such as the United States, the EU, Japan, Canada, and Australia, and some of its authoritarian members who see preventive diplomacy as a threat to their sovereignty, such as China, Myanmar, and Vietnam. The agreement to move forward with a preventive diplomacy work plan in 2011 was so conservatively worded that the decision-making ability of this diverse body has been seriously compromised. Rather than flexible consensus the requirement for any agreement is non-negotiable unanimity (Emmers and Tan, 2011; Tan, 2017).

The ARF's primary achievement has been to create a forum for the member countries to convene and regularize dialogue on various political and security issues, including the regional powers, China and the U.S. This worked well in the immediate post-Cold War era under Chinese leadership of Deng Xiaoping's "Bide our time" strategy and while the U.S. was focused on the War on Terror and its foreign policy objectives in the Middle East (Tan, 2017). There was an increase in cooperation on non-military security issues such as anti-terrorism, humanitarian assistance, and disaster relief in the immediate post-9/11 era. However, the ARF was not efficient in addressing other security issues such as North Korea's nuclear proliferation, rising tension between China and Taiwan, as well as territorial disputes in the East and South China seas. The period since 2009 with China's increasingly assertive foreign policy and the U.S. foreign policy pivot toward the Asia-Pacific region has brought the two great powers on a collision path and created more disunity and polarization amongst the ARF members. This constrains the ability of the ARF to move forward towards increased security cooperation to mitigate security threats that have arisen from Covid-19 to the War in Ukraine. In fact, both of those events have increased the tension and rivalry between the U.S. and China and minimized the ability of the ARF to serve as a forum for dialog and consultation, as members feel pushed to choose sides.

Another challenge to the ARF as an effective forum for security cooperation has been the creation of the Asian Defensive Ministers Meetings Plus (ADMM+) in 2010, which consists of 10 ASEAN countries plus Australia, China, India, Japan, Russia, the U.S., New Zealand, and South Korea. While its design is similar to ARF, to create cooperation on various security issues, a major difference is the scope and frequency of its military cooperation. There have been numerous military exercises held between the group's 18 members since its inauguration. Despite the level of coordination and cooperation, it has been unable to address the tensions in the South China Sea. The difficulty in curbing tensions between the maritime members and China, as well as the tension between China and the U.S., emphasizes the limits of regional security cooperation, despite the complex web of multilateral institutions at the regional and international levels.

Looking ahead, there are several areas where the ARF may become more of a battleground for great power-sparing than a forum for a peaceful resolution. There are already several examples of this. In 2010, China asserted the South China Sea represents a "core interest" that clashes with the U.S. foreign policy dedication to the free use of international shipping lanes, with specific reference to the South China Sea. Another example in 2014 was China's reclamation and militarization of the Spratly Islands. Both of these examples demonstrate the difficulty for ARF to create dialogue and consultation. While the idea of binding countries with opposing interests in networks of agreements can foster communication and cooperation, it can also have the opposite effect and stifle the ability of these organizations to create peaceful forums for resolution. Defensive realists would argue that to overcome these pressures, the best way forward would be to accommodate China as a rising power and look for ways in which the U.S. can create a power-sharing agreement with China on critical issues. Offensive realists would argue that there is no accommodation that can constrain Chinese ambitions and that the only way forward would be to assert American primary through bilateral agreements. The question remains whether the concept of security governors can provide a different approach to security governance at the regional and international levels in the current political climate of great power competition, the challenge to Taiwanese autonomy, and the tension in the South China Sea.

APEC

Economic security is at the heart of the APEC mission, but also one of the hardest areas to control due to the nature of the global economy. Take, for example, the 2008 financial crisis. The United States was at the heart of the crisis, while the APEC economies were for the most part spared. Yet, no country was completely spared due to the interconnectedness of global economies and international trade. Likewise, the Covid-19 pandemic, which brought about restrictions on travel and production, had a huge impact all around the globe. Thus, while multilateral institutions and cooperation are important for the function of the global economy, national economies are the key component of each state's national security. A state's ability to project power, regardless of size, rises and falls with its economic strength (Forman, 2012). There is one advantage here. Most of the APEC countries have a specific reference to the linkage between the economy, security, and power in their national security doctrines, thus facilitating their collaboration and dialog in this area. Nationalism in this sense can actually help push the APEC countries to cooperate on issues of economic security in their quest for national security objectives and their ability to project national power. Some scholars note the opportunity to frame climate change within this concept of economic power because climate change narrows the pathways to achieving sustainable development. Economic insecurity in turn diminishes national power. It is further argued that APEC is well situated to address the problems posed by climate change in the region due to the leadership role it has in addressing economic security (Hauger, 2012).

There are in fact many opportunities for APEC to go beyond its traditional focus on trade liberalization and economic cooperation to other areas of non-traditional security threats, such as public health and human security issues. APEC is well situated to address issues related to disaster management, food security, and health security all in the name of the negative long-term impacts all of these challenges have on regional economic development. There has been discussion about needing to provide a more formalized economic union, akin to the EU, as the natural next step for APEC to develop its economic cooperation. However, there are many obstacles to this idea, including the "Asian way" with its focus on sovereignty, non-interference, and preference for consultation over rules. Some have suggested other scenarios. An "OECD model" would focus on helping member states find suitable policy solutions while also coordinating a number of domestic and international policies for all members. This would create an opportunity to widen and deepen the partnership between member states without imposing an EU-like rule structure, as enforcement would be through peer pressure (Park and Lee, 2009). Another option would be for APEC to become an institution for security cooperation under the auspices of the human security agenda of APEC (McKay, 2006; Park and Lee, 2009). The idea would essentially entail creating a fourth pillar to represent these issues in addition to the existing pillars of Trade and Investment Liberalization and Facilitation (TILF), Business Facilitation, and Economic and Technical Cooperation (Ecotech). Formal adoption of security issues may face significant obstacles due to the highly sensitive nature of these issues and how it may clash with the preference for non-interference in the internal affairs of the member states. Human security is another issue that will be difficult for the APEC members to agree on.

Regardless of the challenges in finding an adequate approach to increase the scope of cooperation within APEC, it certainly still has the potential to be the most successful organization to increase areas of cooperation among member states, because the underlying focus on economic well-being speaks to both national, regional, and international agendas whether focused on power or security.

China and the U.S. are members of both organizations, which will likely lessen the ability of these organizations to effectively increase security cooperation in areas like the South China Sea and Taiwan. It could very easily have the same inability as the United Nations to come to binding agreements. So far membership in the ARF and APEC has not kept Chinese ambitions in check, it may actually have helped China, because of the emphasis on voluntary action and the principle of non-interference. However, APEC with its focus on economic security may fare better at providing pathways for cooperation, consultation, and dialog, as opposed to ARF with its focus on political issues.

Conclusion and Future Prospects

In conclusion, the "Asian Way" has been successful in a limited scope. Regional cooperation has been unable to find solutions for security challenges in a few key areas, such as the South China Sea, counterbalancing of Chinese foreign policy ambitions, and human security related to human rights abuses at the hands of authoritarian regimes. There have been no efforts to address the plight of the Rohingya people in Myanmar, the Uighur people in China, or the plight of political prisoners in Cambodia, to mention a few examples. While Asia faces a multitude of traditional and non-traditional security threats, the complex web of multilateral institutions designed to create a forum for dialogue and consultation has been most successful in addressing economic and environmental security threats.

On the negative side, the principle of non-interference leaves issues of human rights and human security outside the reach of these institutions. On the positive side, it does seem as if the principle of non-interference has lessened the risk of military confrontation between states. ASEAN countries have held joint military exercises with US, China, and Russia separately in recent years in pursuit of their goal to remain non-aligned and maintain stability in the region by not antagonizing foreign powers. The ASEAN-Russia Summit in Sochi in 2016 was part of the rapprochement ASEAN has pursued to enhance its bilateral relationships with powers outside the region in its continued quest for peace and stability. Thus, depending on the conception of security and the theoretical lens, multilateral institutions will appear either effective or ineffective.

The story of Asian multilateral security cooperation does not end here. In fact, there are many future challenges awaiting. Whereas optimists would have hoped that the move towards increasing security cooperation at the regional level would delimit security concerns to NTS issues, the analysis here demonstrates this is not the case. In fact, due to the rise of China and the hegemonic tension between the U.S. and China, the ARF and APEC along with the myriad of multilateral organizations within the ASEAN system face a number of traditional security challenges. Thus, future challenges for Asian security cooperation include:

1. How to balance their relationship with China and the U.S. as tensions rise. Can they remain non-aligned?
2. How to stay relevant if China takes on an aggressive role as the primary security actor in the Pacific, particularly if the relationship between China and the U.S. continues down the road of a "Cold War" framework?
3. How to keep the "Asian way" relevant to counter both NTS and TS issues?

The answers to these questions in part depend on the outcome of the Russian war in Ukraine. Many scholars and policymakers are drawing a direct line between the outcome for Ukraine and the possible Chinese invasion of Taiwan. The small and medium states in Southeast Asia have no available action in the War in Ukraine, yet the outcome can have an impact on the future of security cooperation in the entire Asia-Pacific region. Thus, the age of globalization has consequences for the range of actions available to East and Southeast Asian states in negotiating peace and stability and moving toward greater regional security cooperation.

Notes

1. The Association of Southeast Asian Nations was founded in Bango, Thailand on August 8, 1967. It consists of 10 member states: Brunei Darussalam, Cambodia, Indonesia, Lao PDR, Malaysia, Myanmar, Thailand, and Viet Nam. Its primary purpose is to facilitate effective decision-making and peaceful relations amongst member states and the ASEAN bodies. ASEAN also strives to develop friendly relations with external partners at the regional, sub-regional, and international levels.
2. The current participants in the ARF are as follows: Australia, Bangladesh, Brunei Darussalam, Cambodia, Canada, China, Democratic People's Republic of Korea, European Union, India, Indonesia, Japan, Lao PDR, Malaysia, Mongolia, Myanmar, New Zealand, Pakistan, Papua New Guinea, Philippines, Republic of Korea, Russia, Singapore, Sri Lanka, Thailand, Timor-Leste, United States, and Vietnam.
3. APEC countries are: Australia; Brunei Darussalam; Canada; Chile; People's Republic of China; Hong Kong, China; Indonesia; Japan; Republic of Korea; Malaysia; Mexico; New Zealand; Papua New Guinea; Peru; the Philippines; the Russian Federation; Singapore; Chinese Taipei; Thailand; the United States of America; Vietnam.

References

Al Jazeera. 2023. "Russia-China Ties Enter 'New Era' as Xi Meets Putin in Moscow." *Al Jazeera*. https://www.aljazeera.com/news/2023/3/21/chinas-xi-says-ties-with-russia-entering-new-era (May 1, 2023).

Almonte, Jose T. 1997. "Ensuring Security the 'ASEAN Way'." *Survival* 39 (4): 80–92.

Annan, Kofi. 2005. *In Larger Freedom: Towards Development, Security and Human Rights for All: Report of the Secretary-General*. UN. https://digitallibrary.un.org/record/550204 (April 26, 2023).

Avant, Deborah D., Martha Finnemore, and Susan K. Sell. 2010. *Who Governs the Globe?* Cambridge, UK, New York: Cambridge University Press.

Bosello, Francesco, Giacomo Marangoni, Carlo Orecchia, David A. Raitzer, and Massimo Tavoni. 2016. "The Cost of Climate Stabilization in Southeast Asia, a Joint Assessment with Dynamic Optimization and CGE Models." *MITP: Mitigation, Innovation and Transformation Pathways 251810*, Fondazione Eni Enrico Mattei (FEEM). https://ideas.repec.org/p/ags/feemmi/251810.html.

Buzan, Barry, and Ole Wæver. 2009. "Macrosecuritisation and Security Constellations: Reconsidering Scale in Securitisation Theory." *Review of International Studies* 35 (2): 253–276.

Buzan, Barry, Ole Wæver, and Jaap de Wilde. 1998. *Security: A New Framework for Analysis*. Boulder, CO: Lynne Rienner Pub.

Caballero-Anthony, Mely. 2018. *Negotiating Governance on Non-Traditional Security in Southeast Asia and Beyond*. New York: Columbia University Press. https://go.exlibris.link/T6cHzblM (February 10, 2023).

Caballero-Anthony, Mely. 2022. "The ASEAN Way and the Changing Security Environment: Navigating Challenges to Informality and Centrality | SpringerLink." *International Politics*. https://link-springer-com.hal.weber.edu/article/10.1057/s41311-022-00400-0 (February 10, 2023).

Darmawan, Aristyo Rizka. 2021. "ASEAN's Dilemma in the South China Sea." *Policy Forum*. https://www.policyforum.net/aseans-dilemma-in-the-south-china-sea/ (March 17, 2023).

ASEAN. 2012. "Declaration on the Conduct of Parties in the South China Sea." *ASEAN Main Portal*. https://asean.org/declaration-on-the-conduct-of-parties-in-the-south-china-sea-2/ (April 27, 2023).

Emmers, Ralf, and See Seng Tan. 2011. "The ASEAN Regional Forum and Preventive Diplomacy: Built to Fail?" *Asian Security (Philadelphia, Pa.)* 7 (1): 44–60.

Fleitz, Fred et al. 2016. *Warning Order: China Prepares for Conflict and Why We Must Do the Same*. Washington: Center for Security Policy Press.

Forman, Lori. 2012. "Economic Security in the APEC Region." In *From Apec 2011 to APEC 2012 American and Russian Perspectives on Asia Pacific Security and Cooperation*, eds. Rouben Azizian and Artyom Lukin. Asia-Pacific Center for Security Studies.

Harris, Paul G. 2003. *Global Warming and East Asia: The Domestic and International Politics of Climate Change*. Richmond: Routledge. https://go.exlibris.link/Rr8BczWJ (June 8, 2023).

Hauger, Scott. 2012. "Climate Change and Environmental Security in the Aisa-Pacific Region: A Role for APEC?" In *From Apec 2011 to APEC 2012: American and Russian Perspectives on Asia Pacific Security and Cooperation*, eds. Rouben Azizian and Artyom Lukin. Asia-Pacific Center for Security Studies.

Hebron, Lui, and John F.Stack Jr. 2016. *Globalization: Debunking the Myths*, third edition. Rowan & Littlefield Publishers. https://rowman.com/ISBN/9781442258211/Globalization-Debunking-the-Myths-Third-Edition (May 1, 2023).

Hettne, B. 2002. "Globalisation, Regionalisation and Security: The Asian Experience." *European Journal of Development Research* 14 (1): 28–46.

Jayasuriya, Kanishka. 2004. *Asian Regional Governance: Crisis and Change*. London: Routledge.

Jones, David M., and Mike L. Smith. 2001. "The Changing Security Agenda in Southeast Asia: Globalization, New Terror, and the Delusions of Regionalism." *Studies in Conflict & Terrorism* 24 (4): 271–288.

Kipgen, Nehginpao. 2020. *The Politics of South China Sea Disputes.* Taylor and Francis. https://go.exlibris.link/9RHLQlG0 (April 26, 2023).

Kirshner, Jonathan. 2012. "The Tragedy of Offensive Realism: Classical Realism and the Rise of China." *European Journal of International Relations* 18 (1): 53–75.

Kremlin. 2022. "Joint Statement of the Russian Federation and the People's Republic of China on the International Relations Entering a New Era and the Global Sustainable Development." *President of Russia.* http://en.kremlin.ru/supplement/5770 (April 25, 2023).

IMO. 1982. "United Nations Convention on the Law of the Sea." https://www.imo.org/en/OurWork/Legal/Pages/UnitedNationsConventionOnTheLawOfTheSea.aspx (May 1, 2023).

Lane, Jan-Erik, and Florent Dieterlen. 2017. "Climate Change in Asia and the Pacific: Challenges and Perspectives." *Asia Pacific Journal of Public Administration* 39 (4): 287–296.

Lee, Zhi Hua et al. 2013. "An Overview on Global Warming in Southeast Asia: CO2 Emission Status, Efforts Done, and Barriers." *Renewable & Sustainable Energy Reviews* 28: 71–81.

Loke, Beverly. 2005. "The 'ASEAN Way': Towards Regional Order and Security Cooperation? - Document - Gale General OneFile." *Melbourne Journal of Politics* 30.

McKay, John. 2006. *"The New Security Agenda & Emerging Concepts of Regional Resilience."* Presented at the Australian APEC Study Centre Consortium Conference, Vietnam. https://www.yumpu.com/en/document/view/31370218/the-new-security-agenda-emerging-concepts-of-regional-resilience (April 28, 2023).

Mearsheimer, John J. 2010. "The Gathering Storm: China's Challenge to US Power in Asia." *The Chinese Journal of International Politics* 3 (4): 381–396.

Mearsheimer, John J. 2014a. "Can China Rise Peacefully?" *The National Interest.* https://nationalinterest.org/commentary/can-china-rise-peacefully-10204 (April 26, 2023).

Mearsheimer, John J. 2014b. *The Tragedy of Great Power Politics.* New York: Norton.

Nesadurai, Helen E., ed. 2012. *Globalisation and Economic Security in East Asia.* Routledge. https://www.taylorfrancis.com/books/9781134190447 (April 25, 2023).

Park, Sung-Hoon, and Jeong Yeon Lee. 2009. "APEC at a Crossroads: Challenges and Opportunities." *Asian Perspective* 33 (2): 97–124.

Raditio, Klaus Heinrich. 2019. *Understanding China's Behaviour in the South China Sea: A Defensive Realist Perspective.* Singapore: Palgrave Macmillan. https://go.exlibris.link/DHTt67Kg (April 26, 2023).

Ruengkitkrisin, Supansa. 2019. "The cooperation of Thailand and China under the Belt and Road Initiative: A Thai Perspective." 对外经济贸易大学.

Sawasdipakdi, Pongkwan. 2021. "Thailand's Engagement with China's Belt and Road Initiative: Strong Will, Slow Implementation." *Asian Perspective* 45 (2): 349–374.

Schofield, Clive. 2016. "Untangling a Complex Web: Understanding Competing Maritime Claims in the South China Sea." In *The South China Sea Dispute: Navigating Diplomatic and Strategic Tensions,* ed. Cheng-Yi Lin. Singapore: ISEAS Publishing. https://hal.weber.edu/login?url=https://search.ebscohost.com/login.aspx?direct=true&db=e025xna&AN=2030468&site=ehost-live (April 27, 2023).

Song, Yann-Huei. 2016. "The South China Sea Dispute: In U.S.-ASEAN Relations." In *The South China Sea Dispute: Navigating Diplomatic and Strategic Tensions*, ed. Lin Cheng-Yi. Singapore: ISEAS Publishing.

Tan, See Seng. 2017. "A Tale of Two Institutions: The ARF, ADMM-Plus and Security Regionalism in the Asia Pacific." *Contemporary Southeast Asia* 39 (2): 259–264.

Index

Page numbers in **bold** refer to figures.

Abe, Shinzo 72, 76, 76–77
Abu Sayaf group 99
Aceh 5, 54, 58
Acharya, Amitav 8
Action-reaction model 37
AEC 79
Afghanistan 20–21, 23, 57, 58–59, 59, 60, 61, 65, 89, 95, 97, 118, 124
Ahmad, Mobin-ud-Din 119
Ahmad, Mumtaz 56
Alagappa, Muthiah 34–35, 52, 57
alliance politics 40
al Qaeda 10, 59, 60, 61, 65n9
American Institute in Taiwan 42
Amul, Gianna Gayle 140
An, Brian Y. 141
Annan, Kofi 150
Anti-Access Area Denial (A2AD) 38
antiquities trade 97
anti-OC campaigns 90
anti-terrorist measures 10, 60 61; and human rights 62–63; international cooperation 61–62; kinetic 60–61; militarization 63; negotiated peace 63–64
APEC Business Advisory Committee 73
arms race 9, 37–38
artificial intelligence 36, 64
ASEAN+1 79
ASEAN+3 72, 73, 75, 84, 101, 102n2
ASEAN+3 Economic Ministerial Meeting 74
ASEAN+6 73, 74, 75, 84
ASEAN-centrality 77–78, 79
ASEAN Defense Ministers Meeting-Plus 153, 157

ASEAN Ministries Meeting on Environment 124
ASEAN Regional Forum (ARF) 11, 72–73, 146–147, 155–156, 156–157, 160n1
ASEAN-Russia Summit 159
ASEAN Senior Officials on Environment 124
ASEAN State of Climate Change Report 124–125
ASEAN Summit, 2011 77–78
ASEAN, Treaty of Amity and Cooperation (TAC) 75
ASEAN Way 21, 23, 146, 148–149
Ashraf, ASM Ali 63
Asia 14, 16–17, **18**
Asia-Pacific 11, 17, 33, 36, 37, 40–41, 44, 57, 70, 71, 73, 75, 77, 146, 149–150, 152, 154, 156, 160
Asian Financial Crisis, 1997 22, 72, 149, 151
Asian Infrastructure Investment Bank 2, 12n6
Asian landmass 16
Asian Monetary Fund (AMF) 72, 151
Asian Pacific Economic Cooperation (APEC) 11, 84, 146–147, 155–156, 157–159, 160n3
Asian Security, definition 1–2
Asian Tigers 19, 100
Asian Values 58
Asian Way 11, 147–148, 154, 158, 159
Asia-Pacific Economic Cooperation (APEC) 10, 70, 71, 73, 74, 75, 82
Association of Southeast Asian Nations (ASEAN) 19, 22–23, 36, 37, 53, 75, 101, 102n1, 143, 150, 152;

anti-communist interests 57; anti-terrorist measures 62; China FTA 72; corporate culture 146; COVID-19 epidemic responses 140–141; environmental threat response 124–125; expansion 21; limits 140–141; members 160n1; members economic growth 57–58; negotiations with China 27; Our Eyes Initiative 62; and piracy 99; regional institutionalism 28; regional security cooperation 147–148, 148–149, 155; strategic network 46; unity in diversity principles 56
Asuncion, Ruben Carlo 121
AUKUS 25
Aung San Suu Kyi 35
Australia 2, 25, 40, 72–73, 80–81
authoritarian regimes 17, 56
authoritarianism 58
Autonomous Region of Muslim Mindanao 58
Avant, Deborah 148

Ba'asyir, Abu Bakar 56
Babbar Khalsa International (BKI) 54
Balakrishnan, Vivian 104
balance of power 4, 24, 37, 155
Bangladesh 109, 111, 117
Bangsamoro Autonomous Region in Muslim Mindanao (BARMM) 63
Bangsamoro Islamic Freedom Fighters (BIFF) 63
Beijing Consensus 2, 12n7
Belt and Road Initiative 2, 12n5, 26, 46, 94, 153
Beydoun, Khaled A. 63
Bharat Raj Paudyal 118
Bhutan 107, 109, 117–118
Bianchi, Sarah 82
Biden, Joe 14, 25, 82
Bill and Melinda Gates Foundation 125
bin Laden, Osama 59
biocapacity, decreasing 107
biodiversity 106, 117
Bollyky, Thomas J. 137
Booth, Kenneth 39–40
borderless landscape 1
borders, transparency 7
BRIC Plus 80
BRICS 40, 79–80
Brunei 153
Buddhism 54
Burma 1, 5, 10, 35, 88, 92, 94, 97, 101

Bryja, Thomas 7
bubonic plague 133
Bunge, Mario 15
Busby, Joshua 104, 105, 106
Business Facilitation, and Economic and Technical Cooperation 158

Caballero-Anthony, Mely 132
Caliphate 58–59, 64
Cambodia 20, 94, 97, 109, 116, 117, 117–118, 153
Campbell, Joel 10
Canada 2
capacity building 138
carbon dioxide (CO_2) emissions 105, 106, 107, 109, 125n3
Catholicism 54
Center for Strategic and International Studies (CSIS) 26, 45
Central Asia 2
central authority, absence of 4
Chellaney, Brahma 58
chemical, biological, radioactive, nuclear and explosive weapons (CBRNE) 62
child trafficking 98
Chile 2
China 23, 66n12, 155–156, 159; accession to CPTTP 80–81; anti-corruption programs 101; Anti-Foreign Sanctions Law 83; and APEC 159; and the ARF 155–156, 156–157; arms race 38; ASEAN Free Trade Agreement 72; assertiveness 45–46; attitude toward multilateralism 143; authoritarianism 26; Belt and Road Initiative 2, 12n5, 26, 46, 94, 153; Blocking Statute 83; Blue-Water Navy 3, 12n9; Center for Disease Control 136; China-Central Asia Summit 26; coercive governance 35; COVID-19 epidemic 140, 141–142, 152; economic growth 19; economic policies 24–25; economic reforms 19, 21; economic security 150; emerging technologies 40–41; Entity List registration provisions 82; environmental degradation 107; export control laws 82–83; Five-Year Plan 45; foreign policy 14, 152–153, 155, 159; Free Trade Agreements 72, 73, 82; GDP 19, 22; globalization and environmental quality 107; globalization level 109; Global Security Initiative 26; greenhouse gas emissions 7, 109, 111, **111, 112**, 115;

Index 165

health assistance 140; human rights abuses 159; human trafficking 95; imperialistic ambitions 3; Indo-Pacific strategy 40; industrial strategy 24–25; intellectual property theft 95, 95–96; Made in China 2025 industrial strategy 24–25; Military-Civil Fusion (MFC) Development Strategy 41, 45; military power 3, 9, 12n9, 21, 23, 33, 46; military spending 33; Ministry of Commerce 81; NCD governance 138; Nine Dash Line 27; nuclear weapons 33; One China policy 42, 45; Open Door policy 93; opening 19; organized crime 89, 90, 93, 94, 95, 95–96, 101; priorities 10; rapprochement with USA 20; regional posturing 155; relations with Japan 72–73; relations with the Philippines 27; relations with USA 22, 22–27, 27–28, 30n8, 33, 36, 38, 44–45, 72–75, 75–77, 82–83, 84, 147, 150, 152, 153–155, 156–157, 160; relations with Vietnam 27; rise of 2–3, 11, 14, 19, 21, 22, 23, 33, 37, 40, 72–75, 84, 147, 149, 150, 160; Russo–Ukrainian War role 152; SARS epidemic 133, 134–136; and sea-level rise 120–121, 121; Sino-Soviet Split 20; Taiwan policy 26, 41–45, 153; tariff reductions 79–80; territorial claims 149; threat 3; transport revolution 100; water disputes 124; wolf warrior diplomacy 46; WTO accession 21, 72
China-Central Asia Summit 26
China Sea Level Bulletin 120–121
China Threat Theory 3, 12n8
Chinese Civil War 17–18
Chinese sweeteners 93
civil approach 6
Clash of Civilization
Clausewitz, Carl von 34
climate change 11, 104, 105, 123, 125, 151–152, 158; and food security 116–117; and sea-level rise 11, 119–122; and water security 119
climate financing 125
Climate Risk Assessment (World Bank) 117
Clinton, Bill 23, 71, 83
Code of Conduct for the South China Sea 153
Cold War 5, 6, 14, 17–21, 22, 37, 38–39, 40, 52, 57, 84, 96, 150
collaborative culture 2
collective defense 37

collective security 37
Colombia 89
colonialism 20
communications 7, 36
communist influence 19–20
communist insurrections 19–20
community security 8
Comprehensive and Progressive Agreement for Trans-Pacific Partnership (CPTPP) 80–81, 81–82, 84
Comprehensive Economic Partnership for East Asia (CEPEA) 73
comprehensive security 52
confrontation, culture of 22
Confucianism 54
Confucius Institutes 3, 12n10
Congress Party 56
constructivism 92, 148
constructivist 148
cooperative security 21
corruption 89, 92–93, 98, 100–101
Costa, Antonio Maria 89, 96–97
counterfeiting 90
counterforce (Chinese term for A2AD) 38
counter-terrorism 62–63, 73
counter-terror 53
COVID-19 epidemic 10, 11, 14, 24, 25, 27, 94, 98, 139–142, 152, 158
Criezis, Meili 64
crime-terror-insurgency nexus 95
criminal justice theories 91–92
crisis escalation 38
critical terrorism studies 52
cultural conflicts 2, 7
Curley, Melissa 132
cyberattacks 64
cybercrime 96

Dabla-Norris, Era 105
Daniel, James 105
Declaration on the Conduct of Parties in the South China Sea 153
decolonization 19–20
de-globalization 22
deep institutionalization, lack of 155
defensive realists 147, 157
deglobalization 9, 14, 15, 22–27, 27
Democratic People's Republic of Korea (DPRK) 18, 96
Deng Xiaoping 94, 156
deterrence 6, 35–36, 38–39, 41
deterrence theory 91
digital disinformation campaigns 64
digital trade 80

disease surveillance systems 135
diversity 149
Doha Agreement/Round 61
domestic strife 5
drone strikes 59–60
drug trafficking 88, 89, 94, 97–98

East Asia 1
East Asia Free Trade Agreement (EAFTA) 73
East Asian Economic Caucus (EAEC) 71
East Asia Summit 75, 153
East Timor 35, 55
Ecological Threat Report 60–61
economic cooperation 23, 33, 71, 77–80
economic development 34–35, 53, 100, 121
economic disparities 70
economic elites 150–151
economic growth 22–23, 57–58, 94, 121, 150, 151; China 19
economic interdependence 6, 37
economic power 9
economic problems 7
economic security 8, 10, 82–83, 84, 150–151, 155, 157–159
economic strength 158
economic threats 10, 70–83; and economic cooperation 77–80; Future Prospects 84; and globalization 82–83; rise of China 72–75; U.S. East Asia policy 75–77; U.S. foreign economic policy 81–82; U.S. hegemony 71–72, 84
Economy 139–140
Eisuke, Sakakibara 72
emerging technologies 40–41
End of History 21
environmental quality: and globalization 11, 106–107, 108; and greenhouse gas emissions 109, **110**, 111–112, **111, 112, 113, 114**, 115, **115**
environmental security 8, 104, 105–106, 151–152
environmental standards 80
environmental threats 7, 11, 60–61, 104–125, 151–152; containment 123; climate change 11, 104, 105, 116, 123; climate financing 125; floods and flooding 118, 119, 121; to food security 115–117, 122–123; future prospects 122–125; and globalization 106–109, **108, 110**, 111–112, **111, 112,**
113, 114, 115, **115**, 122; levels 123; and military security 121–122; natural disasters 124; persistence 124; sea-level rise 11, 119–122, 151–152; as security threats 105–106; theoretical orientation 105–106; to water security 117–119, 122–123
ethnic conflict 5
ethno-nationalism 10, 54
European Union 141
Europe, Cold War 19
EU Way 146

Facal, Gabriel 63
Federally Administered Tribal Areas (FATA), Pakistan 60, 61
Fidler, David P. 132
Financial Action Task Force (FATF) 61–62
financial crisis, 2008 23, 157–158
Finkelstein, M. David 38
Finnemore, Martha 148
fisheries 117
flexible consensus 21
floods and flooding 118, 119, 121
Fog of War 34, 46
food security 8, 11, 115–117, 122–123
former Soviet Republics 2
Freedman, Lawrence 38
Free Papua Movement (OPM) 55
free trade 7
Free Trade Agreements 72, 73, 77–78, 82
Free Trade Area of the Asia-Pacific (FTAAP) 73–74, 75
Fukushima Daiichi nuclear accident 124
Fukuyama, Francis 21
Fukuya, Shu 10

G8 132
Gates, Robert 154
General Agreement on Tariffs and Trade (GATT) 77
GDP 19, 22, 24, 57, 60, 78, 121
general deterrence 39
geoeconomics 1, 3, 6
geopolitical calculations 9
geopolitics 1, 3, 6, 57
Global Footprint Network 107
global government, absence of 4
globalization 1, 3, 5–6, 10, 14; characteristics 6–7; definition 106; dominant trend 22–23; and economic threats 82–83; and environmental quality 11, 106–107, 108; and environmental threats 106–109, **108,**

168 *Index*

110, 111–112, **111, 112, 113, 114**, 115, **115**, 122; and health threats 131, 132–133; measurement 107–108; organized crime, transnational 89, 92–96, 100; regional security cooperation and 148, 149–150; security threats 7; and terrorism 53–54
globalization scores 107–108, **108**, 109, 111–112
Global Security 8
Global Security Initiative 26
global supply chain 17, 21, 26, 27
global village 8
Global War on Terror 10, 23, 59–60, 62 globalization
golden triangle 92, 97–98
Gorbachev, Mikhail 20–21
Gourevitch, Peter 28
governance, coercion in 34–35
Great East Japan Earthquake 124
great power competition 38, 41
greenhouse gas emissions 7, 105, 107, 109, **110**, 111–112, **111, 112, 113, 114**, 115, **115**, 122, 125n3, 151
Gutierrez, Antonio 119, 123
Gygli, Savina 106

hard power 4
health care 138
health development assistance 137
health governance infrastructure 143
health security 8, 11, 131, 132–133, 136, 142–143
health threats 2, 7, 11, 131–143; conceptualization 131–133; costs 136; COVID-19 epidemic 10, 11, 14, 24, 25, 27, 94, 98, 139–142; disease surveillance systems 135; economic effects 133; future prospects 142–143; and geopolitical competition 140; and globalization 131, 132–133; historical 133; infectious diseases 137; misinformation 135; non-communicable diseases 11, 136–139; SARS epidemic 11, 133, 133–136, 140, 142; state capacity framework 141; structural issues 139; vulnerability 131
Hebron, Lui 146
Hekmatyar, Gulbuddin 57
Hinduism 54–56
Hindu nationalism 56, 62–63
historical context 9
Hong Kong 95–96, 101; rise of 19; SARS epidemic 134, 136

hub-and-spokes bilateral security structure 46, 47n5, 71
human condition approach 6
Human Development Report (UNDP) 8
humanitarian disaster relief 35
human rights 58; abuses 149, 151, 159; and anti-terrorist measures 62–63
human security 8, 54–55, 106, 132, 148, 150, 151, 158–159, 159
human trafficking 89, 94, 95, 97, 98–99, 100
Huntington, Samuel P. 37
hydro-politics 124
Hyun, In-Taek 105–106

illegal businesses 87–88
illiberal democracy 17
illicit trade 89–90
immediate deterrence 39
imperialism 20
independence movements 19–20
India 54, 55, 57, 66n15; anti-Sikh riots 54; GDP 19; globalization and environmental quality 107; globalization score 111; and Global War on Terror 59–60; greenhouse gas emissions 7, 109, **111, 112**, 115; health assistance 140; Hindu nationalism 62–63; Indo-Pacific strategy 40; Islamophobia 62–63; nuclear-weapons 59–60; occupation of Kashmir 58; partition 56; Public Safety Act 63; and religion 56; and rise of China 72–73; transport revolution 100; water disputes 124; withdrawal from RCEP 79
Indochina 20
Indonesia 20, 27, 54, 55, 58, 60, 148; anti-terrorist measures 62, 63; economic growth 57–58; environmental security 151; GDP 19; greenhouse gas emissions 7, 109, 112; organized crime 95; piracy 99; radical Islamic fringe 56; rise of 21; and sea-level rise 120; South China Sea claims 154
Indo-Pacific 2
Indo-Pacific Economic Framework (IPEF) 80, 81–82, 84
industrialization 22–23, 151
infectious diseases 137
Institute for Health Metrics and Evaluation 137
Institute of Economics and Peace 63
institutional capacity 151

Institutionalists 147
intellectual property theft 80, 95, 95–96
intelligence, surveillance, and reconnaissance (ISR) capabilities 33
interconnectedness 6, 8, 11, 27, 131, 146, 158,
interdependent 8, 22
Intergovernmental Panel on Climate Change 123
internal colonization 54
internal disturbances 5
internal security 20, 55
Internal Security Act (ISA) 55
internally driven threats 5
international cooperation, anti-terrorist measures 61–62
International Health Regulations (IHR) 135
International Monetary Fund 105
international political economy 1, 3
International Relations 1, 3, 15, 30n2
"International Situation and the Military Strategic Guidelines" (Finkelstein) 38
internationalist perspective 6
Inter-Services Intelligence (ISI) 57
Iraq 23
irredentism 2, 5, 7
Ishigaki Strait 17
Islam, Md Monirul 117
Islamic State (IS) 59, 60, 61, 64, 66n10
Islamic State-Khorasan Province (ISK) 60
Islamization 55–56
Islamophobia 62–63

James, Patrick 9
Janatha Vimukthi Peramuna (JVP) 55
Japan 152; Asian Financial Crisis, 1997 72; and CPTPP 80–81; economic miracle 19; economic security 151; economic stagnation 21–22; GDP 19; globalization and environmental quality 106–107; Great East Japan Earthquake 124; greenhouse gas emissions 7, 109, 111, **111, 112**, 115; Indo-Pacific strategy 40; organized crime 90, 101; priorities 10, 70; relations with China 72–73; relations with USA 71–72, 76–77; tariff reductions 79; Trans-Pacific Partnership Agreement (TPP) 75–76; transport revolution 100
Jemaah Islamiyah (JI) 56, 60, 63, 64
Jervis, Robert 37, 40

Jihad 57–59, 65
Johnston, Alastair I. 23

Kamphausen, Roy 16
Kashmir 58, 60, 64
Keo, Chenda 98–99
Kim, Sung-Han 105–106
kinetic measures 61
Kirby, Mac 119
KOF Globalization Index 107–108, **108**
Korean Peninsula 17
Korean War 18, 19, 20
Krishnan, Nisha 104, 105
Kwok, Sharon I. 93

labor standards 80
Lally, Mike, Lally, Mike 122
Laos 20, 94, 97, 116, 117–118, 153
laser technology 40–41
Lashkar-e-Taiba (LeT) 60
Law of Sea 154
Lebow, Richard 39
Lee, Minsoo 121
legal codes 55
Leon, Joshua K. 140
lethal autonomous weapons 36
Levin-Banchik, Luba 11
liberal
liberalism
liberalist
liberalist/internationalist perspective 6–7, 147–148
Liberation Tigers of Tamil Eelam (LTTE) 54, 58, 59, 63
lifestyle diseases 136–139
Lin, Hen-I. 116
Lionel, Baixas 54
Liu, Zongyuan Zoe 10
Li, Yitan 9
Lo, T. Wing 90, 93
Lombok and Sunda Straits 17
Loong, Lee Hsien 120
Luzon Strait 17

Maastricht Globalization Index 107
Maddock, Rowland Thomas 105
Made in China 2025 24
Mafia 7, 88, 90–91, 100
Magnusson, Roger 137
Malaysia 20, 55, 57–58, 60, 62, 71, 153
Manila Pact 19
Maoist Communist Party of India (CPI) 55
Mao Zedong 20

170 Index

Marcos, Ferdinand Romualdez 104, 116
Marawi siege 64
maritime piracy 10, 87, 92, 99
maritime security 26, 26–27, 28
maritime trade 17, **18**
market capitalism 10
Marxist OC theories 91
Maute Group 63–64
Merkl, Peter 53
Mexico 2
Middle Eastern Respiratory Syndrome (MERS) 140, 142
Middle Eastern studies 2
middle income trap 24
Military-Civil Fusion (MFC) Development Strategy 41
military deterrence 4, 38–39, 41
military influence, expansion of 35–36
military power 4, 9; China 3, 9, 12n9, 21, 23, 33, 46; and cross-strait conflict 41–45; defensive capabilities 36; emerging technologies 36; emphasis on 34; rise of 36; role 35; and statecraft 35; status 34; theoretical background 34–36; threat 37; United States of America 35–36
military spending, China 33
military threats, traditional 9–10, 33–46, 37–38; action-reaction model 37; arms race and weapons proliferation 37–38; background 33–34; cross-strait conflict 41–45; deterrence 4, 38–39, 41; future prospects 46; inadvertent escalations 36; key issue areas 36–41; preparedness model 38; spiral model 37, 38; theoretical background 34–36
Modi, Narendra 62–63, 66n15
Moïsi, D. 6
money laundering 62
moral panics 99
Morgan, Patrick 39
Moro Islamic Liberation Front (MILF) 58
mujahideen 58–59, 65n6
multilateralism 10, 21, 70, 143
Muslim
Muslim League 56
mutually assured destruction 39
Myanmar/Burma 35, 54, 64, 94, 97–98, 107, 140, 149, 151, 159
Mykhalovskiy, Eric 134

National Footprint and Biocapacity Accounts 125n1
national identity 56
national interest 35
National League for Democracy (NLD) 94
National Liberation Front of Tripura 58
nationalism 4, 20, 24, 26, 42, 58, 71, 94, 158
national security 3, 4, 7, 37, 46, 52, 92–96, 151
national security doctrines 158
Nationalist Socialist Council of Nagaland-Isak-Muivah (NSCN-IM) 58
national unity 54–55
nation-building 61
natural disasters 2, 7, 124
Nepal 109, 111, 117–118, 124
New Cold War 22–27, 27, 28, 33
New People's Army (NPA) 55
New Zealand 2, 140
Nikai Shock 74
Nikai Toshihiro 74
Nine Dash Line 27
Nixon, Richard 20
Non-Aligned Movement 20
non-communicable diseases 11, 136–139
non-interference 11, 56, 75, 141, 143, 147, 149, 151, 155, 158, 159
non-state actors, rise of 6
non-state political threats 10
non-traditional (contemporary) security threats 5–8, 8–9, 11, 14, 150–152; regional security cooperation 147–148, 149
North Atlantic Treaty Organization 37
North Korea 18, 20, 21, 87, 96; nuclear weapons 39, 71, 156
Nozaki, Masahiro 105
Nuclear Non-Proliferation Treaty 60
nuclear weapons: China 33; India 59–60; North Korea 39, 71, 156; proliferation 39; United States of America 35–36
Nye, Jr., Joseph S. 4

Obama, Barack 14, 74, 75, 76, 154
official development assistance 132
Olomi, Ali A. 57
Olsen, Cameron 10
One China policy 42, 45
open markets 7
open regionalism 21
Operation Searchlight 55
organized crime, transnational 2, 7–8, 10, 87, 87–101; activities 88–89, 94, 96–99; anti-OC campaigns 90; China 89, 90, 93, 94, 95, 95–96; and COVID-19 epidemic 94; crime-terror-insurgency

nexus 95; definition 88; drug trafficking 88, 89, 94, 97–98; external actors 95; film and TV images 87; future prospects 100–101; globalization 89, 92–96, 100; human trafficking 89, 94, 97, 98–99, 100; illegal businesses 87–88; illicit trade 89–90; images of 87–88; levels of analysis 92; and national security 92–96; patron–clientelism 91–92; piracy 88, 89, 99; security threat 89, 92–96; seriousness of problem 89; theoretical approaches 91–92; traditional gang organizations 87, 88; transformation 89–90
Ortuoste, Maria 10
Our Eyes Initiative 62
overfishing 7

Pakistan 55, 56, 60; anti-communist stance 57; Federally Administered Tribal Areas (FATA) 60, 61; food security 117; globalization score 111–112; Inter-Services Intelligence (ISI) 57; population 119; water disputes 124; water security 117–118; water stress 118–119
Panayotou, Theodore 106
pandemic 2, 7, 8, 14, 24–25, 27, 94, 98, 132, 140, 142, 148, 152, 158
Parashar, Swati 52
Patel, Jay 140
partition 56, 63
patron–clientelist studies 91
Paul, T.V 39
peace dividends 21
Pelosi, Nancy 26, 42–43
people-centered focus 6
Peoples, Columba 53
People's Republic of China (PRC) 4, 18, 41, 141, 160n3
personal security 8
Peru 2
Peterson Institute for International Economics 24
Pham Binh Minh 104
Philippines, the 20, 25, 55, 59, 63–64, 148; anti-terrorist measures 62; Autonomous Region of Muslim Mindanao 58; counter-insurgency operations 57; COVID-19 epidemic 140, 152; environmental security 151; food security 116; greenhouse gas emissions 115; military uprising, 2001 35; organized crime 95; piracy 99;

relations with China 27; and sea-level rise 121; South China Sea claims 153, 154; US security alliance 30n7
piracy 88, 89, 99
pivot to Asia 14, 75, 83
policing 87
policy cooperation 33
political elites 150–151
political instability 5
political security 8
political survival 52, 53, 54–55, 65
political threats, non-state 10
political violence 51–54, 58; *see also* terrorism
pollution 107
population growth 105
post-Cold War 9, 11, 14, 23, 33, 46, 71, 83, 94, 146, 150, 156
post-colonial states 20–21
post-Soviet communist regimes 17
Potter, Lyman 88
poverty 12n12, 12n13, 151
power alignment 10
preparedness model 38
Price-Smith, Andrew T. 133, 141
primary health care 138
Proliferation Security Initiative (PSI) 62
Protestantism 54
proxy wars 19–20, 20
public disobedience 5
Pun, Ngai 133
Putin, Vladimir 156

Quadrilateral Security Dialogue 37, 40, 46, 72

Rajah Solaiman Movement 63
Ramakrishna, Kumar 64
rare earth mining 97
Raymond, Gina 82
Reagan, Ronald 42
realism 147
realist
realpolitik framework 4
Regime de la Terreur 52
Regional Comprehensive Economic Partnership (RCEP) 73, 78–79, 81–82, 84
regional focus 1
regional institutionalism 28
regionalism 22–23, 84; emergence of 10, 72–75
regionalization 10, 22 101, 149
regional organizations, web of 149

regional security cooperation 1, 8–9, 11, 146–160; APEC 146–147, 155–156, 157–159; ARF 146–147, 155–156, 156–157; conceptualization 146–147; COVID-19 epidemic 152; economic security 150–151, 155; environmental security 151–152; evolution 148–149; future challenges 159–160; future prospects 159–160; globalization and 148, 149–150; moving towards 150; non-traditional security threats 147–148, 149, 150–152; security governance 148; South China Sea Dispute 153–155; theoretical approaches 147–148; traditional security threats 152–155; relations with USA 157–159; *see also* Association of Southeast Asian Nations (ASEAN)
religion 55–56
Republic of China (ROC)
Republic of Korea (ROK)
Ricardo, David 77
Rim, Hyun Ji 9–10
risk management 27
Roberts, Brad 36
Roberts, Sean 66n12
Rohingya 5, 35, 159
rule-based partnership 149
Russia 36, 66n12, 89, 153, 155–156, 159
Russian Mafia 95–96
Russo–Ukrainian War 14, 26, 45, 150, 152, 160

San Francisco System 19, 21
SARS epidemic 11, 133, 133–136, 140, 142
Savoy, Connor M. 7
Schori Liang, Christina 64
Schulte-Bockholt, Alfredo 91
sea lanes 17, **18**
sea-level rise 11, 119–122, 151–152
security: definition 8; key issue areas 36–41; theoretical background 34–36
security actors, proliferation of 148
security architecture 17–22
security community 70
security cooperation 159–160
security dilemma 10, 38, 39–41
security environment 8–9
security governance 148
security governors 148
security reconfiguration 14
security structure 37
security threats: conceptualization 3–4, 148; environmental threats as 105–106

Sell, Susan 148
semiconductor 40–41
September 11, 2001 terrorist attacks 14, 23, 54, 73
Severe Acute Respiratory Syndrome (SARS) 2, 7, 11, 12n3, 131, 133–136
Shanghai 95–96
Shangri-La Dialog, Singapore 154
Sharia Law 56
Shaw, Rajib 121
Shwe Kokko Yatai New City project 94
Siddique, Mohammad Abu Baker 117
Siegel, Dana 93
Sikh 54
Singapore 27, 55, 101, 106–107; economic growth 57–58; economic security 150; globalization score 111–112; greenhouse gas emissions 109; rise of 19; and sea-level rise 120; Shangri-La Dialog 154; water stress 118
Singapore Strait 89
Singer, J. David 38
Sino-Soviet Split 20
Snyder, Glenn 39, 40
So, Alvin Y 133
social disorganization theories 91
social media 64
social network theory 91
societal threats 2, 7
soft power 4
soft regionalism 21
solidarity 54
South Asia 1
South China Sea 25, 26–27, 27, 28, 36, 99, 122, 153–155, 157, 159
Southeast Asia 1
Southeast Asian Regional Center for Counter-Terrorism's (SEARCCT) 62
Southeast Asian Treaty Organization (SEATO) 19, 20
South Korea 18, 21; COVID-19 epidemic 152; economic stagnation 22; food security 116; GDP 19; globalization and environmental quality 106–107; globalization score 111; greenhouse gas emissions 7, 109, 112; Indo-Pacific strategy 40; organized crime 101; rise of 19; water stress 118
sovereignty 4, 26, 26–27, 53, 54, 135, 149, 158
Soviet Union 20–21
spiral model 37, 38
Sridhar, Devi 140
Sri Lanka 54, 55, 59, 63, 107, 118

Index 173

stability 35
Stack Jr., John F. 146
Stalin, Joseph 20
state-building 52
state capacity framework 141
state-centric perspective 1, 4
statecraft, and military power 35
The State of Food Security and Nutrition in the World 2022 (United Nations) 115
state, the 51; monopoly of legitimate violence 51–54; political survival 52, 53, 54–55, 65
Stein, Janice 39
Strait of Malacca 99
Stramer-Smith, Janicke 11
strategic competition 36
strategic flexibility 27
strategic interest 35
strategic terrain 16–17
structural problems 65
structural violence 63–64
succession theories 91, 92
Summers, Lawrence 72
Sungkar, Abdullah 56
supply chain 17, 19, 21, 26, 27, 79–82, 152
systemism 9, 15, 15–16, *16*, 28, **29**

Taipei Economic and Cultural Representative Office 44
Taiwan 18, 18–19, 19, 26, **43**, 154, 159, 160; anti-OC campaigns 90; Chinese policy 26, 41–45, 153; COVID-19 epidemic 140; crime rates 90; economic security 151; national security 151; organized crime 90, 101; rise of 19; SARS epidemic 134; strategic value 44
Taiwan Air Defence Zone 41
Taiwan Relations Act (TRA) 42, 44
Taiwan Semiconductor Manufacturing Company (TSMC) 25
Taiwan Strait 21, 26, 42, 45
Taliban 59, 61, 65, 95
Tang, Shui-Yan 141
tariff reductions 79–80, 82
territorial disputes 45, 53, 122, 156 *see also* South China Sea
territorial integrity 26
terrorism 2, 7, 10, 51–65; 1950s to Mid-1990s 54–57; September 11, 2001 attacks 14, 23, 54, 73; conceptualization 52–53; and counter-terror 53; crime-terror-insurgency nexus 95; economic costs 60; financing. 62; and geopolitics 57; global deaths 60, 66n11; and globalization 53–54; Global War on Terror 10, 23, 59–60, 62; mid-1990s to the current time 57–60; motivations 52–53; negotiated peace 63–64; political violence 51–54; and religion 55–56; resilience 64; soft targets 52; solutions 54, 60–64, 64–65; state narratives 57–59; transnational 51
Thailand 35, 55, 58, 60, 65n4, 97; counter-insurgency operations 57; economic growth 57–58; economic security 150; food security 116; greenhouse gas emissions 111; military power 36; and sea-level rise 120
theoretical foundations 3–4
Terik-e-Taliban 60
Thomas, Nicholas 132
timber exports 89–90
Timor-Leste 55, 160n1
TPP-11 77
Trade and Investment Liberalization and Facilitation 158
traditional security threats 8–9, 11, 14; conceptualization 4–5; regional security cooperation 152–155
Trans-Pacific Partnership Agreement (TPP) 74–75, 78–79, 84; U.S. withdrawal 75–76, 79
transnationalism
transport revolution 100
Treaty of Amity and Cooperation (TAC) 75
Triads 7–8, 87, 88, 93, 95–96
Trilateral Cooperation Agreement 62
Trump, Donald 14, 24–25, 30n8, 76–77, 83, 84, 140, 141
Tsai Ing-wen 42–44
Tsugaru Strait 17
tsunamis 124
Turkey 97

Uighurs 62
United Kingdom 80
United Liberation Front of Assam 58
United National Security Council 119
United Nations 53, 62, 64–65, 94, 115, 119, 125
United Nations Climate Action Summit 120
United Nations Development Program, Human Development Report 8

United Nations General Assembly 104, 116, 150
United Nations Office on Drugs and Crime 89
United Nations Security Council 96, 132
United States of America: America First trade policy 77; and APEC 71, 159; arms race 38; Asian Financial Crisis, 1997 72; Asia-Pacific policy 57, 70; bilateral alliances 40, 70; bilateral trade agreements 73–74; CHIPS Act 83; Cold War security strategy 19; COVID-19 epidemic 140, 141; domestic perceptions 71; dominance 21, 23, 84, 149; East Asia policy 75–77; emerging technologies 41; Export Control Law 77; export regulations 83; export restrictions 82; financial crisis, 2008 157–158; foreign economic policy 80, 81–82, 84; Foreign Economic Sanctions Law 77; foreign policy 157; globalization and environmental quality 107; Global War on Terror 10, 23, 59–60, 62; greenhouse gas emissions **112**; hegemony 3, 71–72, 84; hub-and-spokes bilateral security structure 19, 37, 46, 47n5, 71; Indo-Pacific strategy 40, 41; military intervention 20; military power 35–36; National Security Council 89, 93, 95; Nikai Shock 74; nuclear deterrence (umbrella) 35–36, 39; nuclear weapons 35–36; Philippines security alliance 30n7; Pivot to Asia 14; rapprochement with China 20; relations with China 3, 22, 22–27, 27–28, 30n8, 33, 36, 38, 44–45, 72–75, 75–77, 82–83, 84, 147, 150, 152, 153–155, 156–157, 160; relations with Japan 71–72, 76–77; role 46; and sea-level rise 121; security guarantees 39, 46, 47n5; South China Sea dispute 153–155; subprime mortgage crisis 74; Taiwan policy 26, 41, 42, 42–43, 44–45; Taiwan Relations Act 42, 44; Trade Expansion Act 77; trade policies 10; Trade Act 8383; Trade Expansion Act 83; Trade Promotion Authority Act (TPA) 76; Trans-Pacific Partnership Agreement (TPP) 75–77; TTP 74–75, 79, 84; unipolarity 21; withdrawal from TPP 76–77, 79
United States Trade Representative, Office of (USTR) 76–77, 81, 82

urbanization 137–138
US–China trade war 24–25
U.S. Department of Commerce
US Indo-Pacific Command 16
U.S. Institute of Peace 97–98
U.S.–Japan summit, 1993 71
US National Defense Science and Technology Strategy (US Department of Defense) 36
US-ROC Mutual Defense Treaty 42

value-added chains 17, 57
Vaugh-Williams, Nick 53
Vietnam 96, 111, 115, 116, 120, 134, 138, 150, 153, 154; relations with China 27
Vietnam War 18, 20, 97
violence, state monopoly of legitimate 51, 51–54
Visual International Relations Project (VIRP) 15–16

war 35; avoidance of 36; potential threats 4–5
Washington Consensus 37
water disputes 124
water security 7, 11, 117–119, 122–123
water stress 7, 118–119
weapons of mass destruction (WMDs) 62
weapons proliferation 9, 37–38, 156
Weir, Lorna 134
Westphalian State System 53
Western Asia 2
wildlife smuggling 97
World Bank 109, 115, 116, 125, 125n3; Climate Risk Assessment 117
World Health Organization 134, 135–136, 136–137, 137, 138
World Trade Organization 21, 23, 72, 74, 77
WTO+ 74
Wu, Cheng-Feng 106, 107

xenophobia 26
Xi Jinping 14, 26, 45, 142, 156

Yakuza 7–8, 87, 88, 90, 93
Yen, Wei-Ting 141
Youde, Jeremy 11

Zhang, Enyu 9
Zia ul-Haq 56

9780813344607